Child Soldier

Child Soldier

by

China Keitetsi

Souvenir Press

Dedication

I would like to dedicate this book to all child soldiers who are still alive, and those who couldn't make it. May God rest your souls in peace.

I would also like to take this opportunity, and say goodbye to my son's father, late Lt-Colonel Moses Drago Kaima. And to Major-General Fred Rwigyema, Uncle Caravel, my sister Helen, my sister Margie, my sister Grace, my mother, Lt-Colonel Bruce, Lt-Colonel Benon Tumukunde, Major Moses Kanabi, Major Bunyenyezi, Captain Kayitare, Afande Ndugute, Corporal Kabawo, Private Sharp, and all the other brave soldiers of the NRA, who decided to give their lives for the sake of Uganda's people. It is so hard that you all have gone, but I just have to stay strong and try to prevent this from happening again.

Publisher's Note

Child Soldier, China Keitetsi's heart-rending story of her early years, is told entirely in her own idiom. The language she spoke as a child was Kinyankole, and she learned English after she escaped from Uganda to South Africa.

Contents

ILLUSTRATIONS
(between pages 82 and 83)
China Keitetsi, 2002
China's sister Margie
Lieutenant-Colonel Moses Drago and
    Lieutenant-Colonel Bruce
China in battledress, Kampala, aged 18
(between pages 178 and 179)
Chinar, reporting for duty
China with football fans, Denmark
China with Nelson Mandela, Bill Clinton and
    Whoopi Goldberg
Freedom! China in Copenhagen

Foreword

I am China Keitetsi, a former child soldier from Uganda, in East Africa. My country is bordering Kenya, Tanzania, Sudan, Rwanda and the Democratic Republic of Congo. In 1999 I was resettled in Denmark by the United Nations. My story is about my life as a child soldier in Yoweri K. Museveni's National Resistance Army (NRA) now known as the Uganda People's Democratic Front (UPDF).

This is how it all started for me writing this book. The head of the integration office of my Danish Commune, Birgitte Knudsen, suggested that I wrote down all the pain that I felt, assuring me that that was the way to help myself through. She said this, because every time I was sad and frightened of the nightmares, I always called her, and it did not matter whether it was at night or the weekend. I did as I was told and, as I wrote, tears seemed to run with no end. I wrote as I cried. The more I wrote, the more I felt a little bit relieved, and I could not stop. When the pages were more than 150, I told Knud Held Hansen, the man who is like a father to me. He said, 'Oh! You are writing a book', and for the first time I realised, that it actually could become a book, but one question remained. I could not imagine that I, China, who looked upon myself as something that didn't matter, like an unwanted piece of paper that you wouldn't want to read and would just throw away, could write a book. I didn't think about the book, I just wrote for the sake of emptying myself of the stones that I could feel breaking my shoulders.

The book has helped me come to terms with my past, and helped me come closer to myself. Because of this book, now I see so many things that I always passed without noticing. Even the plants in my home made me realise the innocence of the trees and the grass that I have left behind in a place that I once walked as a soldier. This made me feel good, because now I hoped that in my dreams, I might begin to dream the dreams of the innocent: the dreams of a normal child.

The reaction I have got [after publication of my book in Denmark] is beyond my expectations. Actually I never felt any reactions at first. People write to me from around the world through mail, e-mail, or by signing the guest book at my website. Everyone seems very touched and ready to save someone's child from walking along the same long road as mine. My story seems to reach everyone disregarding rank in society. So far I have met presidents, actors and top national governments and UN officials, like the Secretary-General of UN Kofi Annan, Olara Otunnu of 'Children in Armed Conflicts', Nelson Mandela, Bill Clinton, Whoopi Goldberg, Harrison Ford, Robert De Niro, even Graca Machel, and Queen Sylvia of Sweden. My meeting with Nelson Mandela was unforgettable. When I entered I found myself holding my mouth, speechless, and my head dropped to his chest, and my tears had already begun to drop. I can't find more words to describe how I felt at that moment but the answer is felt by my heart. Mandela said: 'I have written a poem for you' (for my friend Ishmael and me). 'Now you have to listen as I read it to you.' I watched him as he read words of love and peace and my tears just dropped. And now I couldn't work out whether I was extremely happy or whether I was remembering my every pain. They were feelings that might have remained inside of me for ever, feelings that I could not express in writing, because me and the pen had been kept apart.

In Denmark, life is treated differently. Every living thing has rights. When I arrived here, I learned my human rights, but still I was afraid to say: 'No!' I thought I would be punished as before, so I had to say: 'Yes, sir' without a question. Later my psychologist and doctor helped me to stop calling people 'sir'. Now I'm no longer ordered who to kill or hate, as in the army, but the most beautiful of all, is that I no longer had to live my life for others, and no force makes me act against my will, but most of all, I didn't miss my gun, because everything in Denmark is peaceful.

Despite all this new freedom, my fear seems to be permanent. I still feel the abuse and humiliation, scars which my body still carries, scars that sometimes make me feel like washing off my skin. It feels like a mark for life. In my sleep, I still see the shadows of my fellow child soldiers and friends, who ended their own lives with their gun in order to escape the torture of the enemies, the torture of suspected civilians, and the unmarked graves of my fallen comrades. I still see the dark rooms of the military police and those we tortured there; I still see their eyes. The dreams are real. I still see the same gun, the same uniform, and the same faces; the fear I had to carry every day of the desperation I saw in almost any soldier. That desperation often betrayed the innocent, as everyone struggled to find favours among their superiors.

Now I am like a child who needs nice stories before falling asleep. I'm sure that my dreams will never be free before the 300,000 other child soldiers are free from the orders of their creators. The love I have is mostly for the kids, because innocence is love to me. Now I'm left in the world to count the loss. It's us who lost our childhood, and the dignity of a woman, and it's us who lost our clear dreams, it's us who remain hating our skin and it's us with no thoughts of a child;

or grown-up thoughts, yet we are already mothers and fathers to the child given to us by men the same age as our fathers. I used to smoke with my friends, but here I am smoking alone, and the cigarette doesn't taste the same. My eyes look up in the sky, and all that I see is the moving clouds, and not my friends, and those that I loved. My childhood is long forgotten. Sometimes I feel as if I am six years old, and again it's like I am 100 years old. With the love of the world, let me hope for a day where I will dream, and feel, as you.

C.K.

(Email: ck@xchild.dk Website: www.xchild.dk)

2003

Acknowledgements

My gratitude goes to: The Danish people and their government, my new family the Hansens, United Nations staff in South Africa, N. Omutoni, Richard, Robert, Emanuel, Lucky Dube, Thor Kujahn Ehlers, Jens Runge Poulsen and his family, Melissa Stetson, my teacher Søren Jesperson, Birgitte Knudsen, Eskil Brown, Søren Louv, Pia Gruhn, Dennis Hansen, Kenneth Hansen, Lisa and Kenneth, my doctor Lill Moll Nielsen, Lars Koberg, and my late mother.

C.K.
2003

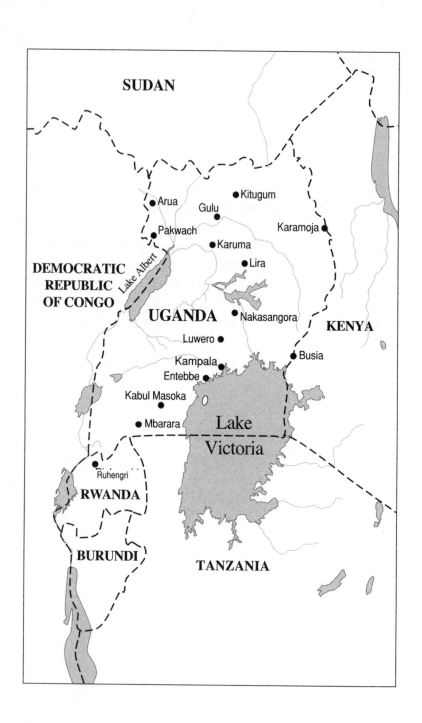

PART ONE
My Early Life

My Birth Mother

My father was born and studied in a small village of western Uganda, and his first job was as manager at the coffee marketing board. Later, after meeting my mother, he decided to study law.

When I was born, everything changed because I wasn't a boy, so my father divorced my mother, and she left the family home when I was six months old. Looking upon the world with the eyes of a young child, I didn't have much chance of knowing what the future held for me. My mother was forced out of her home and forbidden ever to return, and if ever she tried, her life would end. At those times whoever was the most powerful between the man and woman decided their fate, and my father had the power and he would not share it. My mother had no other choice but to leave me, though she knew well that I would never get a chance to grow up like most other children. I was too young to understand my loss, and I do not remember much from those times. Sometimes now, I sense a feeling of extreme loss so different from other emotions, and a flood of sadness and powerlessness flushes away my every thought. When I gain my senses back, and try to track through my life of memories and emotions, I always meet the swamps of forgetfulness – the loss of my mother, I suppose.

Madness in the House

I could not know that I was only a poor kid left with a father who had more resemblance to an animal predator than to a human being. I was a nuisance, I suppose, having to be taken care of, every minute of the day, so my father got rid of me by sending me to the farm where his mother lived.

My grandmother was not pretty as other old women I had seen. She was a big and short woman, with one eye crying all times. Her mouth faced to the east and whenever she opened it to talk, it seemed to struggle to escape by flying away, but her old muscles always held it in a firm grip. I was less concerned with the way she looked, as long as no one made me kiss her, but still, I never needed her relentless words.

I had learned now that my father had a huge land with banana plantations, and all the farm animals you can think of, but the one animal I loved most was the goat. The farmhouse consisted of five rooms, built with clay-bricks and covered by a tin roof. At the end of the house in the fifth room was what I considered my grandmother's biggest asset, the banana store, and through the window you could see a grass field full of pumpkins, that in my eyes seemed just to grow there by coincidence, and I do not remember the taste because we never ate them. I guess that one can say that I had a huge playground. Remember that these were my first years in my life, and I got a bit 'savage' in those surroundings – a feeling which I never really got rid of.

During those days another old woman, my father's aunt Florida, came to live with us, and when I compared her face with my grandmother's, I found her charming and with a beautiful face, that made me want to be a boy and grow older. My grandmother was always shouting at Florida, and I was confused not knowing why grandmother was so aggressive.

Whenever my grandmother started swearing at her, Florida would just stare back, and she showed no sign of defending herself. That made me dislike my grandmother, and I was convinced that Florida would have far more power if she defended herself. I knew that, if I wanted the two to fight with their fists, I had to make it my responsibility. Soon I was busy searching for the perfect idea of how to start it all.

One fine morning I woke up, and no nobody was home. I went to the corner in the living-room where the milk was stored, and filled a pot until it became heavy. Then I went to my grandmother's room and as I was pouring the milk on her bed sheets, I thought of how she would react if she caught me, and quickly I ran to hide in the bush. After some time I asked myself: 'Why am I hiding, when no one has seen me? This is stupid,' I said aloud, and left the hiding place. But when I was about to reach home, I remembered that they would ask me who had been drinking the milk, 'Should I go back to the bush?' I questioned myself. 'No, go home'. On my way, I passed where the goats and the calves were, and stood there for a while staring at them. Then I went home, sat in the garden, and waited for Florida and Grandma to return. After a while I heard Grandmother asking me about the missing milk, and with my red sleepy eyes I told her that the goat had asked for it and I gave it to her.

'Which one among them?' she asked with her big voice.

'The white and black,' I replied with my little one.

'We do have many, which happen to have those colours,' she said.

'Jaah, the one with four kids.'

She busted into a rusty laugh and, if I had not covered my ears, I would have lived without them today. When she laughed I said to myself: 'Laugh now! because you will cry later,' being sure that Florida would beat her.

They began preparing supper while I sat beside them, like a dog waiting for a piece of meat. Yes, my eyes might have been looking at the meat, but my mind was at my grandmother's mouth, thinking of how it would look after the fight, maybe then it would face to the west for a change. In the evening Grandmother was outside in the kitchen, busy calling my name. When I got there she told me to help her hold the lamp, because the moon which normally lit the open kitchen was not clear that evening. Our kitchen was of an ancient design, without chairs and with a fire site made of three stones which held the cooking pot above the burning wood. My grandmother was sitting down on a little piece of cloth, while I sat on the dusty ground, giving her light from the fuelled lamp. When the oil was ready, she began cutting the onions, and now her other eye too dropped tears. I felt like laughing, but I got angry at the same time, thinking that her tears might fall in our food. Accidentally one of the tomatoes fell down, and I was told to point the lamp where it had fell so as to locate it. With my head down to the ground, I saw the tomato between her legs, and when I was about to pick it up, I looked up and saw something, which looked like a small animal with black fur. 'Au!'

'What is it?' she asked.

'It's an animal with black hair!' I replied.

'What are you waiting for, burn it!' she commanded, and in a flash I grabbed a big fire stick and burned it. She jumped, while singing 'Stop!' in a high-pitched voice, but I continued trying to have another go, because I wanted the animal which was stuck to leave. She smacked my cheek and stopped, but she told me to leave the kitchen anyway.

After supper, I sat in a corner like a shadow and stared at them, until Grandmother ordered me to bed, and reluctantly I went, but feeling disappointed because I had wanted her to go to bed first, so I could enjoy the war between them. As I lay in my bed, I began to question my actions, and suddenly I found them mean and ugly, but still I didn't blame myself, because I believed that it was the right decision. Few moments later I heard my grandmother moving towards her bed, and I became frightened, so I covered my head with the blanket, and waited for her to turn into a screaming monster. I waited for some time, but still nothing happened. I woke up and it was already morning, so I jumped out of the bed fearing that I might have missed the fight which I had arranged, and hurried to see if they had fought in silence. When I was about to reach the living-room, I remembered that I had no clothes on, so I ran back to my bedroom like a rat with a broomstick at its tail and dressed myself up. When I finally reached the living-room, I couldn't decide whether I was disappointed or relieved. I discovered that no changes were made through the night, even when I observed them carefully I could not see any scars. I kept wondering, but I could not figure out what had stopped Grandmother from raising her anger. 'Maybe I didn't use enough milk,' I thought.

The next day, my grandmother went to the banana plantation, leaving me with Florida. She was sitting down in the little garden beside the house, where I went and sat myself down very close in front of her. 'If I tell you a secret, would you keep it to yourself?' I asked. She smiled beautifully, but her eyes were blinking as if she was about to cry.

I began telling Florida about my feelings towards my grandmother, but I did not stop there, I also told her of what I had done the day before. Then she moved closer, I suppose, to hear more, but I was already busy with something else, sneaking with my eyes to see whether she also had 'the black furred animal'.

'Don't look there. Stop it!' she said. Then she warned me about my grandmother, telling me that I never should do such a thing again. I could not understand why her eyes were becoming wet, since I expected her to be happy of what I was trying to do for her. After her words, she took me to bed leaving me there to sleep. When I woke up it was already supper-time. We ate our beans and then I went back to sleep.

Few months later Florida fell sick and spent most of her time in bed. I was sad all the time, seeing my grandmother shouting at her whenever she asked for something to eat or drink. One evening I went and sat beside Florida's bedside waiting for her to hold my hand as she used to, but her hand remained by her side. I took her hand and began shaking it, but she remained still. I went outside and told my grandmother, but she ignored me and continued washing the dishes. I started crying, thinking that my tears might move her, but instead she shouted at me to keep quiet. After she had finished she went inside the house and I followed after her. She went to Florida, so I decided to stay away. The next thing I remember was my father coming in a white car leading in front of several other cars. Inside the house I saw my father cry while the rest of the people were quiet. Then people started one by one to visit Florida in her room. When they came out of the room they were grey and sad, crying, or just even quieter than before. I became angry when nobody could tell me what they were crying for, but then my grandmother began to cry too. At first I was shocked, but then, after a second thought as I had a closer look, it could as well be spit that she had put there below her eyes, because I couldn't imagine her crying for real. After many tears, Florida woke up and suddenly the whole place got another tune. People who had been crying were now happy, all laughing and drinking while singing. My confusion was total, and I thought that my father and the rest had turned mad. Then my father ordered the workers to slaughter some goats. I stood near them while their throats were cut and looked at the blood as it flushed away. I loved those goats: they were like my children, I even had names for them. I began crying and ran to my bed, leaving the madness for Florida.

I woke up the following day and found Florida in the living-room, still looking sick. I went and sat beside her and asked if she had heard people crying. She told me that she must have been in deep sleep and heard nothing, but when I looked in her eyes I saw tears. Then she told me that she was leaving with my father to the town house and she felt sad to leave me behind. I almost panicked as I begged her to stay, but she told me that she only would be away for a few days. A few days was a long time for a small child, and I could not convince my broken heart. So I ran away, to the stables of the goats and calves, and after some time there, I heard myself singing for them, while my tears wetted the fur of the goat I embraced. After a while I got angry. I couldn't accept what Florida had told me, and now was the time to stop my father from taking her away from me. I ran home as fast as I could, but found that she already had been taken. I turned to look at my grandmother and thought about Florida, asking myself if I would ever see her again, but my tears clouded in my eyes, and found no answer. I cried many times over the loss of Florida, but they never brought her back to me.

The Lion's Mother

Now that Florida was gone things started getting tough for me. The love that had been surrounding me had left. It felt as if my heart lost some of its life, making the days long and grey. Even before I got over the hardest time of missing Florida, my grandmother started turning everything around me. She stopped changing my bed sheets, and one day she

7

told me that I had to learn how to wash them myself, 'Stop peeing on them!' she had shouted, making it sound like I did it on purpose to annoy her. I asked myself why she had to change after Florida had gone, but I could not find the answer. That night I went to bed and tried to stay awake as the only solution I could find to my new problem, because she had told me that she would punish me if ever again she found a wet bed. During my sleep at night everything was quiet and warm. I dreamed of peeing on the toilet and felt nice as my pee left me in slow motion. I sat on the wet bed for some time, trying to find how to escape the punishment. I went outside and poured some water in a cup. I poured the water on the already wet bed sheets, and screamed for help. My grandmother's old legs came running to my bedside and she asked me of what had happened. With the cup in my hands I told her that I drank some water, and then the cup slipped right out of my hand. She looked me in the eyes for about five minutes without blinking and said in a low voice: 'Tell me the truth.' I felt a strange cold creep upwards from my tailbone to the back of my neck, making me change my statement. With a dizzy head and pounding heart I told her that I had peed on the bed, and I was afraid of her. Even before I could shut my mouth, she grabbed my arm with her strong old hands, and dragged me outside, still without my clothes on. In the surrounding bush, she plucked a stinging nettle with her other hand, and beat my whole body with its burning leaves. She left me there screaming and crying as I tumbled around with my skin on fire. I cried half the day and refused to put on my clothes, thinking that I was punishing her back. But I soon realised that I only punished myself. The punishments only made me more nervous, and I had a hard time understanding my grandmother's reasons for treating me like this, and her punishments just kept on getting worse.

One evening my grandmother came to wake me up, discovering that the dress I wore was wet. She grabbed my arm like an angry lion and threw me on to the floor. I heard a sharp snap, followed by a strong pain tearing me apart from my elbow to my neck. Still I struggled to get up, but when I looked at my arm I stayed down. A white bone had penetrated my skin, but the worst shock hit me when I saw my own blood. The amount of it brought the memory of goats being slaughtered as breathtaking flashes before my eyes. I saw the blood coming and their life fade away. I cried in a loud voice while screaming at the same time, and my heart was beating at a scary pace, convincing me even more that this would be my final day. My grandmother shouted at me to keep quiet, and then set my bone in its right place. The pain came back as hard as before, but I feared the woman more than my pain, so I remained quiet. When she had finished, she took me to bed again, and without a word she left me alone to cry in silence.

It must have been Thursday when the old woman broke my arm, and she knew that my father would be coming on Saturday. I remember him always coming with the sunset, to check on his livestock and pay the workers. Saturday morning, my grandmother ordered me to lie, by telling my father that I had fallen from my bed. She warned me to comply because, if not, she would beat me again, after my father's return to the town house. She left me at home and went to the field for a few hours, before she returned and began cooking. When we finished eating, I went outside, and sat where the goat kids were jumping around in wild games. But my smile faded, when I started remembering the good times that I had had with Florida. After a while, I stood up and walked to the road, sat myself down with my arm on my lap, and began singing in silence.

Suddenly I heard the sound of a car, I stood up and listened intently, and I hoped to see my father. A blue Suzuki car that

I never had seen was driving towards me. 'That's not my father,' I thought, with excitement. I remained, waiting to see who it could be. A tall beautiful woman stepped out, and my eyes caught up with her smile. Her teeth were white as the snow, and when she smiled the second time, I hoped her to keep on smiling. When she came closer, I noticed something in her arms bundled in white cloth. A man stepped out too, and it was my father. I stood there with my teeth in the air, waiting for him to hold me, but he seemed too busy exchanging jokes with the woman. I was puzzled by the way my father looked at her, it seemed as if he was about to bite her. When we were about to go into the house, I took off my long-sleeved T-shirt and showed him my arm, and before he could ask, I told him the lie. He held my arm looking at it with intense eyes, before he asked who had tied the sticks on.

'Grandmother' I replied.

'You'll be alright' he said, and went inside.

I followed from behind and went to a corner of the living-room, where I remained standing, as I hoped to capture his attention. No one seemed to take notice of me, so I decided to go outside. Before I could get to the door, the woman called and asked if I wanted to hold the baby. 'Is she mad,' I thought. 'Where's the baby?' I remained standing, so she turned and looked at my father, and both looked back at me. I told them that there were no other children but me. Sadly they smiled, and she told me to come and see what child she meant. Sitting down like she had told me to, she put a child on my lap, while she kept her hand supporting the head. I was about to ask her whether it was a boy or a girl when it threw up on me. I got a little upset and told her to take her baby. She did so while telling me that it was a boy. Then I asked her of who she was, and she told me that she was my mother. I went back to my kids with a contented heart and renewed hope, leaving the four of them inside.

10

Mother

She was the one, finally here to free me from the grip of my grandmother. I smiled. She asked me if I was happy about her coming to live with us, and there was no doubt in my voice when I had replied: 'Yes!'

I had a good time with my mother, but I became more excited when my father and the workers began building a new house for my mother and I. The new house was about two kilometres away from Grandmother's and it had more rooms, but the surroundings looked pretty much the same. The cows and the goats were moved from Grandmother to our new place. My mother seemed to control everything, apart from one banana plantation, which remained in my grandmother's care. My father returned to the town house, leaving my mother and me at our new home. I trusted her, and told her everything about my grandmother. She seemed to take my side, and I was overjoyed. I thought that I was pleasing her, and as any other child, I was jealous of my position, trying to find favour in her eyes. I exaggerated, even lying when telling her about things my grandmother had never done. I do not remember my mother being pregnant, and I don't know, how and where, she gave birth to her second child.

All I remember was me taking care of my mother's little girl named Pamela. I was pleased about this because now I had a child to be with. But one day, she went somewhere unknown to me, and I was puzzled when she had demanded me not to let her daughter cry. At first I had a good time with the baby until I tried to make her sleep. It went on fine, but it didn't take long before she woke up and began to cry. I tried to feed her with milk without success. I tried everything, but she just kept on crying until her mother returned, and before I could say a word she grabbed the baby and blamed me for not having fed her. Though I was very hurt by her accusation, she scared me too, as I saw her face twisted with anger, so I remained silent.

After having finished feeding the baby with her breast milk, and put her to sleep, she came back for me. I was shocked and unable to defend myself as my mother turned into a biting dog, all over me, pulling my lips and ears for then to push me to the ground. I laid on the ground quiet in suspension as I tried to understand the meaning of it all, but when I tasted the blood from my lips, it didn't matter: a hate against my little sister was sown. I was certain that if she had not cried, this would not have happened. Every time I looked at her, I felt like pulling her ears and lips like she had made her mother do to me. My sister became my enemy, and whenever she cried my heart would beat with fear and hate, because I knew that my mother would punish me. The love which I had thought would last for ever between my mother and me was fading.

Some time passed, and my father returned from the town house. During supper, she told him that I was wetting the bed every night, and she was getting tired of changing the wet sheets every morning. I watched her telling these lies to my father, and it hurt me to accept the fact that she was trying to put the knife in my back. I was the one who made my own bed, making my mother a liar! But the look on my father's face changed my mind from telling him this.

After supper, my father told me to sleep on the sofa and, if I wet it, he would beat me the following morning. I went to bed with fear and promised myself that I would not fall asleep, though I doubted myself. The first thing I did, when I woke up was to check the sofa, and to my disappointment it was wet. 'No!' I cried in a whisper with my arms on my head. I went and sat in the rising sun as I waited for my father to wake up and do what he had promised.

After my father had beat me, he told me that I was not allowed anything to eat until supper. The lie from the woman's mouth stirred my expectations of what a mother was, but again I was confused, as I saw the love she showed to my younger sister and brother. I was getting jealous, because the place which I took as my home was being turned into a nursery school: when one of them would sleep, another one would wake up crying.

In that same period, an old woman named Jane came to our farm, and I was told that she was my grandmother on my mother's side. I became nervous, wondering if she also would live with us, adding on to my misery. But I was relieved when she left a few days later, and I wished her never to return. Shortly after the old lady's departure, my mother left for a brief visit to the town house where my father lived. Through a month or two my mother's mother returned with her belongings, two daughters, a son and a few cows. Not only was I forced to call her two girls 'Aunt', but I also had to call her son 'Uncle' though he nearly was my own age. Everything about them annoyed me. They were wild with food, eating each and everything that came in their way, and I wondered if it was their first time to see food. But I could not find an answer to my questions, because I was afraid of in which way they would answer. Every day I hoped they would go back to wherever they came from, and leave our food alone.

Around three days after the new family had arrived, my father returned to show them where to settle. I became torn between two families, because both grandmothers required my services. All the time I was sent with parcels of food and other appliances, and soon parcel became parcel. It turned really bad, when the two old women began questioning me about what the other had got. Jane was a lazy old woman, who preferred me to stay and do a little extra work while her children played around. When I got back, my mother would beat me for being late. What annoyed me most was that there never was any 'thank-you'. I felt that everybody had begun spinning around me giving orders, and I urgently needed to stop it, as my strength and sanity began to fail.

We had many different kinds of poison, but I had no idea of how they worked. Once in a while the cows needed to be cleaned of parasites. It was a demanding job, which required all the family to go out and spray some disinfectant liquid on the skin of the cows. And that's when I found a possible escape of the torment.

I pretended to be sick so I could stay home and try some of the poison. When everybody had left, I took a stick and put on a glob of poison, pointed the stick to the cat, who because of the colour mistakenly thought that the poison was milk. After the cat had finished to lick it, it started to spin around and then went darting out of the door. I followed behind realising with fear and sadness what I might have done, as I looked at the cat's new-born playing around, tumbling after me with happy voices as I passed. I went in the bush and began a search with tears of regret as I hoped to find her, while condemning myself of my thoughtless action. I simply could not find her, so I stood still for a while not knowing what to do, as I zoomed in on everything that catched my eyes. My heavy breathing and tired mind had dried my eyes and they found a place for me to relax. On the grass I sat myself, and burned in the sun. I remembered how the cat lived her life and what good times we had together. I remembered her yellow-green eyes surrounded by a black fur, which covered a fat but strong body. She was only fed with milk so that we were sure she remembered her job. She never went far from our house because of the armies of rats always camped there. She was always welcome indoors and she spent a lot of time there with her kittens. Often when someone got home she would look at the person and pretend that nothing had happened, but when you sat down, her eyes would open wide. If she were not already near you, she would try to approach in a nonchalant manner, a little too eager to get the act right. Then she would wait until seeing a good place at your lap to sit, and you just had to say one word while looking at her and she would jump right up to you. If we had been away too long she would take a bit longer before even looking in anybody's direction. She would then make sure to turn you her back, or if there were a high place she would jump up there and look at you from afar, still wanting your attention. Her tail would then be twisting randomly around in an annoyed and restless manner.

Suddenly I became spooked: 'If I give them the poison, would they spin around and disappear as the cat did? and, if so, would they come back?' The fear of their return made me abandon the plan. My mother and Jane returned, they found me where I had left myself after the search. I was very hot from the sun and my sadness gave me an ill look, so they were convinced even more about my illness. Later they discovered the disturbing cries from her kittens and they wondered what had happened, so I told them I didn't know, because I had been asleep. But still my heart felt the guilt as it made me want to tell what I had done, and my hope of possible return of the cat remained in my mind.

Dangerous Mind

We had two small lakes, and the one furthest away through a vast line of bush and trees was the only one the cattle could drink of; the other one was very close and was therefore easy to get to, but its water was unclean. It was torture to go to that lake because of the many trees that dropped their spiky branches, especially for me who didn't have any shoes to wear. That very evening I returned with the calves, while having a good time singing for them, but I came to stop when I saw Stepmother standing with her hands on her hips in front of the little calves' shed. 'Why did you take them to the bad lake? Do you want us to lose them because of you?' she began questioning me.

I tried to defend myself by denying her accusation, even though she was right.

With an angered voice she started walking towards me. I noticed a stick in her hand, so I took a few steps back. 'Do you want to kill them all?'

I told her that I loved the calves and I could not do anything to harm them, but her madness only increased, so finally I had to tell the truth.

She said, 'You are not afraid of eating, but you are afraid of hurting your feet. I'm sick and tired of feeding you. It's better to feed a pig!'

How can this woman say this? She came without anything but her son and a cloth wrapped around him. How then could she think this way as if she owned the food that I ate? I thought she didn't know what she was talking about, but of course I kept my mouth shut. Otherwise I knew that I wasn't going to eat for another day or two. So I turned my face like a hungry dog, hoping that she might feel sorry for me and forget what I had done.

'Go to bed! No supper for you, and don't think I've finished with you,' she said.

Slowly I walked away, like an unwanted dog with its tail between its legs, hoping again she might have some compassion and say 'Come you dog, and eat,' but she didn't.

That night I couldn't sleep, because of my stomach which kept on crying for food. About two in the morning I finally got up. I was surrounded by darkness so I kept my eyes closed as I slowly moved towards the door that led to where the leftovers were kept. I got hold of a pot, and started to gobble down the food as I listened for any sounds that might cause me trouble. I was back in my bed with a smile, as I thought that now I would be able to sleep. But my worries took over where my stomach had left, as the thought of the food I had been eating crossed my mind.

Early in the morning I hurried back to the pot and smoothed away the marks of my fingers, but then I noticed the sides of the pot still revealing that somebody had been eating of it. I realised that my worries of that pot had no end, so I decided to go outside to await for my lesson. 'From now on you will be doing each and everything that is needed to be done.' Then she went back inside, leaving me still wondering if she was going to find out about the missing food. I stood there waiting for her to return, and when she didn't, I went inside to check if she had gone through the back door to her mother's, but she heard me from her bedroom and told me to cook some milk. I was hungry, but I was afraid to ask for breakfast, so when I had finished cooking the milk, I took a cup myself and began pouring the hot milk, but as I had to hurry in fear of being caught, I forgot the heaviness of the pot and suddenly I missed the cup and poured the milk on one of my legs. The pot fell to the ground as I in pain started to scream. She came, looked at me and said: 'Your big stomach would bury you one day', before going back to the house while complaining about the spilled milk. I went to a tree, picked some leaves and covered my burn, but they wouldn't stay on, so I began to cry. While calming myself down I ripped a piece of my clothes and tied it around my leg. Then I sat myself down against a tree watching the calves play with each other.

It did not matter what I had done to myself. My mother's feelings towards me stayed the same, insisting that I still was capable of working.

Three days after, she told me to go and check on the calves which were down in the field. Before I could reach the place, the cloth fell off my leg, I picked it up and told myself to check the wound later. When I reached the place I sat down slowly and untied my wound and discovered white little things. At first I thought they were strings of the cloth in which I had used to bind my wound, but when I tried to remove them I discovered it wasn't cloth, but maggots! I screamed while running home as fast as I could, crying, thinking that my leg was rotten. My mother helped me to remove them and covered my wound with cotton wool. It didn't help me to get rid of the fear that I might lose my leg, so I checked it each minute of the day. The next day I had to bring some milk to my grandmother. She was not home when I got there, so I sat myself down in the garden and waited, while thinking about my pain back home. I felt sad and didn't want to return. Then my eyes came across a machete lying in the garden. I took it in my hands and looked at it for a while as flashes of blood met my eyes. Suddenly I laid my thumb against a piece of wood, closed my eyes and chopped it in the middle. When I opened my eyes, a piece of flesh was hanging from my finger with blood already beginning to cover my feet. I tried to cry to ease my pain, but the sight of it remained. I was in pain but happy at the same time, being sure that now my grandmother would let me stay at her home. I laid myself against the wall, as I watched myself bleed, and my wish to stay was so strong that I even squeezed the wound when the blood showed signs of stopping.

Soon one of the workers named Byoma (meaning metal) came to fetch me. Byoma was a funny-looking man just like his name, with muscles all over and his hanging lips made him look like a waking-up cow. When I told him that I could not walk, Byoma only shook his head and went back from where he came.

When she finally came, and asked me what had happened, I told her that a man passing by had taken the machete from the garden and chopped my finger. She asked me if I knew the man. 'No,' I replied, as I noticed the wrinkles on her face increase. She panicked, before getting a basin of water and began washing my finger, and I just managed to hide a happy smile as she bandaged it. As soon as she had finished she looked at me and said: 'Now you can go back home.' Alone, I walked through the grass and woods feeling sad, thinking of the machete, my finger, the blood and pain wasted for nothing.

When I got home. my father had returned from the town house, but he had gone to check on the cows. In the evening he returned, and I went to greet him as if I was dying, while holding my arm. 'Take off the cloth,' he demanded, and gently I did so. I noticed a change on his face, a face of pity, which made me feel secure, and I approached his lap where I then laid my arm. He turned my hand around before asking me of what had happened, and with tears in my eyes, I told him: 'Grandmother did it!' as I managed to squeeze out another tear. He looked down for a while, still holding on to my hand, then he stood up all confused and began walking around the house. Soon Byoma walked in and before he could say a word, my father told him to go and call Grandmother. My tears dried fast as I in fear realised that he actually had decided to ask Grandmother about this. I thought of telling him the truth, so I went outside to where he was standing with the calves, but his shouting scared me back to the sofa where I remained seated until my grandmother arrived. She had sat herself beside me, and as she was about to greet him, my father started shouting at her that she was nothing but an evil old woman who only thought of herself. Grandmother didn't have any idea of what was going on, so she asked him to calm down and explain. 'Go away from my house,' my father told her, before he went back outside. She turned to look at me and asked whether I had any idea of what might have made my father so upset. My answer to her was to shake my head and I didn't wait for more questions, so I ran to my bedroom, leaving her alone in the living-room. I heard her talking with herself before she left, and I was satisfied with my revenge for not letting me stay at her home. I had to stay in my bedroom to be able to control my excitement.

Now that I had injuries, I no longer could watch over the goats and calves, but I had to take over the duties of my mother's sisters, bringing food and other supplies to their mother every night. There were no roads from my father's house to Jane, just a path with wild grass and other plants. I felt very afraid of being out there among the wild animals. And she always sent me in the evening after the cows had been milked and the food had been cooked.

Weeks went by without any problems, until one day I heard what sounded like a scream of drunkard people. Shocked, I stopped and listened intently, but heard nothing more. Just convincing myself that it was just my imagination I went on. But the next day, I heard a hyena howl and it made me very afraid. It was dark, making it impossible to know if they were near me or not. I stopped for a long while, arguing with myself if I should go back or go on. I had to choose between being caught by the hyenas or by my mother waiting at home. I waited for the hyenas to come and get me, but they never did, so I went on. When I reached the house I told Jane of what I had heard, hoping that she might let her daughters escort me back home. To my disappointment, she seemed not to care. I went back to the darkness of the road by myself, while singing in a loud voice to ease my fear. When I reached home, I pretended nothing had happened because I knew she wouldn't care anyway.

One day I heard them howling very close by me, so I ran back home, fearing they were about to attack me. When my mother saw me return without giving Jane the food she demanded an explanation. I told her: 'But I heard the hyena howling near me, and I thought that they were too close and that's why I had to run away.'

She told me for the second time that I knew nothing but to eat, and that I shouldn't return before having delivered the food.

I looked down, feeling the whole world against me, and returned back to the loneliness of the night. I wished that I were a bird, flying high above the dangerous animals, feeling helpless, because I knew I couldn't be a bird, and there was nothing else to do. All I could do was cry on the shoulder of the road. I looked around, seeing the bush covered in nothing but darkness and the sounds of night birds.

As I walked, I suddenly felt pain go through my heel. But I ignored it and kept walking. When I reached Jane's house, pain covered my whole leg. I was surprised by Jane's reaction when I told her. She knew immediately it was a snakebite. Fear gripped my heart; I knew that snakes were dangerous. At once she examined my heel, cutting it with a razor, putting medicine in the wounds they made. Then she put something that appeared to be sucking the blood out of my veins. I was afraid especially when nobody could tell me where the thing was taking my blood.

It was heaven. I got this crazy idea of beating my leg with a wooden stick every time it showed signs of getting better, because I preferred the pain rather than being sent back to the darkness. I never condemned the snake, but the one who sent me to it!

The Bees

One day, my mother went to the town house, so I had to stay with my grandmother and baby-sit my sister Pamela. My grandmother used to go to the banana plantation every morning, but now when the baby and I were with her alone, she had no choice but to take us along. Grandmother was marching in front with Pamela on her back and a hoe on her shoulders, and I with a five-litre container full of water. When we reached the banana plantation I looked up at the sun and realised that it was eleven o'clock. Pamela and I were left under the mango tree, and then Grandmother went behind a banana plant to change clothes. I left the baby and tried to sneak up on her to see how she looked without clothes on, but again the little thing prevented me from having a little fun as she began to cry and I had to run back and hold her mouth. When the baby had stopped trying to bite my hand, we looked up and saw Grandmother as she went a bit further away from us to begin planting the beans. Soon I left Pamela playing and went to the other trees filled with oranges. When I looked up at one of the trees I got a nice surprise. My eyes met with a huge beehive and I could not wait as I imagined the sweet honey dripping on my tongue. 'Should I stand down here with this tongue of mine hanging out of my mouth, or should I do something about it?' I asked myself. I noticed a long stick laying there as if waiting for me, but before grabbing it I remembered my grandmother who fortunately was happily buried in her own glories. I took the stick in my hands and looked at it for some time before I jumped over to the tree and began to swing the stick at the beehive. My low height and thin arms almost failed me, but it was a shame for me just to give up so I fought with it until it landed on top of my head, and busted into many pieces while releasing thousands of furious bees suddenly covering my head. With one arm I swept away the bees from my face as I tumbled over to Pamela and grabbed her with the other, but the bees followed me now, stinging both of us. I tried to run away with the baby but no matter where I ran the bees followed from behind. Pamela started to scream, so I put my hand over her mouth and nose so Grandmother wouldn't hear what was happening. Now I was wildly stung all over as I had no protection from my own hands, and I kept my own mouth tightly closed because it seemed where the bees wanted to go most. When running didn't help, I tried rolling on the ground together with the baby, but still it didn't work, so I screamed for my grandmother's help. We were already stung badly, but at that moment I did not see the terror from the bees but from what would happen to me when my grandmother, stepmother and my father saw us.

Grandmother heard the screams and came to our rescue. She grabbed one of my arms still holding tight around Pamela and we began running away from the spot. When we had reached to the other side she took the baby away from my arms, looked at her and screamed. After she had gained her breath back she took me by my left hand and led us home, shouting at me all the way as if trying to drown the noise of Pamela's breathtaking cries. When we reached home she placed Pamela on the sofa and began writing a quick letter to my mother and father before she gave it to one of the workers who then hurried to the town house. After she had finished everything, she ran back to Pamela and grabbed her from the sofa and began picking the stings off her body. All that I could see from the distance was my grandmother's hand picking and throwing away, and I knew the old woman's eyesight, so I was never sure whether she was picking the right thing. I could do nothing but to sit, being as unnoticeable as I possibly could. My situation was getting worse, but Grandmother seemed blinded by Pamela's swellings. I had never felt so much pain before, but when I finally gave up trying to get some help from her, she just turned away from Pamela for half a second and gave me the eyes of a beast. Her eyes made me think of how they would torture me when they got back, and the thought made me so scared and angry that I started swearing at myself. Finally I felt like an outcast as my grandmother kept on reminding me of the punishment I would get, so I went outside and sat on a stone near the house for a while. My eyes were closing, forced by my swellings, so I went to my bedroom and tried to sleep, but the fear inside me could not let me. When the sleep was about to overcome me I heard my mother scream and I knew she had seen her daughter. Then I heard my father's footsteps towards my bedroom, while commanding me out, but I became so afraid that I hid beneath my blanket as I wished everything else to go away. But he just threw away the blanket, grabbed me by my neck and dragged me to the living-room. He sat himself on the sofa in front of me, and demanded to know what I was doing with the trees. 'I wanted honey,' I said, and he replied with a heavy clap on my fat cheek, saying 'Honey-honey-honey'. Then he went away. I stayed there waiting for him to return with a stick. After having whipped me, he called for the doctor. I heard the doctor ask him why it looked as if I was beaten, but he told him that I had fallen running away from the bees. I listened to my father's lies and wished that I could stitch his mouth together.

Four Beautiful Kids

Some time after my father left, my mother punished me by making me look after the goats, without realising how happy this made me, that I would be away from morning till evening, away from the beatings and insults. I was pretty happy at my new job, the goats obeyed me and gave me no trouble, and I enjoyed to see my mother in the mornings watching me as I walked to the bush pretending to be in misery.

One day with my goats in the bush I discovered white small mushrooms, which mostly grew in rain season. The only thing that made my job a little difficult at times was the fact that goats don't talk, and I needed someone to exchange news or joke with. The mushrooms were considered quite a delicacy, so I thought of going back home and telling them, but then I thought of what they were doing for me so I decided not to. I left the goats alone for a while and went to our neighbours', though I very well knew that they were enemies to my father, and I felt good by inviting them to my father's own field. The neighbour's wife was sitting outside and talking with two other women. 'Young John,' she called me, 'What are you doing here?' she asked, but I ignored her question and invited them to my findings. At once all three smiled and started running around in one big confusion as they grabbed any basket they could catch on their way. 'We can leave now,' one woman said. 'Are you not calling other people?', I asked. 'No!' they replied at once. 'But there is many, and you will get hungry, can't you bring some bananas?' I asked.

When I had showed them the place, I went back to get my goats. Then I sat myself down in the grass with my bunch of bananas and watched them humming around the mushroom-field. That night I went to my bed with one wish: I wished that I would find more and more mushrooms. In the morning my mother gave me a cup of milk and told me to finish up quickly and take the goats to the field, and then she went outside. When I could no longer hear her footsteps, I went to the kitchen and grabbed a piece of meat from a pot and hurried it into my mouth. The meat got stuck in my throat, and when I struggled to spit it out I got tears in my eyes. Just before I lost all my breath I ran and grabbed a cup of water that helped me to swallow the meat, then I sat down and breathed heavily with relief. After I had gained my senses back, I went outside and took my goats to the field, while telling them about my horrible start of the day. We arrived at a nice spot filled with grass where I left them eating, and went to search for mushrooms. When I had walked for some time without luck, I heard the sound of goat's kids, not far from where I was standing. I responded by mimicking their little voices and four beautiful kids tumbled towards me from the thick bush. I felt like crying but when I realised that they all were little girls like me, suddenly my tears dried away and I found myself laughing. The little kids followed me and joined the others and I was thrilled with happiness of my new discovery, thinking that I finally had found something that would be mine. All that filled my thoughts was that now I had my own little family and I would never be sad again. After I was done with my duty for that day, I couldn't wait to give them the good news, because I thought they would be happy for me to find these little friends, and I expected them to give me encouraging words, so I arrived home smiling and proud. But they didn't even smile and my grandmother only said: 'We will see them tomorrow.' When I saw their faces cleared of any emotion, my happiness slowly vanished and I was left confused and sad. The next morning, still nothing was said and I could only wonder about what they were thinking: would the goats be mine or theirs? I did not understand. A few weeks later my father came home, and I forgot all about greeting him as I took his hand and dragged him over to the goats.

'You've got yourself some beautiful goats. That's good! You have to take good care of them because they are still very small.' I told him that I would because of my love for them. And he left me full of happiness, with the confidence that now they belonged to me. But I was proved to be wrong. Maybe I misunderstood his words, but as you read you can be the judge. As time passed my goats delivered and I found myself with twelve kids.

It was holiday, and the whole family gathered at the farm. The day had come for me to be baptised, so I woke up early in the morning, and while dressing up I heard my father through the window telling Byoma to slaughter two goats, and my eyes got bigger when I watched my goats being forced by my father himself, busy pulling them by the rope to take them under the tree where the workers used to slaughter. I knew that I no power had to stop him, and I began crying when Byoma began tying their legs. I was still watching with eyes full of tears, when my grandmother grabbed my hand and we headed to the church, where my mother and father in Christ to be were waiting. We sat there for a while, waiting for Father Robert to arrive, and I felt devastated by the sweet music which only increased my sadness. I saw everybody rise from their chairs as Father Robert approached the altar. The next thing I noticed was my new name being called, and I got a gentle push from my grandmother before I reluctantly went up to the altar. As I came back my mother in Christ gave me a hug, asking me why I was sad, but I am pretty sure that I left that church without saying a word.

As soon as I had gone back to my chair I sneaked out and left the rest to finish the ceremony, with the intention never to go back home. Then I went to the banana plantation to my hiding place with a bunch of bananas, and I thanked myself for not going back, because I knew that if I had done so I would have had to eat of my friends. I wanted to punish my father and Byoma by drinking the poisonous milk so that I too would spin around and disappear as the cat did, but I found the thought a bit scary, so I continued on by thinking what might happen to them if I disappeared. Would the police come and take them? I wished they would, but I still couldn't get around the poisonous milk which finally made me quit my plan and think about home. On my way home I was singing to a flock of birds which were flying around above my head, but just before I was there I stopped by a big tree for a while, thinking about what lie could save me from the beatings. But I couldn't find one, so instead I decided to walk into the house with an angry face. My father, mother and my grandmother were in the living-room. They all turned and looked at me. My father stood up and shook his head, and then he walked towards me. With a firm grip he began pulling my ears, while saying that they had been looking for me everywhere, and soon we were outside.

While beating me, I saw Grandmother and my mother looking from the window. It made me hold back the tears, so that they came to think that I was not in much pain, but what I didn't realise was that my silence had made my father beat me harder. When he had finished I ran behind the house to the garden where I let the tears go.

Later I woke up, and it was pitch black. At first I didn't know where I was until I realised that I was getting cold of the night air. I tried to listen carefully through the night-birds singing, but I could hear nothing else in the lonely darkness, apart from the frogs and the noise of hyenas. I became frightened, and yet it was an even worse thought to go and knock on the door. I thought about what to do, and when there were no other options I decided to sleep with the goats. The smell didn't matter at all, I was more concerned of the goats running on top of me but, when I got in, most of them were calm in their sleep. The next morning, I discovered that my dress carried blood stains and one of my fingers was broken. I went and sat in a corner by the house, folded my arms against the early morning cold, and waited for them to awake. I listened very carefully to my pain, but found only anger. I cried again, wishing to have a shoulder to cry on, but I found only the wind and wished to be free like it.

My father came outside, and when I looked at his face I

wished a big stone would drop down to his head. I saw the guilt in his eyes when he looked at me before lowering his head like an innocent thief.

'Father, my finger is broken,' I said. Without a word, he walked down to the same tree where my goats were slaughtered and looked up at the sky, and after a while he walked back past me and went inside.

A minute after he returned with a knife and a piece of wood, straight he went and sat on a stone and began cutting the wood into small pieces. I wondered what the wooden pieces were for, but I only hoped not to be roasted on them. After he had finished, he took me inside and washed my injured hand, but when he began tying the sticks around the broken finger, I felt pain but I didn't want to show him, so I coughed instead, and as he moved, the smelling air escaped him, 'Can he also fart?' I thought, because I had never heard any sound like that before from the older ones. 'You're full of my goats. Maybe that's why you fart' I thought with sadness growing inside me, and promised to revenge my friends when I grew up. This feeling only grew stronger as I was forced at the end to eat of my friends, one by one.

I was becoming desperate, as I could no longer sleep because of the voices of my goats in my memory. To revenge this I thought of giving all of my father's cows the poison, but I imagined the mess that the cows would leave behind after having spun around, so I had to get rid of that thought.

From Far-off Dreams

I was sitting under a tree enjoying the coolness of fresh wind, and when I turned my eyes down the road, I saw a young man coming towards me at a slow pace. I had a strange feeling as he looked at me with gentle eyes that made me feel completely safe in his presence as he came towards me. I hardly noticed when he was close enough to actually touch me, asking me of how I was. I told him I was fine and kept looking straight in his eyes. He asked me whether my father was in. I nearly said to him that I had no such person, but I did not know the man so I kept it to myself. I told him to wait and that I would call for him. But as I started walking, the man yelled at me to come back, he asked my name, and asked me whether my grandmother lived with us.

'Yes, she is here at the moment, but she has her own house,' I replied. His expression changed and I sensed a brief glint of hidden eagerness in his eyes, as he asked me politely if I could call my father.

My father said: 'Go tell him to come here'. The boy came with me as I bid, and when we reached the doorstep, my father was standing inside with each of his hands resting against the door frame with lowered eyes as he seemingly recognised the man. He told the man not to enter the house, and to wait outside. The way my father welcomed the man made me want to hear more, so I went to a hiding place not far from them. I heard my father ask the man what he wanted in his home, and the boy began to weep, telling him he had nowhere else to go.

'You know I told you never to come near my home! What do you want from me?'

'You are the only brother I have!' the boy replied.

When I heard the word brother, I knew that this man was my uncle, so I listened intensely without missing a word. My father gave my uncle a few minutes to act on his threat, and his brother answered, 'Where do you want me to go? Please help me.'

I could feel my uncle's helplessness, feeling helpless myself. What amazed me most was the look on my mother and my grandmother as my father spoke to my uncle.

My father kept getting colder towards my uncle, who at

the end kneeled down and begged him, and I started to cry in silence. A few minutes later, I saw my uncle leave. I had to know the truth behind it all so I hurried to catch up on him. 'Uncle!' I shouted at him.

He stopped and asked me if my father wanted him back.

'No,' I said, 'He don't even know that I'm here.'

'What are you here for then?' he asked, and I told him that I wanted to help if I could, but he just smiled.

I asked his name, and he told that he was called Nyindo, meaning nose, and that's when I realised his clumsy nose. We sat down and I asked him why my father had chased him away, but he said that he didn't know.

'You're just a kid, you wouldn't understand,' he added with a gentle voice.

I told him that I was sure I would understand and when I looked into his eyes I realised that he was not ready to tell me anything. So I asked him if he wanted to hear my story. He agreed, moving a little closer to me.

'You know, you are not the only one my father doesn't like, he hates me too.' I began telling him how I was treated, but when my tears stopped me from speaking, he reached out his hands and dried them away. Then he told me a little about himself and a story about my family. He told me that my grandfather divorced my grandmother and chased away my father, forbidding him ever to come back. At the age of fourteen my father went to live with a chief not far from his father's home. My father was allowed to continue his studies, in exchange for his work at the chief's farm. My grandfather remarried and had a son, whom he named Nyindo. A few years later my grandfather became sick and before he died he left all his riches to his wife and son, but nothing was left to my father. My uncle was too young to manage the documents so they were left in his mother's care.

I asked him why he came begging at my father's if he

already had inherited these riches. He said that it was because my father took everything. 'When my father died, my brother came to the funeral. He managed to get the documents from his stepmother.'

I remained very quiet now as he talked, because I figured that he had forgotten who he was telling this to. After my father had gained everything, he revealed his true colours by chasing my very uncle Nyindo away, and Nyindo's mother too.

After he finished he began to cry. We sat in silence as I tried find a way to help. Suddenly I remembered my mother in Christ and her husband, who I knew would understand. I was sure that she was aware of how I was treated by my family, so I told my Nyindo that I was going to take him to my mother in Christ. He turned and looked at me with a distant hope in his eyes, and when he followed me up the hill I pointed out the house. I saw his tears vanish like a forgotten dream as he hurried to hug me with a smile. While walking I talked about my mother back home, but when I mentioned the word 'mother' for the second time, he interrupted by saying: 'She's not your mother,' but I found it hard to believe, and I thought that he only said this because of some hate that he had for them.

My mother in Christ was seated in her garden with one of her sons, while sewing a tablecloth, and I was moved by her warm smile as she hurried to welcome us. We were offered milk in her beautiful glasses with flowers decorated on them. I felt excited about drinking from them, even though we had the same at home, because there I was always drinking from plastic cups. I did all the talking, while my uncle prayed for a good reply, I supposed. I asked her if it was possible for my uncle to sleep at her place for a few days, and she agreed while condemning my father. When I turned my eyes towards him, ready to share a smile of triumph, I became shocked for the second time to see him cry. I did not understand, because this time we were on the winning side. Time was running out for me, so I had to say goodbye, though it was hard, I had to hold my heart for a moment, pretending that nothing was happening. I knew somehow that I would never see him again, because I was sure that the hate he had observed from his brother's eyes made him never to return. I left with my broken heart and tears dropping from my eyes like gentle rain.

When I got home, my mother was busy putting food on the table, and my father was home, which meant my mother would give me more food than I could eat, and that night it was a perfect match because I could not eat. I looked at the food, trying to find the appetite but failed. Every time I looked at them I felt something squeezing me inside. I looked at my father with a fearful heart, because of what he had done to my uncle, as I thought of the possibilities that he one day might chase me away too.

My fear became crazy and out of control. I ran outside and began throwing up, followed by my father. There he stood waiting until I had finished, took me by my hand and threw me into the hallway. He began asking me of what I had ate. I heard my mother's voice in the background, complaining that no matter how much food she gave me still I ate things I wasn't supposed to, like mango, oranges and bananas. She threatened to leave my father because of me, and demanded him to do something about my behaviour. My father's face became like the bull's that I used to watch fight among our cows. I closed my eyes and let him please his wife. When he pushed me up against the wall I thought of telling him that I was angered by my uncle's tears, but I shut my mouth before the words came out. Later that night I went to my bed in the silence of my dark room. All I could feel were the tears running into my mouth while thinking about my uncle's words, and slowly I was beginning to believe.

When I woke up the next morning, I realised that I had been beaten badly. My body hurt and I had dried blood on my nose and mouth. I did not change my bloody clothes because I wanted to make my father feel sorry for me. I went outside, washed my face with cold water and started to sweep the ground in front of our house. The sun rose, bringing hot temperatures and I was getting dizzy, but I wanted to try and finish what I had started. I was carried away by many thoughts about my uncle and I stopped working when I saw him being strangled by hungry lions. When I woke up, I was lying under the tree, in front of the house, covered by a wet blanket. I had no idea how I had come to be there, but anyway I continued to lie there, hoping that maybe my father would come and check on me, but he never came, and I realised yet again that he didn't care. I threw the blanket aside and sat there for a minute or two, thinking of where I could go and get something to eat. I told my mother that I was going to check on the calves, but she didn't respond, so I went away. Then I headed for the banana plantation and a search began for ripe bananas. As I walked between the palm trees suddenly I heard the sound of footsteps on dried leaves, but ignored it as I spotted a bunch of ripe bananas. I tried very hard not to make any noise and finally I managed to get it down. I began eating until the sound of footsteps became more disturbing, then I gathered as many bananas as could fit in my dress. When I stood up ready to leave, I saw my father talking with three men, and it appeared as if they were walking in my direction. I ran as fast as I could, zigzagging between the palm trees, as a little rabbit sharply followed by my father and his men, but luckily I managed to escape them without losing any of my bananas. The very same day at the dinner table I looked down at my plate as I listened to my father tell his wife what had happened at the banana plantation. And I nearly busted when I heard my mother say: 'Maybe it was dogs!'

I lacked to dry your tears my uncle, when I watched them run like the mountain streams. I know that wherever you are, the love and care that I tried to give you will always lie in your heart. I see you from far-off dreams with the eyes of my heart. I believe you can also remember me with your open heart, even though I can never know where your soul lies. My heart and my eyes lament on your sadness. My soul is with you and your words are in my mind. The road of his death and the soul is gone.

C.K.

My father was fully aware of suffering, but was too caught up in his own life and the centre he desperately wanted to play in it.

C.K.

Holding on to the Rope

The sisters of my mother came often to visit. She always discussed things with them while she would stare at me. It hurt me, because I thought it was her silent way of telling me what a horrible child I was. I could not understand what she meant and her words greatly affected me.

I was troubled by the evil thoughts that formed in my head because of their rejection. I found no place for me in their hearts. The thoughts reached a climax within me, and I had to find a way to react before I exploded inside. I was getting desperate, finding no one who could give me what I wanted. There were so many things missing in my life that I could no longer comprehend There was nothing more I wanted on this earth than to be free, but where could it be found, the kind of life I wanted? My mother pulled and I pulled, but it never got anywhere. With firm conviction I vowed to myself never to give up and let her take away my soul. I would go on pulling and pulling until my hands bled, for I was certain that the rope would break someday, I often convinced myself, trying to make myself stronger. I carried so much, looking around for a sister on whom I could unload the things inside me, but found no one.

I got to the point where I no longer cared how I was treated at home. I cared for nothing on earth, save to get out of my present condition. That very evening just after the cows had been milked, my mother's mother Jane came and told my mother that she had no one to help her clean where the cows lived. And that she could not make her children clean, because she feared that they would be late for school. My mother told Jane that she would send me to her in the morning. A week passed without me realising what was happening to my feet. I was always too tired to be able to wash myself, and when I finally did, I found my feet in a bad shape, because of the cow's urine had corroded itself into my skin. I tried to do everything I could to take away the black spots, I even used a stone, but when I started to bleed I gave it a miss. Now the hate for my mother's sisters and brother was boiling, and I asked myself many times why I had to work for them.

One Saturday afternoon, my mother gave me a basketful of bananas which she told me to take to her mother's. When I arrived the girls checked the bananas and told me that I seemed to have ate some. I was greatly affected by this, so I swore at them, while calling them poor beings that only came to beg, before I ended up by demanding them to stop eating my father's food. A split second after I had finished, the two girls started chasing me around, while shouting at me, as I tried to run as fast as I could, still swearing at them. I told them that if my father had not helped them they would be dead by now. I just heard their outcry of surprised anger and then I headed for home. My mother was not home and I took a deep breath thinking that now I would get a little time by myself, but when I looked behind me I saw the two tired cows in a slow jog, still after me. Quickly I ran into the kitchen, took a bunch of bananas and hid under my father's bed, as I expected them to wait like hunting dogs outside the door. I started eating my favourite food until I could eat no more, and my stomach had become so big that I couldn't manage to get out from beneath the bed. I woke up all of a sudden to the voice of my father calling me, but at first I thought that I was dreaming, because he was supposed to be at the town house. Then I managed to sneak out from the bed pretending that I had just walked inside. My father and I greeted each other and then I went outside, but I thought a lot about the banana peels and wished no one would find them. The following day, my mother cleaned the house herself for a change and all the peels were revealed. To my humiliation I was the only suspect, because of my brothers and sisters who were at our grandmother's. My father took my hand and went straight to the rubble of peels that my mother had left in front of their bed, but I was surprised to see how many there were and for a moment I suspected her to have added some. We stood there for a while in silence before he looked at me with a surprised laugh and shook his head. Then he demanded that I told him who had ate the banana, but promised not to beat me. I looked up at his face and said: 'It's the people who live in the bush, who have hair all over.'

'Did you see them?' he asked, while laughing. Actually he laughed so much that his eyes began to roll and with wet eyes he let me know that he did not believe me. I told him that the girls had been chasing me so hard, that they succeeded in preventing me from coming home; I hid in the bush and when I finally returned I was very hungry but there was nobody home. My father seemed to have something to say but instead he left me, and I heard him from the living-room telling his wife that she should tell her mother Jane to leave his farm. I watched my mother almost collapsing, suddenly weak and limp, but then her eyebrows tightened a little as she approached him with a trying smile as she tried to persuade my father to change his mind, but he would not listen. I turned and looked at my mother with a visible smile, but my father's anger, which was getting out of control, made me hurry to my bedside. I heard her scream from outside, ran to the living-room and listened. Then I walked to the door and began observing them as they fought, and I learned that my mother was losing, because she was the one on the ground. Her scream somehow made me scared, so I covered my ears, but still I wished the beatings to carry on. My father left her in bed where she stayed until the following morning. In the evening my father returned, while I was falling happily asleep with an empty stomach. When I woke up my father had already gone back to the town house, and as I came to the living-room, my mother was holding a wet piece of cloth to her face. I went and sat outside watching the birds flying beneath the rising sun, and a while later I went down to where Byoma was busy tying a couple of goats. After being sure that he was occupied I left him there and sneaked to where he had left his grasshoppers to dry. To make sure that he wouldn't know that I had eaten them, I started picking them to make it look like a hen, and when my work was done, I gathered a nice handful which I hid at another place.

In the evening when I came back from fetching water I was hungry, and I discovered some food in a pot. When I was about to put in my hand I remembered that I always had to ask permission, so I stood there for a while doing nothing with my eyes on the pot. My mouth together with my stomach agreed not to wait, but my bums said wait. When I could not know which part of my body to listen to, I decided to sneak my hands in the pot, but even before the first bite, my mother appeared through the door. Then she squashed the food out of my hand and smashed it in my face. Hurt and angry I ran outside, picked up a stone and started beating the ground, but still I wasn't satisfied. Now she had hurt me enough, so I told myself that I would not give up before I found a way to punish her.

When I was searching for the grasshoppers from the day before, I remembered the hen which loved grasshoppers.

I forgot everything about my search, and ran to the hen run and began gathering their droppings. As always, she told me to make her tea, so I dried my gatherings on the fire, as I kept an eye on the door. I took a stone and ground it nicely, before mixing it with a speck of tea, because I had heard one time that if people ate chicken shit they would lose their teeth. That day I enjoyed watching her drink, and the more she drank the more my excitement grew, but I became disappointed when she didn't lose any teeth at all.

The next day when cleaning the house, I found a whole bunch of medicine bottles in a box. I took them all out to look for a good one that I could try on her, but as I was about to make a choice, I heard her call my name and in panic, trying to put the medicine back, I poured some on my dress, and it stank like rotten meat. When I was close enough she raised her nose and, before she could ask, I told her that I tried to pull out the box and the medicine spilled on me. She screamed at me that she had told me never to go near the medicine, but her screaming didn't prevent me from trying again.

Later that day she went to check on her children at my grandmother's, and immediately I went back to the medicine box. I finally found what we used to give the calves. It had no smell, so I thought it wasn't too dangerous, even though I didn't know what it would do to her. Now I had to figure out how to give it to her. I couldn't put it in tea because she put in the milk herself. Each morning we drank soft porridge mixed with milk, and a perfect idea formed as I thought of this. She returned home that evening and we ate. I did my daily duties such as bringing her water in a basin, but inside of me I laughed at what I would do to her.

The morning came with the hot African sun and its blue, blue sky. I was standing by the door like a guard dog as I waited for the order and began as soon as possible. When the porridge was ready I took some aside in two cups for me, went outside to fetch my little bottle of medicine, and began mixing it together with her porridge in the pot. After I was done I went to her bedroom and informed her that breakfast was ready. I left her in the living-room as she was about to drink her porridge, and went outside to drink mine. When I finished I started to clean up the dishes, while one of my eyes was looking at the doorway. Two hours went by without any signs, but just as I was thinking of what more I could do, I spotted her running as fast as she could to the toilet. I was the happiest kid in all the countryside! But after a while, when I lost count of her toilet-visits I became frightened and thought of telling her, but my fear of her putting me to death stopped me from saying a word. She was now becoming like a wet rat, and I began shivering as the sweat ran across her face. I heard her tell me in the most calm voice ever that I should call her a doctor, and I ran to his home as fast as I could. On my way back, I decided to tell the doctor every-thing I had done. He asked me what kind of medicine I had given her, and I told him it was the medicine that was given to the calves, when having a hard stomach. After having begged him not to let her know, the doctor looked at me with puzzled eyes and smiled, while shaking his head. 'What made you do that to her?' he asked, and I began telling everything about my family, as I saw his eyes become bigger and bigger. He looked at me for a while before going back inside, and I was left behind with a fearful heart. I folded my arms and began walking round the house, hoping to get rid of my increasing fear. I was beginning to hate myself for what I had done as I realised a possible punishment, and while busy thinking of my next lie the doctor came back and said: 'You should never do that again, do you hear me!'

'Yes,' I replied in a small frightened voice. 'Will she die?' I continued.

'No,' he replied. 'Did you want her to die?' he continued after a short pause, but this time I lied to him as I wasn't sure what I wanted apart from calming him down. Before leaving, he guaranteed me that she would live and everything would be all right. When I couldn't see him any more, I still began crying but believe me I had no idea why I did so.

At the start my mother appeared too good to be true. Good sincerity and intentions. But later I observed her empty promises. I was deceived, she was thirsty for my blood, but death was nothing, as compared to what plans she had for me. Because, it seemed to me, as if I was the only one standing in her way.

C. K.

The Truth about Mother

Later in that year, my father came to the farm, and in the morning he sent me to the men who slaughtered cows. On my way I met with one of the men, and he was happy to hear the good news. I accompanied him to fetch the other man, being asked the whole way of how many cows there were to be slaughtered. The man was so excited that I expected him to drool. I was not surprised by his behaviour because I had been told that other people were not like us, and that they loved meat more than us.

In an hour's time I returned with the two men, and my father was standing outside. Immediately he took over and showed them the cow, but I was afraid to watch animals being killed, so I busied myself with clearing the leaves from the garden. By the time I was told to take the dishes for the meat, the men had already finished. It didn't take them much time before they had a fire, and I stood there impressed, watching the men going wild: one was busy boiling the intestines, while the other struggled with the cow's head, but it didn't take a minute before he had the cow's tongue in his hands, busy looking at it, and it seemed to me that he was about to it raw.

A few hours later the guests arrived. One of the four men was very peculiar, with a skin the colour of light. I watched the man very closely, very sure that I had never seen that kind of person before. I tried to get very close to him to see if it was the cause of a fire burn that made him look so different from us. I loved the way he looked with his big and shiny dark-brown eyes and tall body with big ears and with a moustache under his big nose. I wanted to reach out and touch him, thinking that if I pinched his skin, it would come off in my hands, but because of my father, I did not. Still he left such an impression on my mind to leave me wondering to this day. His name has forever escaped me, maybe because of an ordinary name of our world that he carried so far away from where his soul belonged. I imagined this other world, with no beatings, a world, which would not tell me how and when to eat. If I knew God then, I would have thanked him because I would overcome my enemy! Indeed I would be free, even though it would take me a long time to see the chains fall off from my body, and exclaim in delight: I am free!

When I thought of this other world my tears began to drop like a running stream, and my head became too heavy for me to carry, so I went and sat near our big tree, keeping my eyes on the visitors enjoying themselves. In the evening the guests left, leaving me with a lot to clean, but as I got busy, Father came and stood there for a while. Then he told me that he would take me to the town house the following day, and with a smile he handed me a present. I felt utter joy, and my headache was suddenly forgotten. I stood there smiling, not knowing what to do, and I was relieved when my mother took him away. I went to bed that evening with a clear mind, and my dreams were light and happy.

The next morning, as we arrived at the town house, three girls and a boy were staring at me, and I was told by my father that they were my sisters and my brother. I stared back at them, and noticed their fine clothes that made them look weak and spoiled, and I was sure when we greeted, that I hated them. They were curious, and asked me of how our 'stepmother' treated me, but I did not know that word, so I just looked back at their faces waiting for an explanation, 'Mutesi,' they replied.

'You mean our mother?' I asked.

'No!' they protested, 'she is not our mother!'

'Then where is our mother?' I asked.

They themselves had no idea of where she was, adding: 'But all we know is that, that woman is not our mother.'

I began telling them of how badly she treated me. They looked sad, and I asked them of how they were: 'Does she mistreat you whenever she comes here?' and they replied no. I went and sat alone for a moment, to think things over. I took myself back to the times of my mother's mistreating, and still I found my heart too weak just to accept the fact that she was not my real mother, but despite my disbelief, I silently decided to change her name from mother to 'stepmother'.

After two days yet another one of my sisters arrived at the house, and I was confused of how to address her. Annette was our oldest sister, but from another mother. I accepted her as I did everyone else. Her presence bothered two of my sisters apart from Grace. Grace was a quiet girl with a determined heart which still would make her fight to death if anything wrong crossed her way, and I often created fights between her and Margie, who always wanted us to live under her commands. One day I heard my sisters gossip about Annette, and I couldn't find their reason for this. All I could do was to watch Annette cry every day without being able to help, and I was relieved whenever Marie, our nanny, comforted her. The new surroundings suited me fine. I got along with my brother and Marie showed me that not all women were bad. My sisters went back to the boarding school, and I started my first year at the same school as my brother Richard. He, on the other hand, gave me a lot of trouble at school by introducing me as Baby, and everybody seemed to love that name except for me. Almost every single day I achieved new bruises as I fought somebody who had been calling me that name.

One Friday my father went to his wife at the farm for the weekend, leaving my brother and me in Marie's care. But as the evening came, she went out with her friends without returning. As we reached noon the following day and she still hadn't returned, we began to realise the tremendous freedom we had gained without adults around. Behind the town house my father had a little piece of land with green bananas (matoke) and other kinds. We took as many banana leaves as we could carry to the market and sold them. When we got the money we went to a stand and bought some tasty sweet bananas and ate them while watching the busy crowd of people, with all their different kinds of more or less visible purposes. As we had eaten them we went on to the next stand and bought yet another couple of bananas. We went on like that for a long time, wild with our freedom to do whatever we wanted, so we ate and ate until I suddenly felt a strange sensation in my stomach. We had eaten our last money up, when the noise in my stomach began, I spun around and looked at the woman who had been selling us the banana to see if she heard the noise. Immediately I began pulling my brother towards the nearest exit, as he struggled to get the last bananas into his pockets. In a voice of panic, I asked him if he knew any toilets nearby, but he could only laugh. I began to run towards the only toilet I knew in the area, but I was too late. Before I reached my empty school, I had left a trail of embarrassment and I gave up my race, walking to make sure that no more would leave my body. Still I continued towards our school while my brother shouted so anybody could hear it, that I should walk straight so that he was sure not to step in the wrong place. I left the toilet with a mix of relief and disappointment when my brother had refused to lend me his shirt. On our way home my brother walked in the street while I had to sneak with my bare bums through the bush. Marie was relieved when she saw us, and she hurried to cover my bums. In the evening a man came to the house together with a five-litre can of home-made brew. I met them sitting on the veranda drinking while joking and laughing. I stood there smiling at them and Marie asked me to call my brother, as I was about to turn back to the house. The man slipped her some money and we were told to take it and keep quiet about the man. It had proved to be a good day after all, I thought to myself with a smile on my lips, as my brother and I ran to buy sweets and fat cakes. In our way back, my brother eyed our neighbour's son and he told me to pick a fight with him, and if I would be losing he would take over. As Muhammad was about to greet us, I demanded a fight, but Muhammad told me that he would not fight me because he feared to break my bones. I told him that he was short and ugly like his 'hair-dresser-father' and I was annoyed to see that he was not provoked by my words, so I pulled some hair off his head and the fight began. The fight was not as I expected, he hurt me too much and I began looking towards my brother who was too entertained to remember his promise. I broke off from the fight in a fast sprint while shouting at my brother and crying at my defeat.

The following day my father and his wife arrived, together with my stepsisters and brothers. Now she had brought a little baby boy, which I had to take care of every day after school. I found myself with no time to play or fight, and I was so angry that I almost threw the baby in the privy, but I knew that if I did so I would never get to play again. Instead I started finding other ways to escape the baby-sitting. One day I was sitting in front of the house with the baby in my arms while watching all the others play. They, had been calling me several times to come and join, so I became angry and pinched the baby on the thumb. He cried non-stop and it made me afraid that his mother might see the bruise. I waited for my stepmother to come and get her baby, she didn't, but still I thought that if I kept on making him scream like that, his mother would come and relieve me. This time I had to pinch him on the back so that he wouldn't be able to show his reason for crying. Finally, after a few more pinches my plan worked: she came running and grabbed the baby. But again she proved to be too mean for me to see her next step, and she gave me a new job of washing the baby's nappies. I had become the perfect joke of the neighbourhood, but as their laughs increased, my anger increased with it. I hated all of them and every time I had the opportunity I fought. There was one kid that I left alone, though, my friend Sofia, who never made jokes about me. One day when I found shit in the nappies, I suddenly noticed that it looked like scrambled eggs, so I went inside the house and added a little bit of salt and gave it to my stepbrothers, Ray and Emanuel. I was thrilled when they asked for more, but I told them to wait until tomorrow. Still, I hoped so much for my sisters to return so they could take over my duties. A week or two passed before all of them returned from their boarding school, and I looked forward with excitement to have more time off. Now the town house had become crowded, and somehow my stepmother was disturbed by this. She was always sick, spending most of her time in bed, and when she didn't, she would manipulate my father to beat my sisters. This could have been the reason why Annette and Grace became good friends, and they spent most of the time together.

It was a Saturday morning, as we woke up, Annette and my middle sister Grace were gone. Later that day my father went and searched for them, but he never got them back, and their disappearance made me hope more than ever for my father to clear his eyes of his blindness, and see what my stepmother really was.

Impossible Fight against Unwanted Eyes

Now that my stepmother's kids had started school too, each with two pairs of shoes, I found myself with not even a nice-looking dress. I asked her to buy me one, but she told me to ask my father. In the evening, I went to the living-room where he was sitting with a pipe in his hands, and when he looked at me I noticed an unusual smile, which strengthened me, so I told him of my wishes. His smile didn't fail, as he told me that the following day he would remember to buy me a beautiful dress. I hardly slept that night lying in my bed with butterflies in my stomach, trying to figure out what the dress would look like. The following day went by, pretty much as the night had done, until I spotted Father returning from work. I hurried to greet him, and managed to take the parcel and his briefcase. I went to the living-room where I remained standing, still with the parcel in my hands until Father came to me. Then he told me to open it, and to my disappointment it was a black dress with two white stripes on the chest but it wasn't the stripes that concerned me, but a very low-cut neck and back. I couldn't dare to tell him of my disappointment, as I feared that my old father would resurrect to serve me a new round of beatings. Quickly I ran outside to hide and began crying, as I wished the dress off my body. My sister Margie followed and told me that I looked beautiful in it, and that it was the latest fashion, but what she never realised was that I wasn't concerned of the dress being fashion; the fact was that I almost felt naked. I am pretty sure that dress will never leave my mind because I hated it so much. Even today, I still dream of it, in my impossible fight to cover myself against unwanted eyes.

I went to school with that long dress and bare feet, while my stepsister and brother had everything they desired. Fortunately the schooldays went by without much alarm apart from my own worry. On my way home I was walking in a bad mood and a lowered head trying to avoid the stones picking my feet, while searching for a lie that would make Father buy me a pair of shoes, but I figured that the sharpness of stones would not do as a good reason. Before I could reach home I met Sofia who was attending Newton nursery school. As we chatted I told her of my burning wish. She advised me to tell Father that the school refused to see me again without shoes. I smiled knowing that now he would buy them. I got what I wanted, but I never got what my stepsister and brother had, but soon I was relieved from my worries when I heard that our school had plans for us to wear a school uniform and I looked forward to it. Whenever the break came I went to hide down in the woods, until it was over, because I felt bad watching my stepsister and brother buy whatever they desired. If I stayed as I had done, before looking at them waiting to get whatever they couldn't finish, they would just look the other way, as if I had my own treats, and they had shared nothing with me. But I couldn't find any reason of hating them, because I was certain that their reasons were dictated by their mother who tried to feed their hearts with greed. I had come to think that my worries would have no end, as I still had to be bothered by my friends at school, because of the way I was dressed. My stepbrother and sister had more than three uniforms to change between while I had one that had to last through the whole week. My fellow students didn't know that we had different mothers, and I felt embarrassed, even afraid of what might happen if I answered them, so I just looked down or walked away. I do not remember what made me break the silence. Maybe I was just sick and tired of the same question, and I didn't have a chance to know what this would lead to, that the act of sympathy would soon suffer a terrible accident with the terror of mistrust.

The following day when I returned to school I found one of my friends waiting with a pair of shoes. She told me to try them on, and I was thrilled, as my feet matched the welcoming shoes. I looked at her face with shyness, not knowing whether to thank her or not. Despite of my happiness, I still felt like removing them and put my old shoes back on, but the girl refused to let me, and I wouldn't want her to take them back. When I got back home, my stepmother looked at me with frightening eyes, while asking me of whom I had stolen the shoes from. With sorry eyes I told her that I did not steal them: 'My friend have given them to me.'

She replied with an angry voice: 'You're now begging from people as if you had no father.' She then told me that she would tell my father.

During supper, everyone but me seemed to be enjoying their meal. I just sat there with the food which had decided to freeze in my hand, with my eyes looking at Stepmother's. After she had told him, my father turned like a dog disturbed by the flies.

'What?' my father roared. He stood up, staring at me, before ordering me to bring both pairs. With the shoes in his hands he told me to follow him, and when we reached the sanitation he grabbed my hand and said: 'Look!' as he threw them in. I went to bed sad, with dried eyes, and laid myself down, as I thought about my sisters who had gone back to boarding school.

The morning came with showering rains, but even though, I could not wait one minute to leave for school, so I ran through the rain protected by a banana leaf. As I began telling my friends about last night my tears started tumbling from my eyes, and it became worse as they felt sorry for me. One of the girls, whom most of us took as our team leader suggested that they should tell their parents about this. The following day, in the evening after the class, two of my friends' parents were standing by a car on the school compound waiting for me. One of the fathers reached his hand out and greeted me and my face went limp when he told me that they would try to reason with mine. When I realised that we were about to reach home, I became so afraid that no matter how much I tried to squeeze my legs together I had to let the water go free. My father was stand- ing in the garden with his hands in his pockets. When I got out of the car I was confused on which side I should stand, so I froze for a while looking in my father's eyes to make the decision, so I went and stood by his side. The men greeted him before telling him that I was a friend to their daughters and that I had got the shoes from them. My father seemed not to be interested and I could tell what he was about to say just by looking at his face, 'Go away all of you', escaped his mouth. The men I had thought to fight for me left without any further notice. My father turned as if he was a hungry lion, but I seemed too big for him to swallow. After spitting me out, he left me still on the ground and went into the house. That very same evening, I overheard that my step-mother was going back to the farm. I became excited and my sadness disappeared.

(I might have mixed the years, and the parents, in this first part, and for that I ask my readers to understand, as I was very young then.)

PART TWO
The Purge of the Tutsis

Hunted

In 1982, the Ugandan Government led by President Milton Obote was under siege, and he was more than sure that the rebels who were known as the National Resistance Army (NRA) were being supported by the Tutsis and the people of western Uganda. When his belief became stronger, he made an announcement across the country that his government urged the population to chase out the Tutsis from Uganda. I guess that he believed that the only solution to end the rebels' attacks would be by sending the Tutsis back to Rwanda. In fact, what he didn't realise was that he himself was the sole problem to the country, and I am not sure if he actually was trying to find a solution to the problem, because he was power-thirsty just like any other African statesman, only being concerned about their own wellbeing, always having problems with their pockets, which still seem to carry too many holes. Obote never realised that by sending back Tutsis to the country which once butchered them was not the best way to keep him in power. It was an unwise way to make his dream come true. Now his chances of being able to die happily on his throne faded, as he only gained more resistance from a stronger NRA. Obote was a heavy drinker, who all the time had whisky on his mind, and the bottle was rarely missing in his hand. People listened to him anyway and the government troops and civilians started looting everything that the Tutsis owned. The government of Obote watched in silence as the houses of Tutsis were being brought to the ground, their cows slaughtered and women raped while the children cried in desperation, without anybody seeming to notice what the man was committing.

Many children were displaced as their parents went back to Rwanda while others wandered up and down the streets of Uganda trying to find which way to take as the chiefs raped the girls with the promise of a safe passage out of the country. The Tutsis looked at where Obote was sending them, and they saw death, but I do not suppose that death itself worried them most, the terror lay in which way they would die. As a result, thousands tried to find a way in which to join the NRA. Officially the reasons for Obote's action were all in the name of peace and stability in the region. Obote's neighbours did not object to his brutality, which might have been due to the fact that many other Africans leaders had used similar tactics on a smaller scale and would not have been able to condemn him without raising serious questions about their own regimes. All that they did was to carry on in their own big chairs, while feeding their stomachs. The Tutsis suffered just like the Indian suffered in the hands of Idi Amin.

My family also was of Tutsis origin, and that was the beginning of my family's endless pain.

I watched what was happening to the other Tutsis families and became happy, because I knew that it would, as well, happen to my father and his wife, thinking that the revenge would be on my side. My happiness could not help me from forgetting one incident though, and it can still scare me today. The abuse that I got from the man whom I knew only as the chief, and who threatened to kill me if ever I told about it. It still became harder for me every day to have to think about that evening, with that old man dragging me into a deserted golf field to the half bombed building. My hate towards my family made me realise that there would be similar incidents still to come, as I knew that I couldn't trust telling them of any trouble that I might face. Every day through those times it felt as if somebody else kept on reminding me against my will, to think about in which way my soul would be torn next, and next, until my final ending.

When my father heard that the government had decided to chase the Tutsis away from Uganda, he went to the farm to try and save what he could. On his way he happened to meet one of his workers, who himself was a Tutsis. The man warned him against going to the farm. I was in the garden playing with my friend Sofia, when I turned my eyes up the road and saw my father with a bag in his hands followed by the worker. It made me realise that things on our farm were getting worse, and I was aware of the fact that many of our neighbours didn't like my father. My father had a big land, with a couple of hills and it had lovely sights with its beautiful streams of water. He was a lawyer, so it seemed perfectly appropriate for him to oppress his neighbours by taking pieces of their land by force. Time had come when they used it against him, and now there was no deference between them and my father. They as well acted like hungry lions, and even those that he once helped turned against him, as they were the first to slaughter the cows, and the goats. They looted the households, while the others went down to the field and slashed the banana plants down to the ground while they shouted: 'The Tutsis must never return or they will all face death.' The men's hearts were like those of my own family. They had no sympathy with any living thing, they took the cows in their crying voices which had newborn calves. The calves died of hunger because they were still sucking from their mothers. The stolen cows which tried to return to where they belonged were slaughtered, together with those which only wanted to return for the sake of their little ones.

They searched for my father on his lands and in the house, and when they did not find him, they made sure that the two houses were destroyed to the ground. My father's pride was taken away, and now his bitterness had no end. The neighbours shared our beautiful land, but most of all I was concerned about the goats, and as the worker told the story, I was waiting in vain to hear him mention that my grandmother and stepmother had lost their arms or legs. After the worker had finished telling of what had happened, my father seemed too confused to know where to begin and where to end. I saw him going round the house many times with one hand in his pocket, the other on his head, with eyes to the ground. I observed him going back inside where he then sat himself on the sofa and began to cry. I watched my father from the window, smashing each and everything that was in the living-room as he talked to himself.

When a few days had passed, my sisters returned from the boarding school, and were taken to a home of my father's friends, while my brother and I went with him to the new ranch. We started our journey, and tears of anger could be seen in my father's eyes, and his desperation was turned against us. The journey I had thought to be shorter, became long, as if we were driving towards hell, and every time I turned to look at him, he would spit in my face. He told us a lot about the people who had took his land, but to me it sounded like it had nothing to do with us, because I was just a child observing good and bad. If he was so wise with all his books and property, why couldn't he understand his family, his children? Always troubled eyes, never worried eyes. He kept on swearing at my mother as if she was there with us, saying: 'Stupid woman. She only produced girls instead of boys. Now I am alone because all of you girls.' I was puzzled by his words, because of the four sons that he got with his new wife. Now, as my father's hope had fallen, mine had strengthened. In a weak moment he had mentioned my real mother. My ears couldn't stop listening, so I thought of cotton wool, but when I tried to force my hand into the car seat to take out the stuffing, it froze. I suppose it felt my father's presence.

The new ranch was indeed a different place, not as perfect as the old farm, with its banana plantation. My grandmother was already there, and without bothering to ask us of our journey, she began telling her son that some cows had gone back to the old farm. My father turned towards me, gave me a heavy clap and, as I fell to the ground, I only saw stars. I felt a sharp pain in my stomach as he began kicking me, and he continued until I heard our veterinary shout at him. I got up and went into the house to rinse my mouth. And I was disappointed to see the woman who I hated most standing there, watching. 'There we go again,' I said to myself. 'Am I ever going to be free from this woman?'

The Forming of My Dark Side

On our way to where the calves were grazing, I asked my brother of what we should do when we were not given food.

He turned and looked straight at me, and said: 'In the morning when we take the goats for grazing, we will make sure that we bring the dogs too. We'll make them kill one of the goats and lose it on the fire; then we have something to eat.'

I looked at him with troubled eyes, because to me it sounded like a brutal act. I told him about my love for the goats and I would hate the person who laid a hand on them.

But then he replied: 'Can't you see that our stepmother and father hate us? So why then do you have to love their goats?'

I looked down for a moment in deep thought before I answered: 'Maybe it's just animals, maybe they hate our father too, so let us not make them bleed for our father's mistakes.' I saw the smile of defeat, and it seemed to me that I had changed his mind, but still I was curious about the goats, so I asked him what we should say, when asked about the missing goat.

'We would say that maybe it have been eaten by the lions,' he replied.

Our father and his wife went back to the town house, leaving us with our grandmother, and they took my two worst worries with them, but they left us without proper food. Life on the ranch became harder, we had to live on milk and posho [a cake made of cooked maizena and water] every day and if there were no posho then it would only be milk. My brother and I were not used to eat posho because we thought that people who ate that kind of food were of the other tribe. Each morning we would wake up on milk, and when we were lucky enough we would eat porridge. The milk became ugly to look at and our grandmother had to beat us to drink it, and it reminded me of my old life whereby I had to beg for it.

Each morning we told her that we loved to drink our milk outside. We would then take the dogs' plates behind the house and pour the milk, and wait for them to finish before going back inside the house and tell Grandmother that we had finished. Our dogs became fat and better-looking than the neighbouring dogs. Our plan went on fine until one day when the dogs started fighting for the milk, making so much noise that she came to see what was going on. She screamed at us, while saying that one day we would remember the very same milk. Her words caught my attention, and I found lots of meanings, which made me shake inside. It only got worse when my brother told her that we needed something else to eat, and mentioned a hen as an example. She told us that we were nothing but murderers who wanted to eat everything, even with our father still living. Her words became louder, almost hysterical as she continued saying that when our father would die, there would be nothing left because of us, who would kill and eat everything. She made it clearer for us, that nothing belonged to us, and that we should forget about inheriting any of our father's riches. My fear and anger rose, and I told myself to destroy as much as I could, so that it would be their loss. I became careless and destructive against all that belonged to my father. I knew that I had nothing to lose, and whether the lions ate the cows or not it seemed the same to me.

Early one morning my brother and I took the goats for grazing, and we complained to each other about our grand-mother's words as we walked. When we arrived at the bush far away from any unwanted eyes, we sent the dogs after one of the goats. The dogs caught a young goat by its leg and we provoked it to keep on biting in the wound. I felt no remorse when it began to cry in fear and pain; I saw it only as a part of my father.

The following day a heavy rain shower prevented us from going with the goats, and our grandmother told us to make the wounded stay. There was not much to do on a day like this, and my grandmother and I were sitting by the fire while my brother relaxed on his bed, while the sound of the heavy rain on the metal roof silenced our tongues. Then I saw the wounded goat emerge from the doorway. It was soaked and stood there shaking for a while, before humping towards my brother's bed. As it had placed itself under the bed, my brother reached for its mouth and nose and I went there to help him as it fought for its life. My grandmother continued doing nothing but sitting there with her old back staring at us. The goat gave up its desperate fight, and we ran to our grandmother. When we told her that the goat was about to die she looked happy and told my brother to take it outside and slaughter it.

When I was eating, my fear rose within me as I remembered of how it had been struggling. I told myself then that the only way I could get the fear out of me was to kill more and more. I knew a boy who lived near the main road, and I was certain that he knew some tricks with which one might kill a cow, because his father was a butcher. One fine evening before dawn I went, escorted by one of the dogs, to the boy's home. After he had listened to my wish, he told me that every evening before I went to bed I should put a piece of meat on a stick and make the cow smell it for ten minutes, then after about five days the cow should die. I did as he had told and the fourth day I was excited and ran out to look straight after bed, but to my disappointment, the cow was there playing with the others. In fact it seemed stronger than ever. I thought about his words and came to the conclusion that I hadn't done the job the right way and promised myself to try again. In the afternoon my grandmother went to check on the workers down at their hut. My brother and I started chasing the hens' tail-feathers, trying to find an easy one to catch, then we ran after one cock, beating it with long sticks until we catched it. Then my brother and I took off a few feathers from the neck and wings. When she returned we showed her the cock and told her that we had saved it from the eagle, and I whispered in my brother's ear: 'Now the old, ugly-looking woman is happy too.' I looked at him with a knowing smile as she said: 'OK, now you can take the feathers off.' When she was busy preparing it, we stayed close at her side with the salt, in my pocket, as we waited for her to leave the pot. When she left for the salt I poured some in, but to the maximum of our desire, and a minute later she came back with a confused expression on her face, so I handed it over to her. We knew very well that with much salt she would lose her appetite, and leave it all for us. She had made the cooking, and we made the eating, and when we started eating she shouted at herself as she thought that it was her who had put a lot of salt in the food. The two of us were making signs at each other, as our grandmother called us bad names, complaining that we just swallowed the food without even tasting the unbearable amount of salt.

My brother stayed with his dogs most of the time. I suppose that they gave him good company, they loved him the same as he loved them, they always seemed ready to please him and I often saw him turn into laughter as if one of them had been telling him a joke. One morning I was not feeling well, so my brother had to take the goats alone, and the whole day I was waiting for his return. Around six o'clock in the evening he returned with tired eyes, and he looked as if he wanted to go straight to bed, but he still had to wait for the workers to count the goats. When the man had finished counting, he found one missing, so he went and told Grandmother, she came from the house screaming so loud that even the dogs shivered. She went straight to my brother and started beating him up, while the dogs sat like an audience with their worried faces changing from one side to the other. I was leaning against the wall watching with anger as she hit his head into the ground, but then the dogs jumped in, and started a rescue mission, which turned my anger into happiness, and I started cheering as the drama went on. Two of the dogs jumped on her and started tearing her clothes until the skirt went off her body, and thank God: she had something beneath.

The next morning she prevented the dogs from having anything to eat and milk to drink. She warned us that if we tried to steal milk for them, we would not eat as well. But we knew a lot of tricks in which to feed our beloved long-eared dogs. Today I have come to understand a bit about why my grandmother was like this. My grandmother had no other relatives except her son and daughter. Grandmother's daughter stayed a bit far from us, and she never used to come and visit her. I still wonder on what happened to Grandmother's relatives.

One evening when my brother and I returned from one of our rabbit-hunts, we found our stepmother at the ranch-house. The first thought that crossed my mind was that now we wouldn't be the eagles any more.

After two days my father, too, arrived to the ranch. In the evening he called the workers for a meeting where he told the two of them to find other jobs, because he could no longer afford to pay them on this new and smaller ranch. When eating supper, our father told my brother and me to prepare ourselves for moving to the town house. After having had some glasses of milk as breakfast, our father and stepmother got busy packing their stuff, while my brother and I watched without anything to bring. When we arrived I could not see my sisters Margie and Helen, and when I asked our nanny Marie, she told me that they were at boarding school. My brother and I had a week to resettle, where my brother found his old pals and I, my old enemies. A few days passed before I learned that my old friends, that I had known from my first year, had gone, making my life there a bit more lonely. I had difficulties in making friends, because I often went my own ways, but a week later I got lucky and made friends, with two sisters from third grade. Judith and Mutton dressed smart with shoes of the latest fashion, always carrying lots of pocket-money. They were highly respected at school for reasons unknown to me, but I could see that they felt that not just anyone could be their friends. I had chosen them, not the other way round and they never seemed much interested in me, but still they let

61

me 'hang around'. One day their mother came to our school, I was introduced, and as we talked she asked the names of my father. I saw that she knew of him and, to my surprise, I learned that she knew about my real mother too. Her words snatched my attention, and unlike her daughters she seemed to take a real interest in me, so I dared to ask her if she knew where my mother could be found, but she only smiled and went away. The woman had introduced herself as Patricia and given me her address, but she repeatedly had warned me against showing it to my father. I believed the woman's good intentions, and hid the address so far away from my mind that I even forgot to show it to my sisters, as they came for vacation. My sister Margie surprised us all with the strength of a real woman, and a relentless fight started between her and our stepmother. My stepmother grew thinner every day that passed, along with the remains of her good spirit, but still she managed to create a stand off between Father and his daughters. I watched my sisters being beaten nearly every day, but Margie only got stronger. Whenever the beatings started Helen, our first-born, would scream, telling him to stop, but Margie would bite her teeth until the end. Several times I heard her say: 'Father! Again you beat me for nothing.' I remember the painful times when I watched my stepmother safely from the window move the furniture away so as to create more room for the beatings.

An Innocent Betrayed

Helen could no longer take the beatings. She was tall and well built, light in colour with her big shiny brown eyes, which made her look like an innocent prey. Helen became our stepmother's spy, telling her everything that we said and did. She was desperately searching for a way to escape the beatings. The pain made my sister so blind to the extent of not realising the intentions of the very woman who hated us all. We could not always understand how our stepmother came to know our secrets, and when Margie looked at me suspiciously, I turned my eyes at Helen who started flicking her eyes. In a defensive manner, I told them that I had no idea. Margie thought that it could be the younger sister to our stepmother but I could not believe it, because we were always a little more careful when she was around, but I kept my mouth shut in fear of another confrontation.

My sister Margie suggested that we go steal some bananas, from one of our neighbours' field. When we got there I was told to climb one of the trees, which carried big fruits called fenne. One of my sisters was struggling with the sugar canes, while Helen pulled the ripe banana plant down to the ground. I forgot everything about the fenne and just stayed up, watching my sisters tearing everything apart like wild pigs. In a few minutes I heard Margie say, 'Run.' 'Why?' I replied, but they were already gone just like a wind. I had one fenne in my hands ready to let it down. 'Get down, you thief,' the voice ordered me. When I looked down it was the old woman that we feared most. She had a big stick in her hands, with her face looking up in the tree. I noticed that she had no idea of who I was. I kept on telling her that I was getting down while searching for my target. When her head appeared I let the fenne go and the woman fell to the ground. I quickly came down and grabbed my fenne and joined my sisters in our little secret place. When they saw a fenne on top of my head both laughed, and Margie gave me a nickname, which forever have escaped my mind. Helen asked me how I had managed to escape? I told her that I first had to kill the old woman. They almost scared me away as both of them screamed in terror, and I watched them in amazement as they turned and ran back to the point of escape. I followed them, but we found no dead body.

About the bad old woman. She had only a grandson, but she had lots of fruits and banana plants, down at her property. Whenever one of us kids asked for the fruits, she would run after us with anything that she could manage to grab and that made us steal from her.

A few weeks had passed after the incident without any stealing, and I began to miss the bananas. I had a good eye to the bananas hanging atop in our kitchen, and this very day they were as ripe as they should be. The whole day my mind was occupied in finding out how my stomach could get to them. In the evening as we ate supper the thought of the bananas overpowered me, so I left everybody still eating, and went outside to the kitchen. I picked up a long piece of firewood and began pushing at the bunch until four of them came falling down. I went behind the house and ate, while peeing, and the stars couldn't be ignored that evening. All these three experiences at once took me far away to a perfect world, but Helen appeared as the lightning, and destroyed everything, and I was carried back by the rolling thunder calling my name.

'Here I am!' I answered without hiding what I had in my hands, because I thought that she might want one as well.

'What are you doing?'

'I am eating a banana,' I replied with a whisper. 'Do you want one?' I continued, but she refused, telling me that she was taking me to my father. I just smiled because I was certain that she was trying to scare me. A second later I realised that she was serious as her voice repeated itself with a rumbling sound. This time my reply was true and clear: 'Helen . . . our mother is one. Please don't take me inside.' At the end I begged her, while I cried in silence, holding her hand, but she refused, and took over the grip. I tried to hold on to the wall using one hand, but my fingers were strengthless as I had to accept the betrayal of my sister. She continued pulling me with one hand because she had the banana in the other, and soon I was in front of my father. Our stepmother began crying, while telling my father that nothing she did was appreciated. She became hostile to my father and as her lying tears increased, my father got hotter. Suddenly he exploded by dragging me on to the floor and with his feet on my shoulder he demanded my reasons for stealing the bananas, but I could not answer him because I knew for sure that my answer would be misunderstood, and add more fuel to my stepmother's fire.

The beatings didn't seem to please his wife enough, and I saw him, in a short moment, eyeing her before he continued my punishment. He went to their bedroom, brought one of his coats and ordered me to sleep on top of it until morning. As he put it on my bed he looked at me with warning eyes and told me that the punishment would continue in the morning if I had wetted it. I was crying that night as I had laid myself in bed, not because of the beatings, but because that I always was expected to do the impossible. I tried to sing in silence as I hoped to stay awake.

In the morning I woke up with a pounding heart, as I hurried to feel the coat with my hand, but my hands felt no coldness, and with refreshed hope I brought it to my nose. I felt a strong poison going through my head, that gave me a sad reminder of yesterday's beatings. I became afraid when I touched my unhealed wounds, so I thought of running away, but I had no idea of where to go. Then I remembered who had started it all and I remembered how sad I had become.

On my way through the living-room I crossed Helen and stopped for a moment as I burnt with the hate that rose inside. I walked outside and sat in the garden to wait for my father. Finally he appeared, and without a word I brought the coat to him. He stood there a while with his eyes looking at the ground like a thief, then he called for his big stick. I looked straight at him, while my tears dropped down to my mouth. I saw a shame in his eyes and I could not tell whether he was smiling or about to cry, his eyes continuously blinked, and I kept on looking at him with my small eyes until he slowly turned away and moved back to the house.

That very afternoon, Margie and I called Helen to our meeting place. Margie told her that we all were fighting for the same cause and that nothing could prevent our step-mother from hating us, and if we were beginning to betray one another, she would only laugh at us. When Helen started crying, Margie and I walked away, leaving her in her own tears. A while later Helen followed us on our way to the potato field, and when we were about to dig up some sweet potatoes, she stood herself in front of us and crossed her heart, as she promised never to betray any of us again.

The Trade

The following morning which was Saturday, my sisters and I were in the garden relaxing away from the sun, when we heard the sound of a car. Our ears raised up in the air, like dogs about to catch their victims. We looked up the road and saw Annette for the first time since she had run away. She was in the front seat of an overcrowded Land-Rover with her arm in the window waving. All of us screamed, running towards the road calling her name. We could not wait for the car to stop before trying to open the car door, while one of my sisters cried. With a smile across her face Annette managed to get out of the car unhurt. She had a beautiful little child in her arms, making my sisters fight to hold the child. When our father heard the screams, he came outside, and stood in front of the house with the pipe between his teeth. When the visitors started walking down to our father, he told us to get chairs from the house, and at the door we met our stepmother busy sneaking with her scared eyes. Soon the visitors started introducing themselves, and among them, a man with a long nose like a telephone wire, stood up and presented himself as Mugabo, and he was here to marry Annette. My father told Mugabo that he would have to bring seven cows and four goats. What about the hens, I asked myself. The man told our father that he could only afford four cows and two goats. Our father accepted the cows and the goats, with a smile of excitement on his face. In the evening, the visitors left to get the cows, but Annette stayed with us. The next weekend my brother-in-law brought the cows, and took Annette with him.

With my little knowledge, I figured it out that my stepsister had no love for Mugabo, because he was nearly the same age as our father. After Annette had gone back, our father started telling my sisters and me of how Annette was so special, and he was never sure whether he would get anything from us. Each time we drank milk, he would say, 'Remember that you are drinking out of Annette's cows.' That became his song of every day. I looked at him, and asked myself: 'Is he mad or just greedy? Does he want all of us to get married at this age?' I could not figure out what disease my father carried inside his head. Margie and Helen were bothered by his words, but there was nothing they could do, to make him stop his madness.

At the end Annette never got what she wanted, because her marriage never lasted and her two children were sent to Festo's little brother after the divorce.

One of those days, our stepmother did send Helen to buy meat for lunch, but she returned with nothing. Before anybody saw her she went to Margie. She had lost the money and, crying, she asked her of what to do. A while later Richard and I had been called by Margie, who suggested that we could go to the streets and beg. After some hours of begging, we only had very little money, so Margie told Helen that she had no choice but to tell our stepmother. Helen followed Margie's advice and we heard our stepmother shout: 'What do you want me to do? Wait and tell your father!' Helen cried, begging her not to let our father know but she didn't reply. When he returned and Helen told him, he slapped her in the face and said that the lost money was the money to pay her school fees. My sister kneeled down on the floor with her hands close together, and begged him for forgiveness, but he wouldn't listen. The following morning my father ordered her to work at the banana plantation by the town house, and while the rest of us prepared for school Helen was busy looking for the hoe.

Some days had passed, but still nothing was said. My sister had continued working as if already forgotten, and when we came back from school Helen was gone. Still my father's face remained unchanged, as he said: 'You see, your sister is stupid, just like your mother who is busy selling onions, and no matter how cheap she sells them, still no one is interested in buying them.' He continued by telling us that it meant nothing to him if we all ran away, and I had to realise that he hated us, just like he hated our mother. I tried to see where our lives were heading, and I could only see that all of us were about to go the same way.

Now I was left with one sister and a brother, realising that nothing was on our side. We saw that the woman was nowhere near to give up, so we tried to be careful in each and everything we did.

The Last Vacation

Our school closed down for the holidays, and we were taken by our father to the ranch where we would spend the holiday with Grandmother. On our way my father had a short conversation with Richard, and he told him that he now was a big boy who should be able to take care of us, and compared him with himself when he was his age. My sister and I were eyeing each other. When we reached the ranch, the workers had already slaughtered a cow, and quickly each of us unpacked, while some of the workers made a fire. Then we were told to find ourselves wooden sticks and help ourselves with the meat. Two of the workers were roasting their kidney, but all three workers wanted it, and I felt the tension in the air. The one without waited until the kidney was ready, grabbed it from the stick and ran, sharply followed by the owner. He began eating as he ran, but suddenly he dropped to the ground without a word. We laughed at first but were interrupted by the follower's outcry and learned that the man was dead, with half a kidney lying beside him. The man was 'tugged in' in a blanket, and my father told us that we could no longer go on with the feast. As the meat was brought inside I felt angry at the deceased, blaming him for my father's disappointing decision. After the burial in the evening our father started packing for his return to the town house.

Right after he had left, our brother told us that we should go and search for honey. Margie told us to get plastic bags, which we would use for protection against the bees, and equipped with matches and a hoe, we started out, led by the moonlight. We searched for a while until we found a wasp hill and began digging. The bees went wild and some of them started entering the bags which covered our heads. In desperation we tried to create enough smoke to calm the defenders down. After the struggle with a sweat on our faces, we found that the honey could not be eaten because it already carried young bees.

We returned home and found our grandmother sitting near the fire while cooking milk, and as she turned her angered face towards us, I realised that no word could come out from her mouth. After we drank the milk, we said good-night to each other and went to bed with a smile that we just had developed after Father had gone. In the morning Margie helped the workers to milk the cows, while my brother and I watched over the calves. After having finished, we went on a rabbit-hunt with our five dogs. Soon we encountered the first rabbit, and the dogs started their pursuit, while we followed from behind, but the rabbit ran faster to the hole. Then we began digging, while one of the dogs guarded the hole with its eyes wide open. Suddenly the rabbit came out in high speed through the dog's legs. We turned and looked at each other, before following the dogs who finally catched it. After they had finished roasting the rabbit I watched them fight for legs and breasts, because I only cared about hunt-ing the animals, not to eat them. While they ate we talked about our clothes shortage. Our brother talked about selling a cow, Margie said milk, but I could not find anything to say, so I supported the milk idea.

The old woman was standing near the house with a stick in her hands as we returned. 'Where have you been the whole day?' she yelled, but Margie just passed her, while I stayed there because I knew her better and therefore I was more afraid. She took her breasts in her hands, pointed them into the air, and said to Margie: 'This is the breasts that I fed your father with, and I condemn you with them.' Grandmother told Margie that she would die wandering on the roads before being eaten by the vultures, but I just observed her wornout breasts and shook my head. My sister seemed to ignore the danger in her grandmother's words, as she laughed loudly from inside the house.

The following day we decided to carry out our plan. Early in the morning my brother and I took most of what our sister had milked and poured it into a milk can, which we already had hid in the long grass behind the house. By nine o'clock we rolled the can to the main road and sold it to a truck driver. We handed over the money to our older sister Margie, and the following morning we escorted her to the main road to make sure that she got on the mini-tax. We waited for an eternity before a blue Peugeot stopped at the side of the road, and we ran towards the car as we saw her coming out with a small bag in her hands. When we came closer I noticed the high heels and fine dress that she wore, and I realised that her way of walking had changed. When we asked for our clothes, she reached into her bag and took out a lot of sweets and cakes, telling us that the money was not enough. Then she went in the middle of the road and started walking up and down before asking us: 'Don't I look like a model.' I wanted to laugh as she resembled a new-born calf. As we were about to sit down and eat, she told us that she as well had not been eating. On our way home we told her that we would tell our grandmother. We saw the terror in her eyes, but we didn't care as she asked for forgiveness.

We went straight to our grandmother and told her that Margie had been selling some of the milk. When she had finished shouting at our sister, Grandmother told me to get one of the workers. Then she instructed him to go with her word to our father the following morning. Margie told us that she would leave at night before our father would come. I told Margie that I didn't know that it would go this far, and as I thought of our sisters Grace and Helen, I started crying. We begged her to stay, and promised to tell our father that we had been lying to Grandmother.

'Sister, if you don't stay, you can't go to college, please stay!' I cried.

'Do not be sorry. Maybe I shall be best without it,' she replied, and I realised that she had already made up her mind. When we asked her if she had money, she replied, 'No

I don't. But I will find my way, just like the first ones did.' But these words made me forget about being sorry, as I thought that she had hidden our money.

Margie spend the rest of the day swearing at Grandmother, who for the first time in my life started to cry. That was when Margie told her that her poor eyes already was condemned by God, and when she died no one would care to bury her. At night Margie went to bed without eating anything and the following morning she was gone. We tried to keep each other strong and hoped for our father to search for her. When our father arrived and found us in tears, he just walked inside without asking, and when he found out he acted as if he had lost a hen.

Our holiday was over and it was time for us to return to the town house. When we arrived our stepmother seemed to have a huger smile on her face than she normally would have. I guess that it was because of our missing sister. Our stepmother seemed to be on the winning side, and the war she had started was about to turn into victory, because our nanny, too, seemed tired of the new rules, that our step-mother now dictated. When we saw that she was going away we all started to weep, begging her to stay, because we knew that she loved us like a mother would.

Marie saw us cry, and promised not to leave, and in the morning breakfast was ready on the table. After having finished eating, we went to say goodbye to Marie as we always did before going to school, but she wasn't home. We went to the banana plantation not far from the house, think-ing that she might be down there, but she was nowhere to be found. On our way to school we talked a lot about the things that she had been doing for us, and it made us sad but we could only hope for her to be home when we returned. Now Marie was gone too, and in order to go on without being destroyed, I had to strengthen myself and face any pain without fear, by pretending that nothing wrong was happening.

Now it was only my brother and I, but we didn't see things the same way, making it hard for me to count on him.

It was Thursday around four o'clock in the afternoon and I was confused not knowing what to do, so I went to the golf field to watch the rich men's game. I was sitting on the turf watching, with my cheeks buried in my hands, when a man known as 'Johnson' approached me. He suggested that I helped him to carry the golf bag. 'Sure!' I responded without a second thought, because I knew that he would give me some money. After I had finished the job, he gave me more money than I expected, enough to spend for days. I was so excited that I forgot all the trouble that usually haunted me, and I walked home feeling that I was on top of the world with my teeth in the air, now I had something to show at school just like any other kid. When I arrived, my step-mother was not home and when she returned she didn't bother to ask of where I had been. I supposed that she still was happy about Margie's disappearance.

Early in the morning I got up and did what I was supposed to do, and then hurried to school before anyone woke up. On my way I stopped at one of the stands that was owned by a man, which we used to call Monkey. I bought some bananas and ate them as I continued my journey to school. Before I could reach the school I bought three packets of sweets and stuffed them in my school bag. During the break I called half of my class and we started eating, but we could not finish them, and when we returned to the class, some were still chewing. The teacher asked which one of us had bought the sweets, and all the kids looked at me. When the teacher was not looking, I silently tried to make them shut up. When no one answered, she told those who were caught to go in front. She called Kayirangwa and told him go and fetch some sticks from outside. When the kids heard this, they broke the silence and were sent back to their desks. Now all the blame was on me and she told me to see her before going home.

After class she gave me a letter which I should bring to my father. I nervously looked at the letter and she told me that he was being called to a school meeting. On my way home, I sat by the roadside and tried to read word by word, but I couldn't understand, because of its difficult handwriting. At home my father was drinking a few beers, while talking about law with another man, but when I handed him the letter he just put it in his pocket. When the visitor had gone, he called for me and asked what I had done. 'Nothing,' I said. He told me that he would know anyway the following day, making my heart beat faster, as I thought of the possibility that the teacher might have written about the sweets.

The night was shorter than I wanted, and the morning came with a fast rising sun. When I got to school my teacher asked me about my father, and with a burning hate I told her that he would be coming soon. On the morning parade everybody but me were in prayers, because my eyes were wide open as I fearfully looked in the direction of where my father would appear. Just as the prayers stopped my father came, and I had to concentrate to hold my water. He went straight in front of us to where the teachers were standing, and spoke with my teachers. It didn't take them a minute before he called my name and ordered me in front. My father started telling everyone that I was a thief, and had stolen his money and used them for sweets. All eyes were on me, as I felt the shame across my face and, like a thief, I looked down. He asked one of the teachers for a stick and ordered me to lie down on my stomach. I kept on standing as I thought of telling everyone of how I was treated at home, but before I could decide, he grabbed my neck and forced me to the ground. I struggled to get up, telling him that I wanted to tell the truth. He stopped the whipping and I stood for a while, questioning myself whether the teachers would help me or not when having spoken. At the end I didn't count on anything else but my father's stick, and, with everyone's eyes staring at me, I suddenly gave up. Slowly I looked in his eyes and laid myself to the ground. When I tried to see how the other kids felt, I noticed that most of them looked the other way, some even cried. When he had left, my teacher asked me if the man who had been beating me was my real father, and I looked her in the eyes as she tried to excuse herself. Without a word I turned away, and in silence I wished her hell. In the break I noticed that most of the kids looked at me with sorry eyes. They all wanted to be my friend, and that day, Judith and Mutton gave me all their 'goodies'.

Back home my father demanded to know where I had got the money, so I decided to tell him the truth, and we were just interrupted by a guest when my shameless father was about to whip me the second time.

That day I came to realise that all his power came from others' pain.

A Path of Fear

I had reached to a point where I constantly was fighting for my own sanity. My stepmother's cruelties never stopped, and the word had spread to distant homes of the father beating his children by their stepmother's command. For a while everything had been on me. I guess that she was satisfied with my brother's position, who had no ambition whatsoever except for escaping the beatings. I had arrived from school and while eating, my stepmother approached with an unusual expression on her face. With a smile she told me that she was sending me with her brother-in-law to where her mother lived, so that I could know the way on my own another time.

The following day her brother-in-law arrived from the Kasese district, and when I saw his bike I couldn't wait to go. As we hastily raced through the vast hill area covered by the jungle I came to realise how far it actually would be on foot, but my fear was overshadowed by the excitement of riding the bike while holding the big man's stomach. The old woman lived in a little terrible-built hut covered with grass. There was only one room and the place where they slept looked like the stable-area of a new-born calf. She lived together with her daughter and a boy, and I was surprised to hear them tell me that they were happy with their life. I listened and observed their happiness in the middle of nowhere, living on the milk that their few cows managed to provide. They had to walk four kilometres to a farmer in order to trade their milk for food, that was if they had enough. On our way back home I had to notice the road knowing that I had to return alone some day. The only question I was asked by my stepmother as we halted the bike was: 'Did you memorise the way?'

A few weeks had passed and I came from school, leaving my bag behind, because I was going back for my evening studies. After I had ate she told me that I had to bring some money to her mother, and then the fear rushed through my head. When I thought about going alone through those dangerous hills, the veins in my eyes nearly failed, through the pressure of tears of anger. Slowly I took a bag, packed one pair of underpants and a bottle of water. It was two o'clock in the afternoon when I left beneath the burning African sun that continuously reminded me of the hell I already was in. As I passed my school I looked at it, hoping to be there, and my mind remained there for a while as I walked on alone. When I no longer could see the town I got afraid, and through the savannah I tried to walk as fast as I could. Still I had to stop over and over again to listen, because I knew that the area was overcrowded with monkeys and predators. After I had walked through the savannah, I noticed water coming out of the rocks that had made its own hill, I checked my bottle and realised that I had no water left. I went down to the stream and washed my head and face before I drank out of it, while watching small monkeys playing and having a good time. I looked at them with deep thoughts as I wished to be like them.

When I reached down to the hill, I saw big and black animals with hair all over their body standing in the middle of the road, others up in the tree. When they did not move I went near and observed their movements, one of them was holding its new-born while busy chewing different kinds of leaves and giving it to it. I observed love and caring while looking at the baby monkey enjoying the mother's arms. I kept on standing there, being afraid to move, until I spotted a small made-up road which looked like the animals' path. Before I could think of going through, they moved in it, and just stood there while others sat in the middle of the road and watched me, as if not to make a move.

I was becoming afraid because it was my first time to experience such an event and I was reminded of the story that I was once told by my sisters that the big gorillas ate small children. I became afraid for my life and thought of going back the way I came. But, on the other hand, I thought of my stepmother, and again I thought that if ever I took any step back I would be grabbed and eaten. I became confused not knowing what I should do, I kept on standing, and it was getting late. I started crying, thinking that I was going to die and leave my sisters behind. After some hours of waiting I suddenly saw two men coming towards me, so I decided to hide the money in my underpants, and they were already there before I could get my hands out.

'What are you doing here?' they asked. I told them that I was being sent by my stepmother and finally the men made my day.

I told the old woman that I was tired and wanted to sleep. She did put an old blanket down to the floor where every one of us had to sleep. Even though I was tired, I found it impossible to sleep, because of a smell like old cheese that covered everything.

The following morning the jungle was covered with moisture and the rising sun mixed its red and yellow colours into the morning sky. As I enjoyed the coolness behind the hut, I saw a piece of paper, which looked like a five hundred note. I looked around to see if anyone was looking, and realised that I was all by myself. As they called me for the morning milk I hid the money in my underpants. I drank the milk with the heart in my throat, asking myself whether to give it back or not. The girl started looking for the note, before asking me if I had seen it, and with a smile I denied. But she couldn't let it go, so I thought of putting the money where she could easily see it, but it was too difficult to get it out without being seen. After I had said good-bye, I walked in a slow pace trying not to let the money fall, and all the way I thought about what I should buy. When I could not decide, I let my stomach choose, and before I could reach town, I saw a small shop with a Pepsi-Cola sign on its window. I asked the man how much Miranda orange sodas cost.

'One hundred and fifty,' he replied.

'Give me two,' I ordered.

I drank while the man's eyes stared at me, and after I had finished I told him to give me sweets from the rest of the change. The man seemed to be buried in thoughts when he gave me two packets, and I suppose that he wondered what kind of kid I was, with my feet covered in red sand and a worn-out dress full of money.

I continued my journey, eating my sweets, but when I had walked about a kilometre, I started to feel pain in my stomach. I ignored the warning for some time, until I felt the thirst. I went to some nearby trees and sat down, as I feared that I was about to die, but luckily I wasn't. A huge stone had decided to move into my stomach, making me so heavy that I found it difficult to get up. When my breathing stopped I hurried to put my fingers in my throat. The pain had gone, but now I felt hungry and tired. I managed to get up with great difficulty because of a terrible dizziness that spun around in my head. I hit the road once again, handing out one sweet to each kid that I happened to meet on my way, until I reached school. I went in my classroom and checked my desk, but my school bag was missing. I searched all over, but it was nowhere to be found, and I went on like a mad person, as my tears of desperation run down to my mouth. I asked myself why all this trouble had to happen to me: what have I done to the world? I tried to make myself strong so that I could go home, but my thoughts would not let me. I was left alone crying in the middle of the playground, as the rest of the kids had gone to their homes.

Later I began walking towards home, but I could not think clear until late in the afternoon when I found myself near Mr Monkey's stand. I stood there wondering with my eyes pointed towards my home, and suddenly I remembered my friend Rehema.

I went to Rehema's uncle's home with one set of beliefs: she would be able to help me. Before I got there I saw her from a distance, and called her in a low begging voice: 'Rehema, you have to help me!' She told me to wait down at the banana plantation, so she could find a way of getting me into her room. I walked in the dark to the sound of my own footsteps. I sat myself down and started to look around in fear of what might come to grab me. I had waited for a long time and I was getting afraid that she had forgotten me, but still I had no choice but to keep on waiting. Suddenly Rehema showed up, and together we went to her small room, which was connected to the goat shed. She went into the house and came back with a plate of food. As we were eating, her uncle called her and she told me not to eat until she came back. Rehema came back running, grabbed my hand and took me to the goat shed, I was told to sleep there, because of the visitor, who would be sleeping on Rehema's bed.

Early in the morning Rehema woke me up, and before leaving I told her how much I loved her. I walked through the plantation, crying, to the nearby bush, where I slept for some hours. About midday I started feeling hungry, wishing that I never had bought Miranda. 'But what can I do?' I thought. 'Should I go to the road and beg?' 'Well, let me wait and see what happens,' even though I had no idea of how long I could control my hunger. I went close to the main road, sat there and began counting the cars, as I sang all the songs I knew, hoping to take away my sadness. When my stomach started rumbling, I laid myself down on my back, closed my eyes and began remembering my family and all the people who had ever been good to me. I tried to imagine how my real mother looked like, but my memory of her was too dim. When I was about to be carried away by emotions, I stood up and began begging. I stood there with my arm stretched out, but no one seemed to notice me, until one man driving a coffee-coloured car with 'U.C.B' printed on its side stopped, and asked me why I was begging. I told him what had happened, so he gave me some money, telling me, that if I waited for him, he would come back to help me.

As soon as he left, I went to Mr Monkey's stand and bought some bananas and biscuits. I sat myself in a quiet place, and I got full enough not to eat the peels too. I cleaned my hands in the grass, and returned to the road to wait for the man. As I waited, I remembered telling the man my father's names, and where he worked. I ran as fast as I could, covered by the long grass, until I got to a place where I was sure that no one knew me or my father. I sat myself at the edge of the golf-field and after long hours I realised that my head was being burned by the sun. I went house to house asking for a job, but everywhere people asked me the same questions: how old I was, and who my father was. So I ended up running away from every house, and the day ended without finding any job. I thought of going back to Rehema, but the thought of the visitor came into my mind. It was getting late when my eyes came across the court house. I stood against the wall and began to sing quietly as I cried.

I woke up all of a sudden, looking around, and realised that I had had a safe night. I walked down to the river and threw a few stones in its waters. There was a cool breeze refreshing my fatigued mind, but at the same time I found out how terribly I smelled of the goats from the night before. I thought of jumping in and take a bath, but I remembered that I couldn't swim so I changed my mind. As I left the riverside I saw a house, and decided to try once more. I spend some time standing outside, looking at the door with a pounding heart, and I wondered if I was able to knock at the door after all. 'How long are you going to stand out here? Knock on the door!' I ordered myself. I knocked and a man's voice replied: 'Coming!' The door opened and a man looked at me with a question-mark on his face.

'What can I do for you?' he asked. With a smile he invited me inside to have a seat, and the questions went on again, as if he was reciting what the previous people had asked. The difference was that he had shown his good will and offered me to his home, so I tried to answer his questions. The man told me that I could stay until his wife came home. I asked him of what kind of work he had, and he told me that he was a doctor.

'Why aren't you at work then?' I asked, but he looked troubled.

'Well, I have a little problem with my legs, Infant. One of my legs are crippled, so I have to rest sometimes,' he replied.

'But how? you have two legs like me!' I asked.

One leg was shorter than the other, he explained.

'Which hospital do you work in?'

'Why?' he asked.

'Because I was wondering if you could do me a favour. If my stepmother and father comes to your hospital, could you give them a big injection, so they can cry and scream like I always do.'

He looked straight at me, and shook his head, not as a 'No' to my request, but more like a sad acknowledgement of my situation as a whole. After a silent pause of thoughts he asked me: 'Do you love your father?'

I replied: 'Yes, but he doesn't love me.'

He asked me if I would cry if my father would die and I replied: 'No, I would not cry if he died together with my stepmother, but I would if he died without her.'

He told me that he wasn't a bad person who wanted to harm people, his job was to help. Our conversation was interrupted when his wife came home with a baby-girl in her arms.

'What if she is like my stepmother, and will she make me take care of her baby too?': all my thoughts were occupied by the baby and I felt lost. I just caught its mother's greetings, and I made a sudden reply. She looked puzzled at me and asked what was troubling me, and I replied: 'Nothing, I was just looking at your baby.'

'Do you like babies?' she asked, and I had to take a deep breath before answering: 'Oh, sure I do.'

They all went to the bedroom, and I was left alone. The woman came back, sat down, and asked me if she should

China Keitetsi, 2002.

China's sister Margie in a photo taken in 1999, a year before her death in Rwanda. China couldn't go to her funeral as it took place just as she was on her way to Denmark.

Lt Colonel Moses Drago, the father of China's son. Portrait from Kampala 1993.

Lt Colonel Moses Drago (left) and Lt Colonel Bruce (right). Taken during the yearly Independence Day Parade.

China in battle dress in Kampala as an eighteen year old.

follow me back to my father's. I had no answer because I didn't know if she meant it as a question or an order. I looked her in the eyes, and asked if her husband had told her of my father, and she said yes.

'Are you not afraid of my father?' I asked, but she just smiled as if not knowing what to answer. For the night I was offered a nice bed, in a cosy bedroom. But the surroundings failed to comfort me, because of the woman's last words that kept on nagging me, and I just couldn't find the answers of what the morning would bring.

The following day I was sitting in the sofa like a puppy, waiting for the final answer. The woman came from her bedroom, still dressed in a nightgown. She walked past me and continued into the kitchen, while asking if I wanted some tea, but I refused. She poured a cup of coffee for herself and walked back to the sitting-room. She told me that they couldn't hire me because of my young age. 'You have a family and we think that you should go back home.' I couldn't listen, so I offered her to work for free, but she argued that I had to be strong, and take the beatings even if it was unfair, because of the education I would receive. I shouldn't let my stepmother win, and if she let me stay she wouldn't help me to achieve anything – rather she would be destroying my possibilities, and then I would for certain not win. 'Make yourself strong and let them do whatever they want,' she said. 'This is about *your* life, and it is important that you go back home. You may not be able to understand why I can't help you now, but some day you will. I just don't want you some day to be alone without your family.'

I realised that I had no chance of staying, so I had to prepare myself. With tears and a stuffed nose, I still hoped that she would let me stay. I wished that I had something to pack so that I could delay my departure, so instead I started to wash my face and hands. Too soon I was done and I almost panicked in search for more to do, but I found no more excuses for staying. Then I suggested that I could wash the dishes and clean the living-room, and she said that I didn't have to, but if I really wanted, it was all right by her, so I started right away. As I was cleaning, my thoughts got clearer, so I decided that now I had to leave. I went back to the living-room to say goodbye. 'I'm leaving now,' I said and she stood up. 'Here's some money. Maybe it can help you in some ways.' She said goodbye, but I couldn't reply as I opened the door and entered the streets.

Still I wasn't sure if it was home I was heading for. When I reached within the vicinity of our house, I tried to find a spot where I could get an overview of what might be happening there, but I failed. I continued the walk, and suddenly I met my stepsister, and brother Ray who seemed to have missed me. It didn't occur to me that they might love me, I rather thought of them missing the work I did and the breakfast that I prepared for them. I wanted to know if my father was upset, but they didn't think that my father was upset enough to beat me. There should be no reason for me to be afraid of returning, but I didn't believe them. It sounded like they, by all means, had decided to persuade me to come home. Then Ray suggested that he could go and ask his mother if I could return, and I had to take a deep breath before telling him to do so. He didn't take long, a matter of a few minutes. With the same dreadful suspicion as before, I decided to give in, for what was I now: a beggar with no choice.

My stepmother began questioning me of what had happened. She seemed calm and looked satisfied with my answers, and told me that she would try to ease my father when he returned. I felt relieved and trusted her, because no mad shouting and yelling had come from her mouth. Later that afternoon Father returned from work, and I began preparing for his questions. I expected to greet a father that I hadn't been seeing for some time, but his rudeness stopped me from saying a word. He just grabbed me like a thing and started to punch, denying me to give him my explanation. It went on so fast that I only noticed when my nose started bleeding, and I found myself pushed aside behind a locked door. So there I was, covered in darkness and bad memories.

One of my eyes was injured and shut, and it scared me because I had promised myself always to protect them from the beatings. I tore a piece off my clothes, soaked it with the blood from my nose, and started rubbing my eye as I hoped to open it. I felt a strong pain in one of my ribs and I was seriously afraid. I painted myself with blood to scare him away from beating me again, when I started to kick on the door, screaming and shouting. My father pulled me out of the room and stared at me with scared eyes, before he outburst: 'Oh my god!' He told me to undress, took me to the bathroom, and with warm water he started washing the blood off my body. When I saw his sorry face, I felt secure enough to show him my ribcage, which revealed some bad marks. He told me that he would take me to the hospital the following day. But he made it clear that, if asked, I should tell them that I fell from a tree. He promised that after we had been to the doctor, he and I would go to town, and buy me new clothes. At night I was crying, not because of my body, but my father's words. I could not remember any other time where my father had shown me such affection, and it made everything seem so unreal. I also thought of my sisters, and I cried until the sleep stole me away.

I woke up in a state of alarm, all of my body was in severe pain. I tried to get up but I could only crawl, and despite the terror of pain I managed to reach my father. He told me to come nearer, reached his hand out and felt my face. He then went away and returned with a doctor. The doctor never bothered to ask me of what had happened, because of my father, I supposed, who was standing right beside him. The man did his job though, but it wasn't enough and he explained that, because of the rib, I needed to be taken to the hospital for further treatment. My father looked at the doctor with a pause on his face, and after a while he asked him of what to tell the hospital. To my father's question the doctor answered: 'There is only one way to do this, and it will cost you some money!'

'Like how much?' my father asked.

'Well, I am not sure, but there is a friend of mine, and he can be able to cure the girl,' the doctor replied.

Another doctor came and finally I felt that I had escaped death.

When I got better, my father held his word and took me, for the first time, on a trip to town, and I felt very happy, walking around with him.

When we returned my father gave me a lot of sweets, telling me to enjoy them. I was enjoying myself, but as soon as my father left, my stepmother appeared like the lightning. She chased me out, and told me not to return until I had finished my father's sweets. And I remembered Margie once saying: 'This woman will be buried together with her hate.'

Rejected

My sisters who came back were carrying pain in different ways, and they lived in the same memories as I did. Whenever one of them came, I would think of one thing: 'Now she's coming for me!' But when I spoke with them, they would be telling me of what hard times they were going through. Even though they still pretended to be happier where they were, not letting their father and stepmother know their devastation. And my father seemed stupid enough to believe them. Most of the time I was waiting, with my eyes on the road, as I hoped for one of my sisters to return and take me.

I had just returned from fetching water, at a friend of my father's. Tired I was, laying in front of our house, when I heard a car parking up the road. Helen, our older sister, stepped out of a blue Suzuki, and I could hardly recognise her, being well dressed and with long hair. I was so excited with happiness, that I fell when running to welcome her. My father came out and stood by the door without saying a word. Before Helen could speak, my father wanted to know of who the man in the car was. She told him that this was the man she wished to marry, and my father asked: 'And what language does he speak?'

'Well, he comes from the east,' she replied.

'So what is he doing here, in the west?'

'Because I wanted you to meet him.'

'Don't you understand. I can't approve this marriage, with a man like him?' he replied.

'But he's very good to me, and if I marry him I will be happy. So what is your answer, Father?' she asked.

But he replied, 'If you want to stay as my daughter, don't marry him!'

My sister began crying, and as if being in heavy pain she slowly turned around and walked back to the car. In a sudden before opening the car-door she looked back, and asked my father if he could just greet the man.

'No,' my father roared. 'And furthermore, you should know this, if you marry him, you should never come back again.' After that I observed my father like a snake crawling back to the house as if nothing had happened.

Helen said goodbye to the man, and I was wondering what words she gave to this man that she was so close to marrying, because they parted like they never knew each other. As I watched her cry, there was something in her eyes I couldn't understand, but it made me sad. Then I turned very angry and told her: 'Our father is bad, and you say that this man makes you happy? So why don't you leave, and take me with you!' She told me that she was too scared to live without a father, because of what could a man do, if he knew that she had nowhere else could go. I asked what she would do now, and she told me that she had no idea, because she had nowhere to go. She was not sure if she could cope to live with us, because she wasn't sure that she would be able to obey the rules of our stepmother. I became sad to hear this and begged her to stay for a little while, but she couldn't stop crying and I was getting annoyed, so I went to Sofia's. At night in my room, I told Helen of Patricia, the woman that might be able to help in finding our mother. The next day she said goodbye with a proud face as if she would never return, and I hoped with all my heart that she would find our mother.

The rest of that day my father kept on complaining to himself, and I remember him say: 'They always go, but come back to get my help', and when he turned away I looked at him and shook my head. The following afternoon all of us kids and our father were sitting on the veranda, when two men came and told him that he was wanted by the military police. When he asked them by what charge, they only said that he would find out when they got there. To this he asked: 'Why haven't you come with a car, and where's your uniforms?'

'Do not question us', they said. Get up and you will know everything when you get there!'

My father looked afraid, because in those days it was common news that somebody, somewhere had been taken by mysterious men and disappeared without a trace. I had heard about this as well. I actually didn't care of what might happen to my father. I was only concerned about one of the men, who seemed to fake his appearance by closing one of his eyes. He told the men that they could kill him right where he was standing, because he was going nowhere. The men looked puzzled at each other, and before leaving they told him that they were coming back with more soldiers. As soon as they left, my father ran through the banana plantation, and minutes later he arrived with a group of soldiers.

The military men were very strange, for they were Northerners: with red eyes and a dark skin, and for reasons, I suppose, made us believe, that they were different from us. We lived a cowboy life, they often lived a military life and they called us lazy milk-drinkers. I was standing with a curious mind, as the military men were talking in a strange language which I didn't understand. My eyes got even bigger, when they began chewing on our chilli from the garden. The mysterious men never returned, nor did the soldiers that they had threatened with, but of course my father still had to pay the Northerners for his protection.

After the incident I tried to find the reason, of why this had happened, and when I saw my stepmother's face, it looked as if she had something to do with it. But, of course, my hate towards her could very well have been misleading me. I thought a lot about the strange soldiers, but I never dreamt of that I one day would be dressed in the very same uniform.

A week had passed since my sister left searching for our mother, and a place to stay. I saw her in the corner of my eye, and thought of it as a shadow of my memory, but when I turned she was real. It was impossible for me to wait for her to come to me, so I ran towards her, and asked: 'Did you find our mother?' Before she could answer I saw it in her eyes, and with sadness I had to acknowledge that the journey had been a failure. She told me that the woman I had sent her to was out of the country, and that she had waited together with Mutton and Judith, but she never showed up. While telling me it started to burn inside of me, for I knew what my father would say: 'You go and come back, because the world is burning you!'

What my father said was: 'What made you come back? Did a wild buffalo chase you? Yes, I knew that you would come back before dawn.' Helen looked down with a sad smile, but my father seemed to have more to say, so he went on: 'You go and leave me here, but you will always come back, because this is your home.' That made me think that all my father wanted was the suffering of my sisters whenever they were gone, and to punish them when they got back.

A few nice days passed, free of mad words, and a photographer was about to pass our house. I asked my sister if we could take a photo of us, and our stepbrothers and sisters. Since my photo never had been taken, I was very excited to see how I would look. As soon as the photographer had left, my father came with sad words. He told Helen that there was a son of his friend, and they had been talking about her, and he wished to marry her. I asked myself if my father was happy about my sister staying with us, or if he simply wanted to get rid of her. As I had been thinking this through, I called my sister, and asked her if she could help me with my homework, in order to get some time alone with her.

'Do you know this man that Father have been telling you about?'

'I have never seen the man.'

'Aren't you scared of marrying a stranger? It can be dangerous you know!' As I remembered the old chief with a cold fear I told her: 'Men aren't good. You can't trust them, and if you marry him, be prepared for the worst.'

To my relief she looked at me, and promised not to marry the man. During supper time my sister told our father that she was not marrying the man. The look on his face showed me that the words only provoked his anger, and it scared me seeing my sister not realising that. Every evening as my father had returned from work, he would terrorise her with cruel words, which caused her a lot of pain.

And now that she could not marry the man and had nowhere to live, she was turned into a camel. She had to take over from my stepmother, and now she took care of each and everything. Every day when I came back from school I would start to help her. My stepmother was now reading novels and turned the garden into her private recreational centre. When my father came home he would ask for food from my sister, and I was wondering if he had forgotten that she wasn't his wife. Where I come from the husband is supposed to ask his wife for food, and his children for a glass of water or tea, unless his wife had deceased.

One day my sister had gone with one of our neighbours' girls for a tour. It was getting too late for her to prepare supper, so our stepmother had to make it herself. When my sister returned Stepmother was furious, and yelled: 'Where have you been?'

'Who are you to ask?' my sister replied.

'Because I was looking everywhere for you to cook, but you were gone!' Stepmother continued.

Helen answered her back in very rude words: 'You should learn to cook for your own husband, I'm his daughter and I shouldn't be the one to cook for him every day, so stop questioning me woman!'

My stepmother became even more mad, but she could do nothing because of my sister who had proven herself the strongest. Instead she began to cry until our father came home. He asked his wife of what had happened, and her story was almost unrecognisable. Then my father turned to me and asked of what I had heard, while the woman looked at me with warning eyes. I didn't need to be told of what she would do to me if I told a different story, and to save myself I told him that I hadn't heard any of their discussion. Then he told my sister to lay down, because he had to punish her, but my sister went wild as if she was stung by the bees. She asked him why he only listened to my stepmother's lies, and further-more, she asked him what kind of father he was, to torture and beat up his own children, as if he had nothing to do with them. I was so frightened that my eyes couldn't leave the floor, and when she finished there was a silence like of a bad night. Everyone was in deep thoughts, and in my heart I knew that what my sister had said was the naked truth. At last I managed to look up at my father's face, and I was shocked with what I saw. The wrath was seen all over his face, and it seemed to make him grow to a terrible size. I almost ran outside as my sister broke the silence: 'You're not going to beat me today, because now I'm a big girl, so we are going to fight. The beatings I had from you is enough, that was then and this is now'. My dear sister was the first and last I heard telling him of his own dark sides.

Now my father was struggling to hide his shame as he told his daughter to get out of the house, but she refused with an: 'I'm going nowhere, and if you want to kill me, do it now!' But he only repeated his demand. 'Why did you make me in the first place, or are you not my father? If you're not, then I'll be glad to hear who he is, but you are, aren't you? So I am staying!' she replied.

My father started trying to drag her out of the door, but she was strong enough to resist. Then he tried to beat her, and they fought so hard that some of the doors broke, but again she was strong enough to avoid most of the beating as she shouted: 'I will never let you beat me again, not before the day I die.'

The following day father told her that she should find another place to stay, and maybe take the offer of the marriage, that was if she couldn't live by the rules of his, and his wife. She replied that she refused to live by his wife's rules, and if he liked the man so much, then he could give his own wife away.

She called me to follow her outside, gave me a letter to my father, and then she left. I was confused and powerless as I walked down to the plantation. I dried my tears away to gain my senses, and thought for some time of reading the letter. And this is what I remember:

John.
You made me live my childhood far different from any other children I knew. I am now wandering around in the world without purpose, because of you, Father. You have failed to judge between me and your wife. You have not shown me love, but you still claim that I am your blood. You have buried me in deep thoughts of whether or not you are my father. I am going now, and I will die in pain, but I will never call out for you. The heaven and the earth will be your witnesses and I will not be there any more. You will die with guilt, and never ask yourself why. The pain you have caused me! I wish that it will be felt by your soul.

L. Helen

After I had read it I questioned myself if I should tear the letter apart or give it to him. I tore it apart in small pieces never to be discovered, afraid of what might happen to me if I gave it to him. Now the sister that I called a traitor turned into my hero. I kept the words of her letter, and I am sure to keep them till the end, for she stood by in what she believed in. She suffered a lot in her lifetime, but she never returned to ask for help, before the day she returned to die at his home.

Murderous Lie

I was all by myself again, and the happiness I had gained was taken away from me as sudden as it had come. I was sad not knowing where my sister had gone, and I found it hard to find where to start, and where to end, as I thought of following in her footsteps. My eyes refused to help me sorting good from bad solutions and, as the days went by, the pain grew stronger.

One morning the milkman didn't show up, so I had to bring the milk from the dairy. My father found that he had run out of change, so he entrusted me with a note. I walked down the road, past my school, and, right there in front of the bank, I saw soldiers, and as I came closer they started staring at me. They scared me to the extent of panic when I passed them, as fast as I could. At the dairy I found that I had lost the money, so I went back again, thinking that I might get lucky and find it. I searched all over, even where I most certainly hadn't been, so I just had to walk back home. I was thinking of what my father had done to my sisters, when they had committed similar offences, but I calmed myself down, thinking that he probably would favour me being this young. When I reached home he had already gone for work, and my stepmother left my story for my father to solve. That day I missed school, and whenever I looked at the watch my heart would jump, only wishing that my father would be hit by a car and never return. In the evening he returned, and I heard him talk with my stepmother. Too little time passed and he called for me. 'You bastard, how could you lose the money?'

I told him what had happened, knowing perfectly well

that he, too, was afraid of the soldiers. But my father was not convinced of my story, and told me that he was keeping me out of school. I felt cold all over, as I looked him in the eyes and went to bed. I was lying in my bed staring up at the roof, feeling like crying, but the tears wouldn't come.

Then I remembered of how my father got his education, far away from his own family in the favours of a stranger. I thought of any distant family that I knew, but I found no one who could provide me with what I wanted. I thought of giving up my life, but told myself to wait for my father to feel satisfied with my punishment.

Two weeks had passed, and a call came from my grandmother. She meant that since I was not going to school, I should be at the ranch and help her. The following day my father and I took a mini-tax, back to the memory that I thought was left behind. I watched the road with its tall trees on its sides, that led its way up to the ranch, wondering of how many years of school I would miss. When we got there Grandmother had made a very nice dish, but I didn't feel the taste. My father went back the same day, without any word of when he would return for me. Some days passed without easing my worries, until I met Mike, a man who worked at the ranch. Mike was a very tall man with a beautiful white smile and kind heart, which he opened for me, making me tell everything that troubled me. Soon my brother, too, was brought to the ranch, and whenever the three of us had finished our day of work, we would sit behind the house on the grass, and have a good time while looking at the stars. One night I asked Mike of his family. He told us that he had none, and he seemed bothered by the question, but I wouldn't stop. Mike looked upset and told me that he didn't want to discuss any of this, and then he walked down to the workers' house. After he had left, I asked my brother of what he thought of him, and he just replied: 'Maybe his family was bad just like ours,' and our conversation ended as Grandmother called out that the food was ready.

Days later our father came with a truck, and some people whom he used to sell the cows to. He stayed behind, letting the driver finish the deal in town. The next day my brother returned from grazing the cows, and told me that a cow had hidden its new-born calf somewhere in the thick bush. We asked each other, of who to tell first: our grandmother or our father. We agreed on telling our grandmother, so that my brother could prepare to save himself from being squeezed. When he told our grandmother, I watched at some distance, and a scream almost left the house without its roof. Immediately I ran to see what had happened, and saw grandmother on her way to our father, who was on the other side of the house repairing the fence. My father marched inside the house, went for the chair and sat down, with his face lowered. A few seconds later he jumped up, looking at my brother with flames in his eyes. I saw my brother backing for the door and stood next to it. My father told him that, right now, the lions might be eating the calf, and then he went back to his chair. We spent a quiet moment, and I could breathe again, thinking that everything was over. 'Bastard! You have given my calf to the lions!' he suddenly roared through the silence, as he reached for the machete, making my brother disappear out of the door like a wind, quickly followed by our father with the machete raised, like a madman. And there I was as good as left behind, thinking that my brother would be killed. I kept looking at my grandmother as I thought that she might do something, but she just looked back at me with angry eyes, replying: 'Shut up! Do you think you're crying blood or milk?' I was puzzled by her reply and silently went to bed, and waited there as I feared what the outcome would be.

Some time later my father returned, and ordered me out

of bed, and then showed me the machete which was covered in blood, telling me that he had killed my brother. His words made me strong because I knew that I had no more to save nor to lose. I didn't cry or shake any more, I just felt that the world got a little colder. I went to bed with dry eyes, while remembering my brother's ways and the good time we had. I hoped all the cows to die, because I was hurt to see that my brother had to die for the sake of the cows. But then I came to think of the love that made the cow hide its child, and that stopped my wish. I realised that such love possessed by an animal was tenfold as pure as anything I knew of in people.

I got up early, before anyone else, and went to search for my brother's body. After a short walk I saw the figure of a young boy, standing on top of a termite hill, so I walked towards him hoping he had seen my brother's body. As I got closer I discovered that he was my brother himself, and before I could say a word, he spun around, took his pants off and showed me his bum. I almost laughed my head off, and when he came down, I gave him a big hug, and told him of what happened after the chase. I didn't bother about his escape, because the only thing that mattered was that he was still alive. I told him to stay right there, so that I could go and steal some food. When I reached home my father had gone to the workers' house, and I managed to steal food and milk and return without our grandmother noticing. Later my father returned and I remembered to keep my face sad, until he returned to the town house.

The Whisper

It was hard for me to see the good times that my stepmother gave. Even as I write now, I cannot get my mind to think of any happiness that I might have shared with her, because she seemed to strike down, whenever things started to go the right way. I still find it hard to judge my father who only listened to his wife, and as a result of all this my mind only kept the good times that I managed to give myself.

It was Saturday morning after the cows had been counted, and fifteen were missing, and the two workers quickly ran to Grandmother. I saw her hair rise from her head, and with anger she asked them of where Mike was. As they were about to carry out a search, Mike arrived and it seemed as if he had been out jogging. He asked of why everybody was assembled like this, and my grandmother told him that he shouldn't act as if he did not know what he had done. But Mike seemed unaware of what Grandmother meant, until she told him that he had helped thieves to steal the cows. Mike swore to his innocence, while asking her that, if he had stolen the cows, why then would he come back? But she was not convinced, and told him that he just wanted to make sure that he wasn't the suspect. After having finished intimidating Mike, she sent one of the workers to call for our father. My brother and I told Mike to run away but he refused, saying that because he was a Tutsis too, our father would understand that he had not stolen his cows.

In the afternoon Father arrived with the police, and Mike's words became meaningless as the police only had decided to listen to our father, who was talking as if his feet were on fire. Mike was beaten and kicked by the police, before being dragged into their Land-Rover. In the evening, as we were about to go to bed our father told my brother and me to stop cow-herding, in fear that we might get over-powered by the thieves, but I didn't listen much as I imagined the police still beating Mike.

Early in the morning Father and one of the workers went

to search for the cows, and I hoped so much for those who had stolen the cows to kill my father, but days later he returned empty handed. But still there was one more thing for him to worry about, Mike had been set free, and the only word I could read from my father's eyes was revenge. He began a random search, and bribes were given to the neighbouring ranch workers, and everybody seemed to have seen him everywhere. Very early in the morning when we were standing with our father at the calf shed, a man came and told him that Mike had been offered a job at the place where he worked. Quickly Father ran into the house, grabbed a rope and left with one of the workers. In the afternoon my brother and I returned from the dam, and found Mike almost beyond recognition. His clothes were covered in blood, and he laid on the side of our house with his arms tied firmly behind his back, still surrounded by our father and his men. When Mike saw us he tried to raise his head, while saying that he was thirsty. My brother went inside and returned with a cup of milk, but Father took the cup from my brother and threw it at Mike's face. 'If you hadn't stolen my cows, nothing of this would have happened!' he said. Then he grabbed an iron-pipe and hit him on the back, making him vomit rocks of blood. He frightened me with his screams so I ran into the house, and hid myself. When everything got quiet I came out and Mike couldn't move, and when my eyes met my father's I saw a fright beginning to crawl across his face. He looked away and ordered the workers to put Mike on the wheelbarrow, and dump him in the bush.

The following morning Father brought the police, and I was sure that they were not the ones who had arrested Mike. He told them that Mike was caught stealing the cows again, and when the workers beat him he mistakenly died. When I heard his terrible lie I looked at him, and if the eyes were as they looked surely he would have been burnt. My father went inside the house, and quickly I told an officer the real story, but begged him not to tell my father. When my father returned from the house they handcuffed him, telling him that they were not convinced. Grandmother cried aloud when they took her son, and I smiled a bit, called my brother, and told him that now we could do all we wanted.

A Light in the Darkness

A week had passed without our father and stepmother, which made us have a good time at the ranch. Our grandmother was quiet and she seemed not to pay much attention to our activities, so we were free to do whatever we wanted. One day on our way back from hunting, we met Margie the sweet-buyer, and once again she had brought a bunch of sweets, and this time she didn't bother to ask us of how she looked. Our greetings were brief, as we were in a hurry to tell of what had been happening to us and our father. She believed that he would serve a long time in prison for such a serious crime, and then she asked if our stepmother's children had been removed from school too. When we gave her a negative reply. I nearly ran away, as I saw an anger in her eyes so much stronger than ever.

With a face like a snake who was about to strike, she ordered us to prepare ourselves, and within a few days she had already forced our stepmother to put my brother and me back to school. I heard Margie say that she was going to prison to see our father. I asked her if I could go with her.

'Why?' she asked. 'Well, since you are going alone, I thought that you might need some company,' I replied. But the truth was that I wanted to see how he felt being in prison.

As we walked I thought of telling my sister the real

reason, but I couldn't find a way to explain it without the chance of misunderstanding. When we got there, many prison-orderlies were standing outside the gate, and as we got closer they stared at us. One of the men called my sister, and when she approached him I became afraid, thinking that they might harm her or throw her in prison. I was impressed seeing my sister who faced them without fear. She simply smiled with her pretty face that somehow made the man help us right away through the gate, without having to bribe them. A few minutes later a man brought our father, now wearing grey shorts and a short-sleeved shirt and I was surprised to see him bald-headed. Together we went to an empty room and the prison orderly commanded him to sit, on the concrete floor. Father looked embarrassed, his eyes didn't escape the floor, and he didn't talk much with me, but used most of the scarce time talking with my sister. I observed closely, trying to find any changes in my father, but all that I saw was a smile forced upon his face. At the end he and my sister got into an argument over us not being in school. 'Is this why you're here, to add on to my worries?' I felt sorry for my father, and silently I pinched her, trying to make her stop the argument. But she continued until the prison-orderly commanded my father back to his cell without having time for goodbyes and, as I cried, my sister said: 'Don't make me vomit!'

Soon we were home and right away she began packing before returning to Kampala. Now that she was gone, my stepmother transferred me to a cheaper school, but Richard was sent back to the ranch. The new school was more exciting for me though. The teachers seemed to understand me better, and soon I was appointed to be the class-monitor, but when it came to the other children I felt too insecure. I couldn't tell them of my origin, not because I felt inferior, but I knew that Tutsis were disliked by most people. The children made fun of me because of my different look, and I couldn't find a way of explaining myself out of it. I lied and pretended that I belonged to the same people as them, but I couldn't convince them. I was marked by my face, with my small lips and light tan. Later I learned that no matter how many lies I told, they never helped me to change into their kind.

Some time had passed since Margie left, and my step-mother sold a cow nearly every week. Her excuse for this was that she needed to free our father and pay school fees. I was annoyed to see her sisters come and go, and I was jealous as I thought she gave away my father's money. Even her mother Jane, who hadn't showed up when my father was still present, came that evening with one of her daughters Christina, one of the girls who made Father chase them away from our old farm. I got even more angry when Jane left Christina at our home. I was getting desperate and confused, seeing that Stepmother never visited our father. It made me think that he never would return, so I began to suspect that my stepmother was about to take all his riches, before chasing me away.

At school things got a bit tougher for me. Before, I was known as the kid who had the answer for every question, but now I couldn't concentrate on anything. At the end of class my teacher would ask why I acted this way, but I had no answer. I simply didn't think that she would take my situation seriously. One afternoon I returned home and Margie had arrived. I forgot to greet her as I threw my school bag down and ran through the neighbourhood to tell the great news. Even my worst enemies got the word. I returned from Sofia's just in time to hear Margie threaten our stepmother with beatings, if she didn't stop selling the cows. She stopped all right, but Margie took over from where she had left, and in a matter of weeks, Father was released.

After Margie had left, my major concern was whether Father would take me out of school or not. He spent some time without working, and being a good father. But he began the habit of drinking. He would return at night, waking everybody, as he crashed through the house towards his bed. One of the nights he woke us up: 'All my children, come to the living-room!' He began telling us of what he wanted us to become. 'Look at me and listen carefully!' he said, while managing to straighten his back. He began with Ray: 'You will be a doctor. Pamela! You will be a nurse. Emanuel! You will be a Father. Baby!' he stopped and continued after a break, 'you will be a pilot.' One day I heard him tell my stepmother that she had been sleeping with a boy who was a lodger at our neighbour's, when he was jailed. I do not remember what triggered the fight, but I heard my father say: 'I can even smell sperm all over the house,' before he dragged her out of the door, and they began fighting in the garden. A week later, Father got his old job back, and he even stopped drinking. My stepmother soon began her old tricks, and this time she demanded me to prepare dinner, because she was going to Mrs Derrick.

I tried to imagine how the sauce looked when she made it. It was yellowish and tasty, but that was all I knew. I decided to put in half a litre of fish oil, and a lot of curry, but I was afraid of the salt. When I had finished I looked at the food with a satisfied smile. It looked as it should, and I knew that she would thank me for it. When she returned she went straight to the kitchen, looked at the food and went back to the living-room, without a word. I stood at the door still waiting for her to thank me, but no word came from her mouth. I kept wondering about what she saw in my food. I was proud as any other little girl would have been, and I became absolutely sure that she saved the 'thanks' for everyone to hear during supper time. When my father returned from work, she gave me the food so that I could bring it to the dining table. As we all sat down and were about to eat, my father shouted: 'Woman! Is this the food you have cooked for me?' and my stepmother replied: 'Ask your daughter...'

'Why should I ask my daughter when you are my wife?' Father replied. She told him that she had returned from her friend and learned that I had cooked the food without being told. My father turned his eyes at me, like a biting dog and asked me who told me to cook, but I just looked down without a reply. He told Ray to fetch a bunch of chillies from the garden. He mixed it into his soup and ordered me to eat it.

I looked at him and knew that, even if I ate the food, he would still beat me, so I guessed that it was the same no matter what I did. He repeated his order for some time in a continuously ruder voice until he gave up. He walked to his room and returned with a stick. He stood himself in front of where I was sitting and ordered me to lie down, but I kept on sitting. He sat himself on a chair and held my head in a tight grip between his legs. I decided to fight, trying to make him break the fuelled lamp which was hanging from the ceiling, hoping that the splintering glass would kill us all. My father began beating me all over, and I tried to protect the back with my arms, but a sharp pain in my fingers made me give up the fight. Then I heard my stepbrothers and sisters crying: 'Please Father, stop. You're killing her'. They told the children to go to bed and went too, leaving me to help myself. After a while Ray and Pamela came and helped me to wash away my blood. After having finished they helped me to bed, and it warmed me when Pamela asked me if she could sleep by me. I had a talk with her about our parents, and she told me that she hated our father and her mother for what they had done.

In the morning my father told that I should say that I fell from a tree, when anyone would ask, otherwise he would beat me again. I walked slowly for school, and when I arrived all the children gathered around me asking of what had happened, but my tears just ran down. As I remained silent the kids ran and returned with a teacher. She began asking too, so I told my father's lie, but she would not believe me, and took me to the principal's office. He assured me that anything I said would remain between him and me, but I kept silent looking at the floor. Then he asked me if the woman at home was my real mother. 'Yes,' I replied. But he kept on pressuring me for a different answer, and after some struggle I confessed. He took a pen and began writing with a determined face and a steady hand. When he had finished he told me to give it to my father, assuring me that it was nothing to worry about. At home I gave it to my father, and after having read it he roared. I waited outside for some time, worried, until my father came telling me to deliver the letter that he held in his hand. After the morning parade I gave the principal my father's letter and waited for him to read. He looked up, shaking his head, and looked down at me, before taking me to his office. He then told me that the letter he had wrote the day before was an attempt to persuade my father to let him coach and take care of me at his home.

On my way home, I went through our neighbour's field of sweet potatoes, sat down and looked at my fingers. I dug up a potato with my other hand and started chewing it with a thoughtful mind. I came to think about my sisters: 'Can I rely on them? Do they remember me? Or are they busy struggling for their own lives?' I believed so. I stood up, looked at our house from a distance, and learned that I was gaining strength. This was the time to stand for myself, before my stepmother would destroy my soul.

Stranger in a Strange Land

As my fingers started to heal, my stepmother seemed uneasy, as if things weren't going the right way, and I saw her behaviour as a warning of stormy weather. My father remained peaceful, and I could only guess that he was waiting for me to be healed. Soon my school would close down for holidays, but I didn't want it too, because I hated to stay home. Early in the morning I ironed my uniform and ran for school. I found everyone already gathered in the assembly hall, and later I learned that I was one of a few without a parent at my side. I watched the presents being prepared, thrilled with excitement as I hoped to be number one. Principal walked up to the podium with papers and began thanking those behaving, including us class-monitors and prefects. Then the moment came where he began reading the winners' names according to their position, and my ears were wide open as I expected to hear my name first. Two other names were read before me, but I didn't cry much, because I got presents anyway. As I opened it I found beautiful colours, rulers and a set of twelve learning books with funny pictures.

When our principal set us free we knew that the war was at hand. We ran as fast as we could to get our sticks. We did this every year to get a last good hit at the kids we didn't like. We allied ourselves into small gangs in a sort of hit'n'run warfare, where we would attack in little flocks and flee. Believe me, we were serious! And we knew that all would be forgotten the next year. After the battle my friends and I headed for home, chatting and comparing marks, before we parted. I was almost home when my best friend, Sofia, came running, and before I could ask the problem, she told me not to go home. Sofia told me that my stepmother had been watching me from the hillside, where our house was situated together with her mother.

She had heard a conversation between them, that she would tell my father to beat me again, for not hurrying home.

I stood quiet for a while as I struggled to keep my tears away, before telling her that I would go and try to find my mother. I thanked, but told her not to say anything when she got home. As I had walked a while I looked behind and Sofia was still standing there. Then my tears broke out and I cried all the way to Patricia. She was standing outside with her son and two daughters, all surprised to see me. 'Does your father know that you are here?'

'No,' I replied.

Patricia shook her head when I showed her my broken fingers, but asked me what help I wanted.

'Just take me to my mother,' I answered.

She looked down and said that she couldn't help me, because she feared my father, so I threatened her to drink poison if she forced me to go back. As we sat there in her garden, we saw Pamela and Ray standing up the road. Quickly Patricia told me to run into the house, but I was sure they had spotted me. After a while, Patricia called me back, but she was so afraid that I had to lie, ensuring her that they didn't see me.

She invited me inside with a nervous gesture, as if being afraid that they might return. Judith and Mutton invited me to their bedroom. They had lots of funny and beautiful toys that I never had seen, making me forget all about my troubles. We ate dinner and, after having finished, she showed me a photo of my mother, telling me that I looked like her. She described some guidelines for my Journey, and I was relieved to know that my mother lived at the end of the route.

Early in the morning, that day in 1984, when I was eight years old, Patricia escorted me to the bus, bought me a ticket, and then we parted. The bus continued its journey and I was crying silent tears, thinking of what I had started. As we were half way, the bus stopped all of a sudden at an alien place, and to my terror I saw an army road-block. Everybody were ordered out to stand in a line in front of the bus. They began searching the grown-ups and their belongings. They even beat some of the passengers with their guns. Those who had no identification were accused of being rebels and taken into the bush by two soldiers. We were told that the bus-route was ending where we stood, because of rebel forces, who they said could hijack the bus.

The conductor began refunding people's tickets, but I had lost mine. I begged him, but he refused. The man who had been sitting next to me asked why I was crying, so I told him that I was going to my mother. He asked me if I knew where she was and I answered yes, fearing that he would take me back to my father. I was relieved when the strange man offered me to join him. We all started walking, and the strange man asked my mother's names. But when I was about to explain more, he already knew who she was, because of her husband who was the chief of the town hall, a rich man and influential. When he mentioned this I got angry, and asked myself why she hadn't used her husband's power to rescue us.

We walked for many hours until we at last reached to a Centre, and my friend went to a restaurant but left me outside. I sat there looking at the people eating and drinking, but it couldn't take away my need, so I went for a tour around the Centre. I saw the police station and the buildings adjacent to it, which reminded me of the description that Patricia had given me. I asked some women standing outside the police station if they knew my mother, but they didn't, so I walked back to be sure that the man didn't leave me behind. Looking through the window watching the man eat without me, inside of me I now doubted him as my friend.

Soon people from the bus had gathered outside the restaurant, and our journey continued through the bush, to make a short cut towards our destination. It seemed that we had entered the never-ending wastelands, with scattered bushes and trees on a huge plain of grass, that continued its bulky ways all the way, round into the horizon. The animals were full of life and they made me believe that I was the only miserable creation in the world. As I walked, my mind darkened and I felt that good nor bad mattered no more. Though I was used to walk long distances, this walk burned my legs, but still I kept trying to follow the others, knowing that no one was there to feel sorry for me. At a point I realised that no matter what I did, I was unable to maintain the speed, so I found my own pace, and slacked behind. I fell to the ground tired and sad.

'Get up, now,' I heard the strange man command, as he helped me to my feet. I told him to leave me there, I was going no more. A burning clap on my cheek made me stand, and roused me enough to keep on walking. I forgot about the pain in my legs, the rough ground beneath, and the next thing I noticed was when we reached a house. It was already dark, and before leaving he told me that I had to sleep there until the following day. The old man seemed to live in this big house by himself, but I couldn't know because he didn't say much. The silence of the man made me feel comfortable. He served supper and we ate without saying a word. Then he showed me where to bathe myself, before showing me to bed. I was so exhausted that not even my frustration could keep me awake, and I didn't remember one line of thoughts. In the morning my strength were coming back, and I got a closer look at the old man. He was short, shabby dressed, bald at the top of his head, but around his ears and the top of his neck the hair was white-stained. As we had breakfast, there was a knocking on the door, and I was picked up by the man from yesterday. Before leaving, I thanked the old man and thought of his kindness, as I walked through his green garden which led to the main road.

When I thought of the woman I was going to call my real mother, I got afraid. The only mother I knew of was mean and cunning, so it was hard for me to imagine that any woman would be able to give me love. There was no turning back for me. Besides, I had no choice. Now I was nothing but a beggar, who was prepared to take all kinds of chances. After having walked for some time, we came across two women at the road, and the man pointed at one of them, telling me that she was my mother. When she approached us I almost ran away. He told the woman that I was looking for her, and I froze as she began staring at me. I couldn't recognise her from the photos I had seen at Patricia's, because this woman looked a lot older.

She asked me my names, as well as my father's and sisters'. When I replied, her eyes opened wider and my fear rose when the man said good-bye.

I wondered whether to follow the man or not, when the woman smiled and took my hand. I could see that she was not sure, and it became worse when she didn't know which among her daughters I was. She looked happy to see me, so I just had to walk by her side. She already annoyed me by telling me the terrible things my father had done to her. 'This bastard have kept me away from seeing my own children. I don't even know you!' But I kept quiet, afraid of revealing too much to this stranger I only just had met as my mother. We approached a huge house, surrounded by a beautiful garden with many trees and flowers. Even before we had entered her home she shouted for the workers to slaughter a cow. She forgot me in front of the house, and ran back the way we had come. I went round the house to see if her husband was home, but when I found no trail of him, I entered the house. I walked from room to room, but in a hurry, and in one of the bedrooms, there was some money on the table. I looked at it for a while, and as I was about to walk away, my conscience refused, so I took a few steps back, and took some. I had done this, because I sensed that something might happen, and I knew that, with money, I could find another way.

After a while, my mother returned with a bunch of men and women, and soon all the women was grabbing pots and knives. The men rushed to prepare the fire, while my mother ran around speaking so fast that I could comprehend only when my name was mentioned. The evening came, and we sat around the table, while others sat in the garden eating. Everywhere I looked, I met the same convincing smile, and my heart was fearful, because I couldn't tell if they were happy to see me or happy to eat me. I knew the saying that somewhere strangers ate small children, and that could just as well be these people, as anybody else. Then again, I looked at all the food that was awaiting on the table, and I hoped that everybody would be satisfied. The big feast came to an end, the guests had left and it was already late. I was left alone with the woman, which I still only supposed was my mother. She put me to bed, said good night and went to her own bedroom. As I was laying in the bed I couldn't help thinking about this family and their guests which had left. I feared that they might return to eat me, so I listened very carefully to each and every sound that the house and surroundings provided to my ears, mostly searching for knives being sharpened or footsteps in the garden. When all sounds of living things had ceased, I got up. Very careful as not to make a sound I got dressed. Like a cat, I walked my way through the house and sneaked outside into the night.

Her love and care could not find its way into my heart,
because it was too cold and my suspicion had no end…

C.K.

PART THREE
Child Soldier

A Mark for Life

I stood for a while on the main road, looking around for which direction to take, to go back to the old man. I would tell him of what had happened, so he maybe could make me stay, and work for him. I was already given up with my father and, whatever the price, I was prepared. I felt scared, standing out there in these strange lands, so the moon and the stars were dear to me with their bright light, which shone far brighter than any street light. I walked and walked, but after some time I noticed that something was wrong. 'I haven't seen the old man's house yet! Is this really the same way I walked yesterday?' I questioned myself! 'Maybe the night changes the view,' I carried on. I couldn't think of anything, because of my brain which seemed tired. I had been using it nonstop for two days, and now I was like a zombie, who had no idea where to go, and where to end. I reached to a point where I could not feel my body, all I had to do was to continue walking until I reached the train station.

I stood there trying to think and, when I couldn't find a solution, I entered the train. After having paid, I slept, and woke up when the train had stopped. I got out, and it was still in the night. There were people, but they were sleeping. I stood there, and looked around but there were no houses. I started walking until I saw the end of the road. All my fear was gone and I felt more stronger than ever. Then I saw a flash of light and thought of turning back. I was already exhausted, and the mere thought took away my last strength.

I decided to continue towards the light, but was stopped by a man's voice: 'Stop there! Who are you?'

'It's me!' I replied.

'Come closer!' he ordered, and he acted surprised when he looked down at me. 'What are you doing out here in the middle of the night?' he asked.

'I'm looking for my mother,' I said.

He pointed a torch at me, and asked about my father.

'He's dead,' I lied.

I was still answering questions when a group of men appeared from the bush, with guns on their shoulders. Everybody stood there looking at me, and I was beginning to be afraid of their intentions, but I relaxed when some of the men began to speak my language. All of them were very dirty, and they dressed in torn clothes. The man seemed content with my replies, and I was told to sleep for the night. I was puzzled and kept on looking at him, wondering where the house and bed was. Suddenly he smiled and folded two torn blankets on the ground, and told me to sleep. The blanket was smelling badly, but the swarms of mosquitoes forced me to cover my head.

I woke up to the voice of a man commanding: 'Left right, left right,' and when I looked around, I saw children of different ages marching beside a man in a military uniform. I could feel an excitement growing in my stomach. It was like this brand new game, and I wished that I was there marching along with them.

The man from yesterday approached me with friendly but at the same time strange eyes. Before he could speak I asked to join the others, but he refused me, because of my swollen feet. Shortly after, everyone there, excluding me, had to evacuate from the place, and I couldn't understand the reason for this, but some of the kids seemed to know why. They said that the NRA had just attacked Kabamba military barracks, and therefore we had to leave for a new camping place. NRA had many groups, and each group had its operational zones. We never stayed in one place, always on the run from the government army. We camped at another place.

The third day, I was allowed to join, and I felt excited as I marched, alongside with them. After what might have been two hours of marching, we had a break of fifteen minutes. The grown-ups sat alone and the children sat divided in groups. I sat alone, looking at their faces, and many of the kids seemed to have been there for some time. It became a bit hard for me to join them, because of their language.

After the break, some were lined up behind gun lines at a practice site: twelve children and twelve AK-47s. They got a few seconds to dismantle the gun, for then to put it back together. The following day, we trained in taking cover and charge with bayonets, but the AK-47 was bigger than most of us kids, so we charged with wooden sticks.

The third day of my training an instructor came straight towards my place in the line-up at the morning parade. The hard and tall man stood in front of me, looking straight down in my eyes and asked my name. When the Northerner couldn't pronounce it properly, he became angry, scared and frightened, and when I looked down, he said: *'Look at me China eyes!'* and with a reflex of adrenaline, my head shot up to meet his eyes. Then he pulled me out of the line, and commanded me in front of the others: *'China, left right, China, left right...'* and from that day, my name was changed for ever.

The foreign name had made me famous, and most of the

kids were now my friends, though the languages was a problem. I spoke Kinyankole, and there was a few who spoke this language. There were two languages which I had to learn as fast as I could. Most of the kids were of the Baganda tribe, who spoke Kiganda, but Swahili which belonged to nobody was considered our main language by Museveni.* He seemed to prefer this alien but international language from a belief that it could end tribalism. The differences between us should matter no more, because all of us were fighting for the same cause: 'Freedom'.

For China the training never took long, not necessarily because she was a fine child soldier who would be 'bad' on the battlefield, or because she was a fast learner. The simple reason was that the National Resistance Army (NRA) was still short in men, who therefore could not afford a long training. After getting this little knowledge of warfare, the children were divided into different fighting groups. I was one of those who couldn't carry an AK-47, so we helped carry the leaders' appliances, such as cups, pans and ammunition.

A month had passed since I left the training grounds, and I was picked for a special assignment along with a few other kids. I was excited, because now I would be seeing the action that I had heard so much about from the older kids. We walked through the bush while getting our instructions, and soon we hid in the perimeter of the bush that surrounded the dirt road. The commander told us to go to the middle of the road, sit down and pretend to have a good time playing with the sand. After a while the government troops approached in a huge convoy, but we continued as if being all alone. The convoy stopped with the first cargo truck, right in front of

---

*Yoweri Kaguta Museveni (b. 1945) had from his exile in Tanzania formed the Front for National Salvation which defeated Idi Amin in 1979. He became Minister of Defence in 1979–80 but fell out with Obote who became President in 1980, with the help of Tanzanian troops. When they withdrew, civil war ensued. Museveni would become President in 1986.

us. When most of the soldiers jumped out, we did as instructed: running back into the bush to our fighting group, who then opened fire.

But it wasn't quite as I had been told. The sound was terrifyingly loud and everything on the road seemed to splinter into pieces as rocket-propelled grenades (RPGs) hit the trucks. I was more frightened than ever, and about to run, when the grip from my comrades held me down behind a tree. Our side won, and after the battle everybody ran to the road and began undressing the dead soldiers. Every one of us, except the senior officers, needed something to wear, and it did not matter whether it was the enemy's military uniforms: it was O.K. with us. I stood and watched from a distance, the enemy's underwear and boots being shared. I was getting confused, having been told that I was fighting for freedom, but I had never imagined that to include stealing from the dead. My excitement turned into sadness, as I saw the wounded enemy scattered around crying for help, and suddenly it became hard for me to think of them as my enemy. Those who had surrendered had their arms tied behind their back, in the most painful way, but when I looked around at my comrades, and saw that everybody seemed to enjoy themselves, it convinced me to believe that there was nothing on earth man liked more than to torture and laugh at their prey.

The captured troops were escorted to our camp while being kicked and spat at, and when we arrived, the officers were shot dead. Y. K. Museveni welcomed us with convincing words, and for playing with the sand we became the heroes of that day. We ate supper with the big man himself, outside his little African built hut, where each were given a uniform and a pair of boots, having belonged to the officers. That night we were allowed a good night's rest, while the grown-ups guarded the camp which consisted of three huts.

The following morning, we had to look for a new camp, because we feared that the government would send in helicopters and artillery, in retaliation of the ambush the day before. Our new garments required a lot of skill. The boots went far above our knees, and the uniforms almost swallowed us, making it difficult for us kids to walk through the bush. But there was a woman, who walked alongside with us, somehow making it a little easier. At one point, all of us kids were crying, being hungry and thirsty, so Y. K. Museveni ordered the troops to camp, and cook our dried beans and corns. Some collected firewood, while others searched for water. Y K. Museveni sat in the shadow under a tree, with Narongo and some of the officers.

Among these officers there was a girl nicknamed Mukombozi (The Liberator). She was rescued by the National Resistance Army, when the government troops killed her family. She was there on the soldiers' jeep, when the NRA shot it with an RPG. The soldiers died, she survived, but her names escaped her mind for ever. She was known to be a brave and dedicated girl, who refused to carry anything but the same weapon which once rescued her. Mukombozi and Narongo were best friends and, one night at the campfire, Narongo told us the story of why she was here with the NRA.

One day government soldiers had broken into their house, looking for NRA rebels. They beat up and tortured her husband, and then shot him, still with his hands tied on his back. After this, her two twins were shot in front of her. Narongo was a Muganda, born in Ruwero district as most orphans in NRA. And I believe her living heart towards most of us kids is remembered by those still alive. With tears in her eyes, she promised to get those responsible for the death of her family, when some day we would take over the government. Narongo took her AK-47 as her husband, always by her side.

The Battle

My group and I were at a place near Rwenzori, resting away from the sun which had been draining us since the day before. It was around three o'clock in the afternoon when Salem Saleh, a senior officer and a younger brother to Y.K. Museveni, arrived. In his briefing he told us that it was time for the National Resistance Army to take over the government of Dr Milton Obote. I saw a smile across his face when telling that he and the mobile brigade had captured the weapon called Katusha the day before, bringing the government soldiers low morale. Before leaving he assured us that the NRA would take over in a matter of weeks. Our morale was strengthened by his assurance, and left us singing, and soon after Saleh had left, our battalion commander took over the briefing. He told us to prepare ourselves because we were to attack a government camp, which was about four kilometres away from us. After the briefing, my friends and I looked each other in the eyes, and then down without any comment.

A while later I went on the other side, and had my Uzi gun prepared, and after having finished, I then stripped off the side pockets and shortened the length of my oversize uniform. When I put it back on, I felt lighter and therefore much safer, because I knew that the burden on oneself could decide whether you survived or not. I was afraid but I could not show it, in fear that I would be called coward, as there was always someone looking at the other to see if they were afraid and if you were afraid, many of the kids would laugh at you, and nearly all of us hated that. Many of us kids hated to be looked at as cowards, and we would do anything to be looked at as heroes, and it did not matter whether we were scared, we still pretended to be cool. As we had been sitting by the fire for a while, a woman soldier told us to sleep, and slowly we made our beds on the grass. The mosquitoes and my worries would not let me sleep no matter how much I turned. I gave up and laid myself on the back and I let the sleep go. All night I wondered while looking at the starlit sky, trying to feel the right way, until the time came to shed blood.

Guided by the moon and the stars, we started walking our way through the bush until we found our fellow soldiers already taken positions. Our platoon commander told us to kneel down and wait for the order. Still safely hidden in the shadow of the last trees, with our guns ready as we looked at the sleeping enemy camp, we waited for half an hour with the painful stings of busy mosquitoes draining my blood, and I could not defend myself, because we had been told not to make a sound. So all that I did was to bite my lips. The first rapid fire of AK-47s was heard, which meant that now we should kill each and every living thing in the camp. Men and women began running out, and dropping down in one big mess still naked, and I could see their clothes swing in their hands. The massive fire of our guns turned the wild screaming of goats, hens and people into a faint disturbance to our ears, which slowly declined to nothing for the next three or four hours. When we entered the camp, goats and hens were laying mixed together with soldiers and their women who had been on visit, all laying there dead in the hot morning sun. We collected the weapons and food that we could carry and tied the arms of our captured enemy by the elbows.

When we got back in our camp, the prisoners were ordered to dig their own graves, and some of our officers told us kids to spit them in the eyes. The enemy were told that no bullets would be wasted on them. I could feel tears dropping in my heart, seeing the enemy being told in which way they would be killed: 'After you have dug your grave, I will call for the best men who would then hit you on your head with an "akakumbi"' [a short, heavy hoe]. After all the men had finished digging, they were ordered to stand next to their graves and then be hit on their foreheads and back with akakumbis in shift, until they dropped in the graves and died.

When the job was over, we had to move on because of the better equipped enemy who never left us alone for long. Sometimes we had to walk for a whole day without camping any place, because of gunships [military helicopters] who would pass over our head with loudspeakers telling us to give up or face what they called 'wipe-out'. But we could not give up because we had already crossed our hearts to finish what we had started. We walked with our belongings on our heads, trying to keep up with the grown-ups in a place burning like fire with our small dry lips crying for water.

As all hope had left me, they decided to end our pain and one of the commanders suggested that we went down to a nearby village to ask for water. We never took special care when approaching a village because most of them more or less supported NRA. Just the usual scouting: always with a slow moving head and the eyes looking at an array as wide as possible. At one point as we approached, some of us were alarmed by a faint smell of rotten meat and we discussed it briefly, but decided to ignore it, and carried on. When we came into the village we met a sad sight of our fellow comrades laying dead with moisture leaking out of every opening they had in their body. I shook my head, and closed my eyes. I realised from that point, that there was much distraction to come, but still that I couldn't change the situation I was in. For I tried as hard as I could to care for my presence there. I knew that hardly nobody managed to escape. The ones who tried were captured and suffered terrible deaths, there in front of us, and even those who stole food from the civilians were tied on the trees and shot.

121

Civilians were always good with us, and they gave us some of their cows and other food, but it was always not enough for the low-ranked soldiers. We were still wondering, when a government helicopter emerged with a sudden terror that forced us to throw ourselves into the best possible positions, and await the heaven to fall upon us.

After the terror had ended and we felt safe enough, all stood up in panic, feeling our bodies to see if we were hit. After checking myself I looked around to see if any of my friends were hurt, and to my despair one of them he was laying on the ground. When I walked towards him, he was all quiet like in heavy sleep. I tried to wake him up but he didn't respond, and it was hard for me to believe that he was going away from us. He was this little wise kid who always comfort us with words, telling us to be strong without worrying. A minute or two, our platoon sergeant took us away from him, while telling that the boy was dead. We had no time to cry, but to join the group and carry on our walk. My thirst and hunger was replaced with silent tears and flashes in my mind of the comrades I saw laying dead in the village. I was confused and afraid, because now I had finally realised that the terror I had seen also could happen to me.

We arrived at a place with rain water, and beside it was a bush where we were told to rest. When we had been sitting there for a few minutes, I heard one of the commanders ordering our battalion signal to connect the radio in the air.

After some time, I was awaken by Museveni's presence who came with a group of soldiers. He stood there in front us, and I noticed a stick in his hands which had a few drops of white and black colour, and he was wearing a plain Franklin army jacket. He told us to sit closer to one another so that we could hear every word he was to say. I was seated like an Arab in front, and I looked Museveni straight in the eyes, but he kept looking away, pretending that he did not notice me. I felt bad because I thought that he had forgotten me. In his speech, he told us that we were fighting for freedom and against 'ukabira' [tribalism]. He said that the most important thing for us NRA was to fight with one spirit, so that we could save those who was in government jails for the crime they never had committed. As most kids didn't know what had happened to their parents, he told us that they were killed by government troops, and those who were still alive were in jails, and their hope was us to liberate them. Everybody stood and shouted: 'Yes Afande [sir]!' with our guns in the air. 'No turning back!' and Museveni smiled with his stick in the air as well. But I was different, being with a different background, I knew where my parents were, and I just hoped to stay alive, so that one day I could return home and kill them. I had decided that they pay the price for the pain that I was now in.

When Museveni finally left, we began cooking the dried beans and corns which almost took an eternity to cook. We children were standing against the trees, while others were scattered around in the grass with red eyes which had not had any sleep for days. Everybody was quiet, except for a few low remarks now and then. We just stood there with our eyes on the pots waiting for the food to be eatable.

Suddenly we heard a scream of warning, we looked up in alarm and saw our OP [look-out man] come running towards us with a wild face. He shouted so all could hear that the enemy were at a small distance away from us. Some of us took our hands in the hot water to save some of the food because we knew that this could be the only meal for days. We ran as fast as we could between the trees and grass away from the enemy. When we reached what we believed was a safe place we found that some were missing, and I suppose that, because of hunger, they could not keep up with the rest of us.

There were many comrades that found it difficult to believe that we NRA could win the war. Many soldiers gave up their life because of the intolerable conditions we lived under. They gave up their hope for the day when we would take over, and be offered a promising new life. They saw comrade after comrade die, and it could easily be them the following day. For us kids it was different. Our memory and experience of another life from the past, and our awareness of death, was a lot more limited than the older soldiers'. We fought with one spirit, totally committed to whatever cause there was, with no turning back in contrast to most of the grown-ups. They would always take cover and dodge the bullets because they knew the danger of a bullet, but left us kids to meet them still standing firing back.

Few days later, my five friends and I were transferred to the Fifth Battalion, and when our new commanding officer, Stephen Kashaka, saw us, he ordered two of my friends to join his platoon bodyguard. Many of the officers liked the children to be their bodyguard, because they acted without asking any questions, and they were loyal to their Afandes. We were active in each and everything, killing and torture was the most exciting job for many of the children, and they thought that that was the way to please their bosses. We would increase our brutality towards our prisoners just to gain more ranks, which meant more recognition and authority. But we were too young to realise that our actions against any captured enemy would haunt our dreams and thoughts for ever, no matter where we would be in the world. The children did so much terror to please our leaders, and in return they betrayed us, I guess they never thought of us as getting older, or of what would become of us. I suppose that they 'knew' that we kids never would survive the front lines, which had become our number one enemy. We had to endure a lot that even a grown-up only would expect to see a glimpse of once in their lifetime, and I suppose that our memories as the children we were never could be ripe enough. Our memories were filled up too fast with horrors that only human beings are capable of doing, and an old person grew inside us like a wildfire under desperate control of our commanders. Our own minds were often reduced to that of the very basic feelings of thirst and hunger, cold and warmth, and many acted like robots that only did what our new creators desired. If we were 'out of order', we would be sent to the front line to die, sending our memory into oblivion. So many of us disappeared just like that, and most deeds worth remembering would leave the rest of us within a week. My eyes often looked at the senior officers trying to see whether they gave a damn about us kids or not, and I discovered that most of them only cared for their own presence, trying to figure out of how and when they would take over the government. I couldn't see anything but the promises of a victorious future of wealth and power in their eyes. It was then where I came to think that we kids never existed in our leaders' hearts, not even inside the biggest: Y. K. Museveni, though I guess, he never thought as far as becoming a dictator just like the one that we were fighting.

The Fate of Two Friends

One afternoon I was sitting in the shadow under a tree with my friends, busy talking about our experiences, when a parade was called. A commander from another unit stood in front and two platoons were told to march in front, and I happened to be in one of them. We were told that we would be taken to join a new unit, which would attack Simba battalion, situated in western Uganda.

When we arrived, all my trouble left me when I saw the smiles of my old friends Narongo and Mukombozi. I regained my confidence and strength as I greeted them in their open arms. I wondered what I would have done without these two women at my side, because at that very moment everything else seemed cruel and ugly. The trucks that was captured from the government ministry of works were lined up in front of us, as we were given instructions. I stood there with the gun on my shoulder and listened to our Chihanda [Julius Chihanda] who was buried deep in the glories of war. We were ordered to jump into the trucks,'and soon we began singing and shouting so that we could keep up the good morale that we had gained from his words.

The journey began, a serious one, that gave me the feeling that many of us wouldn't survive. I was extremely scared and looked around trying to find a pair of eyes less scared than mine, but I never found them. Many had tears, some almost bursting, and we were packed closely together side by side, and the air was dense just like our mood. Our overall commander was senior officer Fred Rwigyema, and Julius Chihanda. Rwigyema was loved by most. He was tall, handsome and a great commander, who didn't only persuade us to die for the glory, but also reminded us of the importance of staying alive. On the way we disarmed a police post, which gave up without a single shot. We carried on most of the day, but after Kamwenge we found a place to camp until dawn. Many people came to our camp to greet us, and they spoke sweet words to us. We watched them sing: 'We love you liberators'. Many were excited to see us children ageing all the way down to seven years, and many had brought gifts and food for us, but sadly enough we weren't allowed to accept anything. I felt proud, so did my comrades, and I began to realise that we actually meant a lot more to these civilians, our mothers and fathers, than we did to most of our commanders, and leaders.

It was time to leave again, and our plans had, for some

reason unknown to me, changed. The original plan had been to leave a couple of hours earlier to attack a sleeping enemy camp, but it was now morning with rising sun in the sky. Simba barracks was situated on a hill close to the main road. We arrived, cut the fence and, seconds after, shootings erupted from both sides. We killed most of our enemy who still had been inside the barracks, and it was time to take our victory for granted. Others were busy charging the dead enemies, while we checked on our casualties. As some of us cried over our lost friends, a new surprised attacker came from the other side of the hill, already shooting at us. Fighting against the almost certain, everybody ran to find whatever cover we could find before the next bullet arrived. Many of our comrades were shot in the back in this first confusion, running for their lives, but still we kept on fighting in one spirit.

Mukombozi was not able to take cover because of her way of shooting the RPG alongside her hips, and this day it proved to be fatal. Mukombozi was shot by an anti-tank personnel. When Narongo saw what had happened, she climbed up in a tree, and began shooting. Rwigyema hopelessly tried to order her down, but she refused. No one saw her body falling but, when having withdrawn, we discovered that Narongo was missing.

When I realised that these two women had died, I felt like running away to my father's home, which was miles away from where we were. Then I thought of what his reaction might be, when he saw me in uniform and a gun on my shoulder. Would he scream or kneel down to beg me, I found no answer. So I decided to continue fighting this war until it was over. Many of us were terrified and scared as we walked down the hillside towards the main road, and saw the blood of our fallen comrades that had been running like small rivers now being sucked in by the thirsty ground beneath it.

But, as always, all we could do was to blink one time and swallow the pain. Some of our comrades continued to a place called Nyamitanga, while others were ordered to stay behind and try to take over the Simba barracks. It seemed that there was another more feared front, in a barracks called Masaka. We hijacked some trucks in a small town called Biharwe, and some of us jumped aboard and drove to face the next peril. A few managed to sing, and laugh, while most had given up fearing their near death. My mind was in my hometown [Mbarara] which I once again was leaving behind, and I wondered whether I ever would return in it. When the word death appeared in my mind, I got afraid. I stood up and tried to find a firm grip in the moving truck, with my head spinning in a still increasing dizziness. I, this little girl, began to sing like a proud man with joy in my voice, and soon everybody joined in, and I could see smiling faces all over. We continued until we reached a small trading centre, and all of us were let out.

Few minutes passed and civilians appeared, first slowly and cautious then in a great number. They didn't give the grown-ups much attention, as they tried to give us kids food and money. None of us were allowed to accept anything, because Museveni wanted his soldiers to be different from those of Dr Obote. I was offered some money, but I was afraid to accept it in front of anyone, and instead I told the woman to follow me by the corner. I wouldn't say no, because I was already a chain smoker. I hid the money, and ran back to where the rest of my comrades stood. Hours later we clashed with the government soldiers, which were on their way to Simba Barracks in Mbarara. The government soldiers lost, and made a withdrawal and a day or two later, we joined the Mobile Brigade, commanded by Salem Saleh. Now we were going to attack Masaka barracks.

When we arrived, the enemy was on high alert, ready to

defend their barracks. The shootings erupted, and soon both sides were losing men. The enemy fought as if they were in endless numbers, and because of the barracks situated on a hilltop it gave them a much better shell and eyesight above our heads. I was getting 'drunk' of the gun smoke, making it impossible to see whether my bullets were killing the enemy or not. All that I could see was the dead bodies from both sides, and one thing that I promised myself was never to get up and fight like I was bullet-proof. I took cover, always shooting from the ground, and when an enemy fell I would convince myself that that was my gun. The battle continued much longer than I had expected, even with the much feared Fifth Battalion on our side. The enemy bullets came on us like hail and made us retreat. While running away, each and everything I owned became heavy like boulders, and I thought of throwing my Uzi gun away, but that was a serious offence, so I began with my cap, but it all meant nothing, I still felt heavy. Soon we came to a place where nothing was worth running away from. Some comrades laid themselves under the trees, and those who had cigarettes smoked, while others cleaned their guns. I went and asked one of the comrades for a cigarette, but he told me to buy it. I went for the money in my pockets but I had thrown them away. I thought of telling him but became afraid, imagining they would call me a coward. Instead I laughed at myself while asking in a teasing way, whether I was a coward or not.

Few hours later at our rally point, the briefing began, this time from Salem. He told us that there was nothing else we could do, but to continue until we had taken over the barracks. We would attack again, and this time we could not afford to lose. Within few days, the enemy were losing strength and the NRA, on a national scale, had captured most barracks and other key positions. Through these days, a fast increasing number of government soldiers had wished to join us, but only a few lucky ones were now on our side. Salem was always in the Mobile Brigade, so he left Masaka to go to Colonel Patrick Lumumba.

The NRA wanted to seal off Katonga bridge, so my group and I were told that we were to join Fifth Battalion and First Battalion. When I heard this, my spirit rose, because I was expecting to meet my friends once again. When Fifth Battalion arrived, we were told that senior officer Kashaka had left the unit to get revenge over his father's killers. I was so disappointed, because I could not see any of my friends, even those that I had left in the unit were gone. Though I kept my faith, hoping that one day I would get to see those that were now Kashaka's bodyguards.

Fifth Battalion had now a new commander named Ahmad Kashilingi, who had been appointed by Museveni, after Kashaka had left. Kashilingi was a Munyankole and a former Idi Amin soldier. He was well trained in combat as well as administration work, and tall enough to look a giraffe in the eyes. He had a beard that gave him the nickname 'Kalevu' [goat's beard]. He had a history of being fast and clever enough to escape the most notorious prison in Uganda, called Luzira, where he was kept when Idi Amin's government had been overthrown by Museveni and Dr Obote. Kashilingi was well respected and feared by most other senior officers, who addressed him as a commando. The Fifth Battalion had the greatest fighters that can come to my mind, of them which I can remember were as follows: Moses Drago, M. Kanabi, and Julius Bruce. These young boys were of Baganda origin, and only death one day would separate them. Among these fighters, Moses Drago snatched my attention, and he was one of the youngest ranked officers.

Soon we were ordered to march alongside each other. The Fifth Battalion were ordered to be ready, because soon we would advance and cross a small, but heavily guarded bridge named Katonga, a few kilometres away from the capital, Kampala. At the parade, we were told that the Mobile Brigade was doing such a good job, and soon they would take over the capital. Now that I had survived two major battles, I knew that I had a big chance of seeing this city which most of us kids could only dream of. Before we left for Katonga, we had obtained a lot of brand-new cars. I saw cross-country Mercedes-Benz being knocked over by officers, who hardly knew where to start them. I came to think if there was any purpose with NRA were we for better, or for worse? Was this really what we had been fighting for? I asked myself watching the senior officers, doing the same things, running up and down with women, who were wild with these new freedom fighters. The soldiers had not washed for days, but I suppose that these women were perfectly unaware of that, or perhaps they simply enjoyed the smell. All these crazy things happened, while we stayed in a small town named Lukaya.

I watched all this madness as my comrades and I relaxed under a tree, and three fat grownup women approached us. They invited us to a nearby bar and took me for being a boy too. I enjoyed being looked at as a boy, so I told my comrades while entering the bar to shut up about my true identity and, amused, they agreed. We drank what was offered, and that was the first time that any of us tasted alcohol. All the people in the bar were crazy of excitement about our presence, and we had many laughs looking at their gestures as they eagerly offered us drinks. We didn't care whether we got drunk or not, because we knew our leaders had no time left to see what we kids were up to. We were getting drunk, and the women began to touch us. Whenever my woman got too close to the truth, I removed her hand. She laughed at me, and assured everybody that I was afraid of women. My comrades busted into laughs, but I noticed they were getting afraid too. I wanted to see the minds of these strange beings, so I stayed patient. The women became wild, and tried with more strength to touch us between our legs. When this happened all of us got angry. We stood up, pointed our guns at the shocked women, and forced them to raise their arms above their heads. At that very moment, a soldier walked into the bar. I just noticed his mouth open and close in surprise before he spun around, and like a flash he had disappeared. A minute later he returned with a drunk commander. We began laughing when we noticed him swaying from side to side, as he told us to leave the stupid civilians alone. On our way out, he asked why we had got into that position, so we explained that these women wanted to rape us. He took that as a valid explanation as he knew that children's only strength was the gun. Suddenly he sat in the middle of the street laughing, while pointing at me. 'They even wanted to rape China?'

When he had finished rolling around, we moved on to another bar. The same thing happened, a lot of women went wild with us, though the commander had a good time telling how terrified we were of them. My new woman was busy telling me how cute I was. She was going mad about my smile, but the commander overheard this, and told her that I wasn't exactly the person she expected. What happened next was going on in the same pace as if the enemy stormed our camp. She turned and looked at me with pointy eyes, and her white teeth made her look like an angry lion. Her big boobies jumped violently into the air, and I realised, that if I should avoid to be squashed, I had to jump the opposite way. With my back turned, I heard a scream that almost blew up all glass, and my legs accelerated like a top-tuned motorcycle. When the crying hunter realised that her prey was faster than her, she turned and continued running out on the street, leaving the highly amused bar alone. Back at my seat everybody laughed and cheered at me, but I couldn't see the fun any more. I was stolen away thinking about my mother, if she did the same things as this woman. An anger grew inside my stomach, and suddenly I felt like shutting everybody up with my gun. I left the bar and sat myself against a tree watching the night-life. All but me seemed to have found a partner, and the loneliness seemed to have been made only for me.

We stayed in Lukaya only for a limited time, having a good time away from the war. At the parade we were told to bear in mind that at any time our assistance could be required. After the parade my comrades and I went to a spot and discussed our previous battle. We assured each other that no battle could be as big as the last one. We had survived, and would also survive the last few disputes that remained, such as Katonga. We agreed that no other front line could ever frighten us again, we were real fighters now. Then a message came, I suppose from Museveni or Saleh: Senior officer and full in command of Fifth Battalion, Ahmad Kashilingi, was ordered to take us across Katonga and capture Entebbe international airport. We were briefed and told to prepare ourselves for a morning attack.

I was ready as one of the first, with my Uzi gun around my shoulder. Both worried and entertained, I watched the sun rise while the drivers ran around looking for which trucks to drive. Most of them had glowing red eyes, and I knew they had been drinking booze all night. As nearly everybody seemed ready for going, the worst sight met me. The commanders came from their beds including our battalion commander, all drunk, Muslims and non-Muslims. We went to Katonga but could not carry on the attack. Big guns were lined up behind the bridge, ready to tear us in pieces, and we were ordered to entrench, so we began digging our holes for cover. As I dug, I recalled the words of confidence, and I promised myself never again to judge a situation before I came to it. We were parted by the difficult waters of the river, which only a fool would consider to cross under heavy shelling.

Later that day fire erupted from both sides, but no side took the initiative to cross the narrow bridge which, I am sure, every soldier present considered suicide. We were stuck like this for about four months, until Kashilingi was ordered to cross the waters within hours. I looked at our side, and saw nothing compared to the big weapons on the other side. At first I couldn't believe this order to be true, but I couldn't have heard wrong, and Museveni, the overall commander-in-chief, or his brother [Salem Saleh] were the only ones who could make orders like this. He knew very well how devastating this was, and I started to think that he was careless of our lives. I wondered if he would keep any of his promises, from when he was a hopeful rebel. We started penetrating the bridge, and we were falling like flies, but the commander carried on saying: 'MOVE!' We continued going, through bullets and hand grenades. Suddenly one of my friends nick-named 'Strike Commando' went down. He shouted, begging for help, but none of us could stop. We managed to push the enemy back, but we lost too many lives. I walked among the casualties, but I couldn't find my friend. When I went to the dead, I was interrupted by angry comrades who raged at the bodies of the enemy with fists and boots.

Though I knew he was dead, I could not cry. I simply couldn't, in fear of breaking down. I had come this far, but I never seemed to harden. It was strange to see most other children having a kind of lust for killing and torturing. They could even smile when having made a 'rare killing', as they competed to earn nicknames, such as Commando, Rambo and Suicide. It annoyed me that I always had to feel sorry for others, even the enemy. I had crossed the line, where I had used up both hands to count my fallen friends. Now it was time to decide, from being a broken, but kind and unselfish individual, to being a strong full-blooded killer, if I only could. Soon every child carried more than three magazines tied to the AK-47, and soon many of us had up to six magazines. I guess that we all thought that if we were seen with many magazines, our leaders would be even more impressed. We forgot about our shoulders, and soon many of us started talking like old men. No doubt that all of us kids needed someone to love us, but if your parents have not gave you love, then who will? Others' parents were dead, and those alive let us down. Now we had to search for love from the strangers, but the strangers, too, looked the other way. We were now on our own, and we had to find ways of finding love and compassion. But all the time we searched in a wrong place, and insisted on love, the stranger forced us to find love from the gun. We were told that the gun was our mother, our friend and our everything, and to lose it, we would rather lose ourselves. At night, our leaders would come and steal the gun from us, and the following day, they would approach and ask where your gun was. You would look up and down as you wondered. As they beat you and roll you in the mud, they would accuse you of giving the gun to the rebels, or you have sold it. After the beatings, they would then hand you your gun, and tell you these words: 'You see what happens when you lose your mother.' Whenever I slept, I rolled the gun's belt around my neck, but still I was afraid to fall asleep. I'm convinced that Museveni knew about our treatment, because he, too, had a child as his bodyguard. Fred Kayanja was one of the kids that we were with in the bush, and he became Museveni's bodyguard from when he was about ten, and when I escaped the country he was still Museveni's bodyguard. Many of our leaders behaved like mad people, and they were more loved by

Museveni, while the good ones seemed hated. Many of the good senior officers, who had power to change things, all were dying: in car accidents, or AIDS was to blame. The mad officers were promoted rapidly, and it did not matter what bad things they did. The good officers, such as Lt Colonel Muntu Oyera, Lt Colonel M. Kodili, Lt Colonel S. Mande, J. Ayine, Major Katabarwa were always jailed, and all the power seemed to be in the bad ones' hands.

Once again we had to leave. We were driven on, along the blood-stained main road. The bodies of the enemy were scattered all over, some being eaten by the dogs, but I watched without concern remembering my friend they had just killed. As we took a short cut towards Entebbe, we were attacked by a gun-ship. We were better equipped now, shooting at them with a 37-calibre artillery unit, and soon they retreated towards the Victoria Nile. We carried on fighting and when we were told that Kampala was few miles away, our hope increased dramatically, as we now saw the promised future. We stayed between Entebbe-Kampala road, and blocked the government soldiers from going to Entebbe. After some days, we faced a strong and heavy equipped enemy. They were now bad, and seemed as if they were all prepared to die. Kashilingi begged for reinforcement, but no one came to our rescue. Thanks to Afande Kashilingi, who said: 'Let no one of you die here, fight and defend yourselves.' It was a surprise to see that some of us had survived. The NRA had lost so many great senior officers, and it seemed as if we had killed them ourselves, because we feared them. Weeks later, we marched by the enemy lines of retreat, and I could see a light of glory in every eye. The road was filled with droppings from the retreating enemy, and I was surprised to see everybody passing without picking up any of these precious items. I guessed that now Kampala belonged to us, and a life without guns was about to begin. I smiled as I remembered the words of 'home, and a life of knowledge', a promise made to us children, by Y.K. Museveni.

As we had been on this road for some time, we were stopped by an uneasy crowd of disturbed civilians. They saw us as saviours and, without fear, they pointed us towards a house further down the street. A girl from the crowd threw herself in front of our platoon commander, Julius Bruce, and begged him to rescue her parents. Others followed and a split second later, everyone were shouting, making the situation unbearable. Bruce spoke with a man from the crowd, and shortly after he gave us a short briefing before ordering us to storm the house, and we disarmed the enemy without firing a single shot. A group of exhausted people had been stowed together in one of the rooms, but when told to leave, they suddenly jumped up like a flock of retreating buffaloes, and poured on to the streets. When everything had calmed down, another fear rose inside of me: the enemy soldiers. Only a few of us were even near their height and they had numbers tattooed on their faces: '1 11'. I stood there with my Uzi gun in front of an unarmed enemy, ready to pee in my pants. Some began questioning the hostage takers, while others secured the house. We walked through the rooms stepping over dead bodies, for which some had been laying there for days, and the smell didn't allow us to count the exact amount. We left the enemy being torn apart, without looking back. These men had been hiding behind those walls for several days, killing men, women, and children. With a strong doubt I asked myself, if these men really had a heart, and how could anyone manage to stay in a house with a smell that could even suffocate a pig?

I am still wondering of what happened to these men, but I guess the civilians never stopped beating them, before having killed each of them three times before leaving the bodies for the dogs.

In Kampala, raging civilians were chasing government soldiers, and everybody ran around in one big confusion. The streets were on fire, with screams of our enemy being roasted on car tyres, but there was nothing we could do about it, so we just walked through pretending everything to be in order. When we arrived at the inner city, I couldn't see anything as impressive as the description I had got. I didn't have time to be disappointed though, as we were overrun by thousands of happy citizens welcoming us. Some were crying, while others kneeled down to thank us kids. But we shared our fame with others: for the first time on Ugandan soil, women were armed, and walked proudly as any man. Many looked as if they had forgotten the war, which was replaced by bright eyes of hope, but I couldn't feel that way. I could not loosen up, because I knew that there were more to come. I recently had learned never to feel secure, before I could see the next valley or look around the next corner.

(Bruce would die in 1995 just after having been promoted to the rank of Lt-Colonel, and Major M. Kanabi around 1992, just after returning from France.)

Escaping the Battlefield

To some, the disappointment came as the lightning from above. We learned that we, the Fifth Battalion, had to continue pushing the enemy northwards. I could not tell whether I was disappointed or relieved when Kashilingi handed over the command to senior officer Julius Ayine. He was a Hima coming from the same tribes as Museveni. He was a good commander, and many knew him for protecting his men at the battlefield. Kashilingi was a proud man, known to many as a hard lion, and he was one of those who created NRA. For some reason the Bagandas loved him and his entire bodyguard-platoon was of that tribe. The front line had already moved a fair distance to the north of Kampala. We were transported on the route that led to where Dr Obote was born. The road was in such poor condition that I wondered if the former president never had visited his family.

Kafu bridge, we met strong resistance, and I shook heavily, feeling that I wouldn't survive another battle. Flashes rushed through my memory of the horrors I met at Katonga, the hopeless stand-off which lasted for days, then my friend whom I lost. After some days, we continued to Karuma bridge. I saw a bridge beautifully untouched by war, with thick bush covering a heavy flood passing beneath It. I came to ask myself how was it now we had taken Kampala, I was still fighting. We kids had been promised another life, after having taken over the government, which had been situated in Kampala. I hadn't seen anyone relieved from duty so far, and I sensed, that if I wanted another life, I had to give it to myself. So I decided to live by escaping this fight. I somehow had to get sick, so I asked for a cigarette and ate it, ran to my platoon sergeant and threw up, and I smiled when he too began. When he finished I told him that I had an outbreak of malaria. When he didn't find any difference between his temperature and mine, he told me that I was lying. 'So you want me to send you back to the headquarters? No way!' he added. Not giving up, I went to a friend of mine who was clever at making tricky plans. I got him aside, and he told me that I had to drink my urine, to get a fever. 'He must be kidding,' I thought, as I tried to judge the expression on his face. Desperate, I decided to try. I went to a deserted spot covered by bushes and waited for the cup to be filled. Then I came to the hard part. I thought about it once more, before deciding to drink on the count of three. When the first two drops reached my stomach, I threw everything up. When I was back on my feet, I got overwhelmed by anger. I ran straight to the trickster, to tear him in pieces with my hands. The children around us cheered, while I was biting and scratching him as much as I could. After a while, a mutual and older comrade jumped in between and pushed us apart. I broke down in tears, making the only mistake possible by telling him of what had happened, right in front of everybody. Before I had finished almost everybody had burst; even the mediator himself was laughing aloud. I turned into fire and ran away from everybody, to sit alone with my embarrassment. Everything seemed hopeless. Just before I convinced myself, the trickster came and sat down, being my friend again. As I looked down, thinking about whether to forgive him or not, he apologised and gave me a hug, while saying no harm was meant.

The following morning I learned that one of the trucks was going to Kampala. I approached the driver, and told him of my worries. The man decided to help me, and early the next morning I waited at a safe distance from the base. When I was aboard, I called it heaven, feeling safe for the first time since joining NRA. But in my sleep the nightmare began, and I sensed that I had been screaming, when I felt a gentle push on my head. With my backpack on, I jumped out of the truck, and I was left on the road to wander.

I drifted through Kampala feeling deserted, with sweat across my face. The only relief now and then was the shadows of the hard walls that I passed, keeping any unwanted soul out. I wished more than ever to have a place which I could call my home. A horn honked so I looked up from the pavement, and spotted a car halting. Puzzled, I walked towards it in the same pace as before, with a feeling that the signal was meant for somebody else. But behind the wheel, a fat middle-aged Mugandan woman looked straight at me. I pointed at my chest with my eyebrows raised, and when she nodded I hurried towards her.

I got in the car and watched the sorry streets pass away, but then I turned my head. She had a sweaty face and a big stomach, and I could tell that she had had a bad day as she struggled against the heat. I almost snapped when she said that she loved me, and I was welcome at her home. 'She must be crazy,' I thought, but since I needed a starting point, I decided to accept her invitation without concern. Alone, I sat in one of her sofas looking at a collection of furniture and things that I previously thought only presidents possessed. When she came back from changing her clothes, she asked me to accompany her on a trip in town. I agreed and grabbed my bag, refusing to leave it behind because I didn't want her to know that I actually had a loaded gun in there. As we drove she proudly told me that she was a businesswoman, and we were about to reach her clothing store. The store was medium sized, attended by two beautiful-looking girls, and within minutes they stood ready with a bunch of clothes outside the test room. I looked myself in the mirror as I tried my new clothes on, and every time I left the room to be judged the staff nodded, as they looked at this pretty young boy. Now I felt like a real boy and I felt good seeing that they all were convinced. There was no doubt, and I was pleased. Later at her home we had some beers and listened to some sweet music, while her two house-girls prepared dinner. Now I was sure of what she wanted from me, so I had to come up with an excuse to keep her off me. Enlightened by the knowledge of the screaming woman from Lukaya, and the never-ending stories of my comrades, I decided to make up one myself, but I had to wait for the right moment to serve it. When she finally was about to go on top of me, I began: 'A few days ago I was sent back from the front-lines to get treatment. I had been having a problem with my penis for some time, so the doctor at the hospital was forced to circumcise me, in order to cure the problem.'

It worked and she backed off. Disappointed she went for some photos, and I jumped to a bowl of green bananas. When she came back I was sitting there waiting, now with my legs spread to show what I got. She looked moved, I suppose, by the size of it, so she hurried over to my side and showed me some photos of her, in foreign countries.

I noticed her taking a sip for every photo, and there were many empties on the table already. Soon she was all over me again,so I jumped: 'Get off, woman! You're giving me a severe pain,' and now I was getting angry, but tried to control myself by drinking more beer, and before I got too dizzy, the food was ready on the table. We ate without much talk, but when I had finished my meal, she annoyed me again. She insisted on going to bed with me, though I reminded her of my injury, and as we discussed things I cornered myself towards my backpack. I drew my gun, and the house-girls only screamed once before I ordered all three of them to shut up. I told the 'fat lady' to show me to the money, and in panic she jumped right over to a drawer. I stood with the money in my hands not knowing what to do. This had definitely not been what I wanted, but there was no turning back, so I kept pointing the gun at them, until I realised that I actually could walk away. I warned them not to follow me, making them promise to sit by the gate, and point towards the house until morning. I was trembling with fear when I walked out, and I only stood there for a short while, coughing to assure them that I was still there. Then I climbed the gate and walked towards the city, ready to repel any threat.

On my way I met a group of people, and I asked them of how to find the bus park. They tried to explain the direction of the mini-tax central, but they only confused me with their words. I asked them to escort me and to make sure they would, I changed the gun to my other shoulder. They saw me to the minibus; an old Hi Ace with seats and filled to the brim with people. Just before my home district of Mbarara, the mini-tax was stopped at a roadblock. Bruce, the roadblock commander, knew me well, and wanted to know where I was going but I pretended not to know, so he ordered the tax to leave without me. He invited me to a bar not far from his post, and I agreed with a smile. At the toilet I counted the money and found it enough to help track down the woman I once denied to be my mother. Bruce and I stayed in the bar for the rest of that evening, eating and talking about wars and friends lost in battles. Later we went to the barracks, and I was shown where to sleep, but I could not fall asleep because of my father's house, which was at a short distance away from the barracks. I had had the lust of revenge for quite some time, and it seemed the right moment to take my tormentors out of my life for ever, and I wanted to fulfil my promise the very next morning.

With my gun I went to my old school, and looked up the hill at my father's house, which was a fair distance from where I stood. My stomach was full of knots; my teeth were grinding and whenever I thought of any of them, my trigger finger would itch. My mind was now convinced to walk up the hill, and shoot him and his wife, but when I finally decided to go, my body froze like a soldier disobeying his superior. I became angry with myself. I stayed there for about an hour crying, and finally I returned to the barracks, where I met Bruce looking for me. With anger I told him of my desires, and I could feel my heart hit my chest as if my words was action. After having listened, he put his arm around my shoulder, and together we walked towards a piece of rock and sat ourselves. He told me that he had a bad father too, but that didn't mean that he would kill him. 'Why?' I interrupted. Because otherwise there would be no difference between me and him. Then both of us would be bad men,' he replied. I listened carefully to his words and I found them perfectly sensible. I wasn't like my father, and would never want to be. I assured him that everything about killing my family was forgotten, and he nodded with a sad smile. I told him that the following day I would go and search for my mother. He wished me luck, but I could not tell his mind, because of his eyes which never escaped the ground.

I had run away from my unit, when the war was still on and, to be safe, I decided to wear civilian clothes. I put my gun in a bag, and started the journey.

At my mother's, there was nobody and the place seemed to have been deserted. I was disappointed, and I needed to get myself together before making another move. When I had been sitting there for a while, I realised that I had forgotten my bag in the bus. The only thing which was valuable to me was the gun, and it seemed as if I had lost myself. Now I needed my mother more than ever. I wasted no time, and walked back to the town square, where I had left the bus. Everyone I asked was willing to help, but I seemed to keep on going to people who just had come to sell their goods. I sat down for a while and thought about what had passed, since I had escaped her. Everything seemed to have started that very night when I had left her house, and I couldn't help wondering about what my life might have been like, if I had stayed. I stood up, when I saw a woman coming in my direction. Her face changed into one big smile when I asked her of my mother. She took me by my hand, and assured me that soon I would meet her again. As we entered a house, I saw a girl seated on a chair looking exactly like my sister, Margie the sweetbuyer. She looked at me, and looked back with a thoughtful expression on her face, but as I came closer she looked up again. Suddenly she jumped out of her chair, down to the floor and cried out my name, but I remained standing slightly embarrassed and too proud to fall around her neck. After a while she jumped back to her feet, grabbed my hand out of the friendly woman I had met on the street, and dragged me through the house and out again in a lightning speed. Now I was so confused that I just followed her up the street, but before long I saw my mother in front of us, walking in a slow pace. When we stopped she only looked at us and said: 'Let's go home!' Now both of them started running, and I could only follow from behind.

We sat in front of the house for a while, where the two began questioning me. Margie was more excited about how I got into the army than being concerned with my sudden disappearance two or so years ago (though it seemed much, much longer than that to me). Soon my mother took over. She told me that the only reason for her to stay in that town had been to make sure that I one day would be able to find her. Through all that time, she had been living with the one burning question, of why I had run away that night. For the first time I looked my mother in the eye, and told her the truth. I felt rather silly about that evening at the dining table, and night in my new bedroom, where I never had been sure whether they were about to eat me or not. Now she laughed, and I guess that the reason I had given was a bit too much for her. My sister, though, looked at me with narrow eyes and smiled before she told me that it might have been a wise decision after all, because one never knew what our mother could be up to. My sister and I joined my mother in a silent moment, and I noticed a hen pecking next to us. Before I could ask who the owner was, my mother told us to catch it.

As we prepared the food, Mother whispered in my ear that this very hen had been kept specially for me, and I smiled imagining how old it would then have to be. I didn't really know my mother but I came to accept her faster than most. She had those funny ways of expressing herself, through little stories where the truth always were in question, but they would make you happy. I remember my sister and I laughing our heads off when she told us that the Pope's mother was a Tutsi and his father an Italian. There were certain things that one shouldn't eat when being a woman of her age, but she ate everything. When you asked her: 'Why?' she would only say something like: 'I will eat everything that was created before me!' All the people around her, young and old, were fond of her.

I could still not find more love in my heart, after having met my mother, though she treated me with lots of it. The time from when I had escaped my mother had been hard for her too. Her husband, the former chief of the village, had passed away. Everything they once possessed had been looted during the change of government, when Obote was deposed and Museveni became President (in 1986). Now she was left with a small worn-out rented room, from where she was selling home-made liquor to earn a living. I could not really feel at home there, it seemed as if everybody in the village was sloppy, never knowing what to do, and always talking before thinking. Despite that, I wanted to stay, but people failed to recognise me as the one I wanted them to see. I believed that I was above any civilian, making me to have the final say, but no one seemed willing to let me. Since my gun was lost, I could not return, and my past had to remain a secret.

My sister insisted that I started school, and I didn't know if I was happy with that decision, but I had no choice. My life was in their hands, so I had to do it their way. Margie made sure that I had started school, before returning to Kampala. Every day after school I had to fight, and for some reason it was always the older children which annoyed me. I lost most of the fights, but I didn't know how to stop. My mother would ask: 'Why are you bleeding?' but I never answered, because I thought that she was too fragile to take my pain. I was looked upon as a mad kid, I was marked, which somehow 'closed the case' for me. No one seemed to be able to help me, but of course, I never asked for any. I believed that anything which concerned me was for me to solve. My mother had no idea of how to help, and sent me to live by a couple, who she knew through her deceased husband. There I faced abuse at its worst, but still I kept silent, and endured it for two months. I returned to my mother, quit school and all I could do was to walk around like an animal in a cage. I had to get out, to do something. I could see the confusion in my mother's eyes, and finally I decided to relieve her from me. I started to work as a house girl, for a captain and his wife, but after a short period of time I began to look at myself. I didn't like what I saw. I quit because I felt humiliated, as I saw this as a step down in my life. I was broken, but I hadn't given up yet. Once more I returned to my mother, who took me in with open arms.

Suddenly I realised that I would have to start all over with my life, if I wanted to make it. But there was no turning back, because I saw my childhood long gone. I realised that I simply didn't fit into this community, being a small girl with a vast military experience. I hardly knew anything but the ways of a soldier, so I decided to restart, as a recruit.

I stole some money which belonged to my mother and left without a word. There were trucks driving around recruiting anyone who wanted to join the NRA, and when my truck got a full load, it drove off to Nyachishara. The recruitment time was even faster than I had expected, and in a month's time most were taken directly to the front line. I had learned my ways though, to work around the system, and therefore I managed to avoid this. The instructors had thought I was amazing, because I knew everything they had been teaching us, and before the training was over, the officer in charge had promoted me to the rank of lance-corporal.

I joined the Forty-Fifth Battalion, and stayed there for some time before I let my mother know where I was. My conscience had been bothering me badly, and I felt bad that she had to buy milk when my father had an entire farm of cows. I thought about this for a couple of days, before deciding to pay my father a visit. My stepsisters and brothers seemed to have missed me, welcoming me with lots of love. They escorted me the rest of the way to my father, who was relaxing in the garden on a comfortable chair. For a couple of seconds he froze, apart for his blinking eyes being the only moving thing on his body. I stood there for the first time since I was a small child, and suddenly with a loud and desperate voice he persisted: 'Baby', while he clumsily jumped to his feet and gave me a hug, but I remained still as dried wood. With the face of a desperate man he turned around without looking at me, and went into the house in a dizzy walk. To my surprise he returned with a chair, and placed it beside his as in a ceremony of respect. We sat there for a while without a word as I waited for my uneasy father to begin, and for my stepmother to come and greet me. When she suddenly did, I just managed to control a wrath coming from within my chest, and I greeted her with a forced smile. Now my father relaxed in a 'buddylike' manner, excitedly asking me of when I joined the army, and I caught myself looking at him with angered eyes. He shied away with a fake smile, when I told him that a civilian was not entitled to such information of a soldier, and there was silence for yet a while. I rejected a glass of milk from my stepmother's hands, telling her that I already ate, while the truth was that she still gave me distrust. The very same day I went back, still with an angry mind. I had never forgotten my father's cruelty, when he had chosen my goats first, one by one, to be slaughtered. Maybe he thought that he taught me some kind of lesson, I could not know, but I was going to teach him one anyway, and now maybe I could help my mother out in the very same act.

It was morning and I was sitting outside my quarters on the lawn. My battalion had a good time always hanging around the barracks waiting on 'standby' for whatever might happen. But I had a few problems obstructing my time though, and he happened to cross my way that morning, while I was relaxing by myself with my Uzi gun tossed at my side. This ever-teasing tormentor approached me arrogantly, with his face raised as if he was the president himself. He wanted to sit there on the exact same spot, as where I was sitting, and he told me to move. Distracted and annoyed I looked up at him. I very much wanted to punch his nose real hard, but he was much older and stronger than I. I asked him why he didn't choose one of the many other places there was to sit. He never replied to this, instead he began to pull me up by my arm, and when having succeeded he sat himself down. Then he told me to respect him, even though we shared the same rank as lance-corporal. Now my blood was boiling and my loaded gun was in my arms, but still he added as if he was a wise old man, that more age earned more respect. Through my clenched teeth I told him to move, if he didn't want a bullet from my gun-barrel, but he ignored my warning. I watched him struggle to get back on his feet screaming of pain, without the slightest sympathy, having had enough of his provocations. He had blood gushing all over from the wound, and now the Rally Police (RPs) were all over me. I did as ordered by handing over my Uzi and they took the boy to the sick-quarters, while I was brought to the second-in-command. I told him that this kid deliberately had annoyed me from day one of my service in the Forty-Fifth Battalion. After my explanation he ordered the two RPs, who dragged and rolled me through a mud pit, until I looked like a wild little pig. Then they brought me back through the barracks by the most trafficked route. Now I had even more time on my own. The commander had confiscated my gun for a month without sending me to jail, and there wasn't much to do being a soldier without a weapon, so I decided to pay my father's farm a visit.

I found a butcher who was ready to take the order of two to three cows, and a lorry driver got the address of the farm. I arranged with the lorry driver to arrive early the next morning. When I arrived at the tax park, I happened to run into my father. He was in an unusual mood of talking, but my mind was busy with plans so I tried to cut him off, with as small replies as possible. Suddenly my head was struck by the lightning. He asked me of when I was going to visit my grandmother at the farm, but I cleared up as fast as it had struck me when I saw his sincere face. 'If you could just look into my thoughts, Father,' my mind said, and I left him without an answer. Then I went to the minibus, and waited for it to be filled. I was wondering if I had missed anything in my plan, and as we reached near the farm around twelve o'clock, I was still going through each step. I took off from the main road and walked through the old dust trail, that led to the farm. I could almost see the farm house, when I met the manager of the neighbouring farm. We knew each other from when I was a little child years back, so he came to me, hugged me and pulled my uniform, 'You're a big girl now,' he said, though my rubber boots went far above my knees. 'Hey, you're a soldier now.' He still had his bushy hair that he probably hadn't combed since I saw him the last time, and he was tall as ever, making me wonder if I ever would outgrow him. He asked if my father knew that I had come. 'No,' I replied, not bothering to lie. Just after we had parted, he turned and said that he would return in the evening, but I hardly noticed, because of my mind which only was occupied with one thing. When I was about to step into the grounds of the farm house, I was certain that nothing could go wrong. My brother Richard stood outside the house with a pack of dogs, already looking at me as I eyed him. My heart was beating faster now as I realised how much I had been missing him. The cool way he acted was typical, though he still managed to astonish me every time. He just looked at me as if I just had returned from a trip in the bush. But I didn't mind much, so I hurried to give him a deep hug, holding him until he finally returned my feelings by laying his head down on my shoulder. After having talked for a minute or two, Grandmother came outside and hugged me. Immediately she invited me inside with the same old hanging face, but an unusual smile formed her mouth, and I was almost sure that her forever dripping eye carried real tears. Before I could finish the meal that Grandmother had served for us, my brother already stood by the door. We went together with his dogs to hunt, as we had done so many times before in our childhood, before the war of my life. It felt good to walk beside my big brother again, but as we had walked for a bit I noticed that he was eager of saying something. He wanted to know of why I had returned, and I replied that our mother wanted me to take some cows for her. 'You mean that you came here to steal?' he asked with his ever careless voice.

'Yes,' I answered.

His only reply was: 'Then you are stupid not to bring your gun.'

Clear as air after a thunderstorm, he started our hunting mission and happy with his reaction to my little revenge, I enjoyed every second of it. Half of the day passed and we were getting tired of the bush, that repeatedly had taken its rich offers away, right in front of our noses. The dogs seemed to be disappointed too, picking on each other while looking at their master with embarrassed eyes. Still we debated our hunt on the way home as friends discussing a football match, because we knew that there was plenty of meat waiting for us at the farm. I went straight to my grandmother with a ready mind, followed by an excited and curious brother who sat himself in a corner of the room, as I approached her. She looked up from her dishes and I told her that I was sent by my father to escort a lorry driver to him loaded with eight cows and seven goats. Now my brother laughed, annoying both my grandmother and I. She asked why he didn't come by himself as he usually did, and always ready with answers as my presence in the army had taught me, I told her that a soldier in the truck would save him from bribing the traffic police. Furthermore, I added, that he had told me to choose the very finest animals. It was hard for me to see if she had bought my lie, as she nodded with an angry face, looking at my careless brother still laughing. I knew why he laughed this time, but I hoped that my grandmother assumed that the laughs was meant for her lips and eye as usual.

As we ate supper the manager came as promised. He was more busy talking with my grandmother than with me, and I listened very carefully to their 'chit-chat' just like any other thief would do. Suddenly my mouth refused to chew and my heart jumped a beat. He had met my father in town during the day, and the manager had told him of my visit. My grandmother continued to listen as if the whole thing had escaped her ears, while I forced my mouth and heart to continue as planned, but inside my mind the desperation hid any possible escape. Finally the man stood up and walked to the door, but while his hands grabbed the handle, he turned around and said: 'By the way, he's coming to pay you a visit tomorrow morning.' Then he left and my last desperate hope withered when my grandmother turned to look at me. All the love that she had shown me during the day were now gone. My heart couldn't beat fast enough, still jumping a few beats here and there, while the old woman assured me that my father would kill me as a common thief. I was unable to hide my fear anymore as my lungs continued to demand more air. I knew that if I didn't escape now, I would never escape. She kept on scaring me until my brother, with a sudden attack, shouted at her to leave me alone. He stood up as if nothing had been said, and whispered in my ear once again reminding me of my confiscated gun. Then he went to bed.

After an uneasy night of thoughts, and a few hours of dark sleep I cleared off. It was five o'clock in the morning when I dressed up. My brother was laying in a bed across the room about to wake up, and I thanked him in silence for last evening. A few seconds later I was outside under the sky, just awake before the morning sun, in a fast walk towards the main road. I turned away from the dust trail and headed through the bush, because there was at least two people I did not dare to meet that morning. As I left the trail, I felt the creepy hands of panic in my back, pumping the adrenaline through my chest, and I had to concentrate my walk so as not to run myself to the ground.

At the main road I caught a Somalian petrol tanker who gladly gave me a lift. The two men thought that I was of Somalian origin and trusted that now they wouldn't be bothered by any traffic police. The drivers looked weary after a long drive, speaking to me as if to stay awake, but I could not say much because I was thinking of the lorry driver who soon had finished a distance of sixty miles without being paid. We rushed through the bush on top of the tarmac, that now was being heated by the morning sun. When we were about to arrive at the location of my battalion, a new problem emerged and I had to make up my mind fast. I knew that my father wouldn't back off. He would try everything to have me reported as a thief to the battalion commander. I decided to continue with the Somalians to Kabale, where I knew a detach[ment] commander, stationed to stop the smuggling from Uganda to Rwanda.

Nakasongora

This commander remembered me all right and I was enrolled into his detachment, who stopped and searched vehicles for goods that needed to be tolled. Soon I learned that here the soldiers themselves took the salary that the state never gave us. I began earning a lot of money by letting smugglers cross the border. I didn't know how to use money, because I had never really earned any, but I loved chicken. I ate chicken all the time, using my earnings on these luxurious creatures, without thinking about harder times ahead, because I knew that my stay here would be for ever. I was wrong though, and before I could get used to my new life, all of us were taken back to the battalion headquarters. There we found senior officer David Tinyefunza, who was sent by the army chief, Elly Tumwine.

Tinyefunza told our unit that we were getting fat and corrupt, and to end this he was sending us to a place named Nakasongora, right in the middle of the bush. The only structures in this area were the ruined buildings that once were bombed during the Idi Amin war with Tanzania, and now it was a godforsaken place.

We had left shortly after Tinyefunza's words and was now standing at the location, in line, with him and his instructors in front of us. Speaking in harsh words, without looking at us, he ordered them to give us hard training from six o'clock in the morning until six in the evening. He promised to stay and monitor our training until we would be picked up six months later. After having turned his eyes at our sorry line of faces, he said that this was what to expect for acting like non soldiers. Tinyefunza's words were hard as the place, and I knew that this wasn't just training. It was one of those crucial places of one's life, where one single word could end it all.

Tinyefunza was a very brutal man, and those of us who knew him well, we considered not even to look into his eyes as he spoke. Tinyefunza was one of those senior officers who everybody was scared of. Soldiers and junior officers became even more frightened of him, when we heard rumours that he tied up more junior officers on the tree in a small town called Lira, and shot them to death, accusing them of being cowards. These junior officers were mostly of Baganda tribe. We had many brutal officers, and I remember one called Suicide. Suicide was a war hero, but also a mad one. Suicide had power to do anything. He could rape both civilian girls and army girls, and nothing could happen to him, because he was good at fighting wars. He did everything by force, but I do not blame him. I blame the battles that he fought. Our instructors had been given our souls, and if we wanted them back, we would have to pay a heavy price. The instructors had many ways to make one suffer, but most of their assaults seemed to have been made on female soldiers. The older girls had more problems than any other soldier, because they had to pay with their own bodies. The instructors had power, and since most of the officers were doing the same, then no one was left to stop them.

For us female soldiers, we had to offer sex to more than five officers in one unit, and to those of lower ranks, such as RSM and Sergeant Major. Nearly every evening an officer would come and order you to report to his place, typically at nine p.m. It would have been a little easier on us if it had been one or two afandes, but every day in the week, we had to sleep with different afandes against our will! If we refused our afandes' orders, we would have to say goodbye to our family, because of rejected movement orders. On top of that the abuse would turn violent, and extra duties would be added. I know what I am talking about, because I tried. At the end it just proved to be impossible. After seven days without proper sleep, you could even fall asleep in front of the officer at the parade. It was a day-mare, to have to think about nine p.m. I remember when I had to pray to God, asking him to let the day stay, because of that hour. I have never been to hell, though I am not always sure. Where else can such pain belong? It was so painful, but I could only cry with my heart, because with tears I could never survive. Our afandes were always angry, and they seemed too cold to see the pain they were giving us. Even with them in bed, it felt as if I was sleeping with death, because everything was predicated by the abuser. Male comrades knew about the abuse we female soldiers were going through. They called us names such as 'masala ya wakubwa', and 'guduria', meaning that female soldiers were the fodder of afandes, and the big pot which all the officers ate from. I almost started hating myself. Blaming myself for having nowhere else to go. At some point I was convinced that it was a part of nature, for every girl to endure. It actually made me a little stronger when I knew that I wasn't alone. The NRA gave us weapons, made us fight their war, made us hate, kill, torture, and made us their girlfriends: we had no choice. Museveni had, but his choice was to look the other way. Most of the high-ranking officers behaved like mad people, and now I wonder how Museveni could not have seen this. This should have made Museveni realise what his monsters were doing to us! I guess that, since we were not his own children, he never gave a damn, because if he did, he would not have let them command.

Late in the evening some of us were sitting around the fireplace, resting after a hard day's training. When the training officer came and told me to follow him, I did so with his bodyguards close behind me, and I wondered if I had done something wrong. But when we reached to his place, he sent me to get my belongings. I returned and his chief escort showed me a place to sleep. We called him God, the short name for Godfrey. God was in his thirties. He was a strong man, though a bullet in his leg made him limp. The next day in the evening when I sat on the bed weary and tired, he came into my room and told me that I had to go with him. Scared, I stood up, but I remained standing there. He, too, kept on waiting there for me to follow. In the morning he told me to show up in his room every evening, and with terrifying eyes he made it clear that it was an order. The only thing I could reply was: 'Yes sir,' but my falling heart made my words faint. He asked me, as if he was shouting to a whole line-up of soldiers, if I had understood his command. I could only nod, and with a weak breath I walked to the morning parade.

About three weeks later the battalion got a new commander, Captain Sam Waswa Balikarege, and I tried very hard to become friends with one of his escorts. One day the escort told me that Waswa was going to Kampala, so I begged him to get me out of Nakasongora, and he promised to try his best. In the evening I met God in the doorway to his room, and he told me to go inside. I stood there for a moment eyeing a bayonet on the floor, and after having passed him I grabbed it, and hid it under the mattress. And, at the most terrible moment, I silently told him: 'I wish you die in your sleep, bastard!' All night I was touching the bayonet, feeling angry and dirty, but I feared this man too much, even though I could have done it in a second, but that was if I did it right in the first thrust. The morning came without sleep and without the job done. I went to Waswa's place and found his bodyguards packing. To my relief the escort told me to get in his car, and soon he jumped behind the wheel and led the convoy out of Nakasongora to Kampala.

Finally I was out, and the day after our arrival I went to my mother's. When she saw me my mother started to cry, and I couldn't understand why. I felt a strange pain inside of me, and my anger rose like a charging rhino, making me shout at her. I told her to shut up, that I hated people who cried, especially when it was me they cried for. I stopped and turned away from her, when I saw her shocked and pale face, no more crying, but I still had the same pain inside, feeling low and unworthy.

A month passed, I was gaining back my strength, and my thoughts slowly stopped haunting me with its persisting blame. My mother told me that she knew an officer, Ronald, who she thought was able to 'slip' me back into the army. In the evening I went there together with my mother and met with his bodyguard Kusain, a tiny kid in about his ninth year of age.

Kusain took us to Ronald with small but stout steps, that almost convinced me that he actually was a man in his finest years. Ronald told us that he would soon go back to his unit in 'Kabamba training wing', and that I could join his unit there. He promised to pick me up from my mother's when his time came to leave. It must have been the following Thursday around two o'clock when Kusain, Ronald and his wife Justine turned up at my mother's.

We arrived to Kabamba the following morning after having travelled with bus and train halfway through Uganda. The first week everything was going well for me, but on the other hand not everything was all right. Every morning Kusain, Ronald's bodyguard, was beaten by Justine for wetting the bed, and at least one time Ronald had participated. I felt bad and angry watching Kusain as a soldier, being beaten by a civilian woman. I remember myself in

Kusain, as I had been beaten up for wetting my bed too, so I felt sorry for him. But I was getting a little mad, still fighting with a lot of unwanted memories, and therefore I could not help him much. About two more weeks passed and I began to wonder of when Ronald was going to assign me, but when I asked, he told me that I should stay there as a part of his escort. I was disappointed because in those four weeks that had passed, Justine had given Kusain and me an increasing amount of work, that I felt never was meant for a soldier. There was nothing Justine loved more than to stay in bed. Just staying there and when she finally got tired of that, she would bring a chair in front of the house. She could sit for hours looking at her own pretty face in a mirror, while mimicking different kinds of screams and other ugly faces. I had come to hate her so much, that I sometimes imagined her being shot down. Normally I would have been able to run away to another battalion, because no sort of identification had yet been made on the new government army. On the other hand, this time it was different, in this tiny unit where no numbers was needed to find the one missing. Those thoughts had been turning my head for some time, living as Justine's private waitress, but I still had to learn what kind of a hell it was to be Ronald's escort.

Justine left to visit her parents for some time, and I was happy at first being able to escape her two ugly faces, and I would never have guessed before of how much I would actually come to miss her. Ronald came home from his duty and while staring at me, he told Kusain to go and borrow some sugar from the neighbour. When Kusain left, my heart began to beat in alarm, as he asked me if I ever had slept with anyone. Before I could consider my response, he grabbed me, and threw me on to his bed. I cried in desperation but he stopped me with his dirty hand. It seemed like an eternity while it lasted, but when he left I saw that no time had passed, but still he continued to echo through my mind like a relentless demon. When Kusain came back I found myself sitting in the corner of the bed, crying silent tears as if his hand still covered my mouth. The touch of Kusain's comforting hand on my shoulder made me explode into tears. At first I could not tell him of what had happened, but my head and body was aching of bad memories, that later forced me to tell him. His face turned into something that I still cannot describe, but I could see that he understood more than I had thought. The little Mugandan told me to be strong, even though he was sure that no one would intervene if we spoke of it, because he believed that most officers did the very same. I could not take it any more and told him that I was leaving the next day. I felt sorry to leave Kusain, and advised him to try and find a higher-ranked officer to take him as a bodyguard, because then Ronald would be afraid to claim him back.

The following morning just after Ronald had left for work, I went to one of the instructors, a forty-year-old sergeant of whom I saw as a good man. He looked at me with an increasing troubled face as I told him. I understood why, because he himself was afraid of Ronald. Still, after a couple of minutes, he took me to his wife who he told everything and finally they decided to hide me. For three days I was living behind a locked door, breathing fresh air through a tiny window. The second day the wife told me not even to open the window, because of Ronald who had commenced a search for me. That very same day I heard him at their door asking for me, and I was terrified when I learned that he wasn't content with their word. I heard him walk through the rooms, and the last I saw of him was his boots from below my bed.

Finally, on the third day, the sergeant and his wife gave me some money for the transport back to my mother's. He even assigned a recruit to escort me to the train station. We had to walk through the forest to avoid a meeting with Ronald. After having walked for a while, the recruit's words became strange, and scared I sped up the pace. Halfway through he pulled my arm to stop, and told me that if I didn't make love to him by myself, he would force me. On top of that he tried to justify it, by saying that I had to pay for risking his life. I looked around as to see any sign of hope, but the denseness of the forest held everything to itself. I could only see glimpses of the sun here and there, and the sound of a scream would not get any further than to the next tree. Nobody would hear me scream for help, and the leaves of the trees kept on dripping their raindrops to his face, to this beast which only deserved the desert. The subjects he had put up as we had walked made me question his sanity, so I almost accepted my near-death, but then I decided to fight him with my life and dignity. It was getting too far as we stood there looking at each other with two different sets of eyes, but then, at the last second, I got an idea. I knew that recruits were forbidden to have intercourse before their training was over, and to make him reconsider his decision, I told him that I very much would give him what he asked for, but then he should prepare himself to be punished, because of the syphilis that I carried. When he thanked me for my honesty, I just managed to hide my relief, but I was still shaken as he left me waiting at the station. I cried all the way towards my goal with a smile on my cheeks, thinking of how lucky I just had been.

Womanhood

When I arrived at my mother's she was about to eat supper, with a man I did not know. Annoyed, I took her outside and asked her of who the man was. She smiled and I could see what he meant to her, and I felt disgusted. I told her that if she wanted a man, I could easily force my father to marry her again, but she laughed, telling me that I was insulting her. Her eyes narrowed as I demanded her to chase the man away, and suddenly she shouted that I had no rights to come there and chase her visitors away. Her defending him only maddened me more, so I went into the house and told the man myself. He only laughed and said: 'These kids! When they go to the army, they suddenly lose all respect.' When he had finished, my mother already sat beside him. I had heard enough now and, angered by their determined glare, I grabbed the sigirri [a small grill] and poured the burning charcoal at them. They screamed in panic as they felt the burning coal inside their clothes. They ran outside, jumping, and with a little smile on my face, I closed and locked the door. After a while I heard a knocking, and I got up from where I had been sitting, as slowly as I could. My mother begged me to open the door, but I told her to sleep by her sweetheart. Twenty more minutes had to pass, and then a man presented himself as the landlord. He began explaining to me that everybody could make mistakes, and begged me to let my mother in. She had calmed down and told me that she never really had liked him, anyway. That night I slept like a baby in my mother's arms, and it felt good to rest my chin on her ageing breast.

I did not tell her of why I had come back, because I felt no real confidence between us. Besides I could see that she had already struggled enough.

Around the beginning of 1988, my mother took me to Kampala, to one of her brothers, a man in his twenties. He was the commanding officer of the Twenty-First Battalion, which guarded Entebbe International airport. Caravel seemed very happy to meet me and I didn't stay there for long, before I felt at home. My uncle was a very efficient leader with a sharp mind and mouth, and on top of it all he was a very handsome boy, making the girls swarm around him. He had it all, and now he had a niece too, whom he open-handed shared with, and I became very happy with the way he treated me.

One day my uncle and I were sitting outside his house talking about this and that, while I was playing with his hair. Suddenly a girl approached in full march. In a hysterical voice she asked Caravel if this bitch suddenly was his girl-friend too. He didn't think twice before he drew his pistol from his hip, shot her in the side of her breast and told her that I happened to be his daughter. The ambulance came and picked up the bleeding girl, but there was never laid a charge against Caravel, but at least the girl survived her sustained injuries. As time passed I began to notice that Caravel's atti-tude towards me was changing. He began to look at me with an angry face, telling me that he didn't like to see me dressed up in a military uniform. He only terrified me by saying this, not having any clue to what other life he expected me to have. I only hoped for him to give up, and to make my point I stopped wearing civilian clothes. Some time passed like this, and one day when he returned from work, he told me to change into civilian. It was time for me to go to school like any other kid, and my sister Margie, 'the sweet-buyer', would come and take me to her home. I was not happy with my uncle's decision. Actually I felt devastated. I couldn't trust my sister to take proper care of us, after all she had been through herself.

That same evening she arrived to Caravel's and I was told to pack my clothes. I remembered to sneak in a uniform as well. I came to see that my expectations had been right. My sister had no shower and the toilet was outside; in the night my sister slept in her bed while I had to sleep on the sofa. The landlord made me sure that this was the absolute most miser-able life I could live. She resembled my grandmother down to every detail: she was old and mean, requiring an impossible respect. She shouted every word out at any opportunity she got, when we crossed each other's paths. She kept on repeating one question every time we met: 'Did you remember to greet me?' and I hated her for that. My sister searched in every state school in Kampala, but everywhere she was put on hold, and I was getting fed up with staying home.

I began to gather all the addresses of barracks situated in Kampala, though I had decided to give my sister a second chance. I just had to make sure that I could get out of there when I had enough. A month passed, which to me had seemed like years of misery, but one morning I woke up after my sister had left for work. I went to bathe myself and noticed something strange. After having looked carefully, I was sure that it was blood. I was puzzled because I didn't feel any pain. I tried to think of any time yesterday when I might have sat myself on something sharp, but no matter how many theories I gathered, I could not break the case. At some point I got scared and thought of going to the hospital, but there was no pain. When I could not come up with any reasons, I decided to stick to the facts. It was terribly embarrassing, so I went outside and buried the evidence. After having washed myself I went back to sleep. When I woke up I got a shock: now the sofa was turning red too. My sister could be a hard woman, so I decided to run off. I took my secretly packed uniform out of my bag, dressed myself up and went to the Republic House. There I met with the platoon commander, who I then begged to get me into his platoon. Warakira was a Muganda, and I found him easy to talk to, so I told him of the problem I had. I noticed a mild tremor cross his lips, which turned into a bright smile, and immediately he took me down to buy the proper equipment. I failed to catch what he said to the lady at the shop, but his tone of voice was clearly of a very embarrassed man. Then she took me by the hand, and showed me how to fix my problem.

The Republic House contained offices for the administrative senior officers, and my job was now to guard the gate. I learned that a Mugandan boy of my own age was a part of the platoon. He was one of those people that you just can't help to notice, not because of a loud mouth, but because of this casual ability he possessed to stand where the main attention was. As most people in the army, I didn't know his real name, but his nickname was 'Manager'; he seemed to know everybody, he always had money, lots of girlfriends and he wore a suit as soon as he was off-duty. He knew the place as his own pocket, and gave me a first class tour the first couple of days. To guard the gate proved to be profitable, because for some reason a lot of civilians needed to enter the Republic House without an appointment. I came to know my commander, as the most relaxed of soldiers: even on duty he wore civilian clothes, and he often stayed away from his duty for days. He never shouted his orders as most commanders did, instead it sounded like advice from a schoolteacher. We were the ones who shouted the orders, and I loved to deny the fat and wealthy men to enter the gate, and soon I was able to follow Manager's example by buying myself a suit. Most of us were already off-duty around four o'clock, and then Manager and I would count the money which we had earned through the day. Most evenings we would go to a bar somewhere in town to have a good time with our identical suits, and with enough money to catch attention.

My new post suited me better for each moment that passed, and one day I overheard an interesting conversation of two staff members. Our Afande and President Museveni decided to change the national currency, and give each of us 35,000 to 50,000 shillings to show his gratitude for our contribution to his struggle. Some rumours said that the Libyan leader, Colonel M. Gadaffi, who was a close friend to Y. K. Museveni, had provided him with the money to do so. Soon Manager and I stood at the canteen next to the Republic House, filling out forms, and watching the man who counted up our money.

Never before had I seen this kind of money, and both of us got dizzy just by looking at it. I left him at the gate and ran to my uni-port, where I dug a hole and buried the money. I kept 400 shillings in my pocket, and soon we invaded town in an overexcited frenzy, forgetting all about the 'cool' image that we had been building. When we reached to the shops, a stroke of confusion hit me: I couldn't come up with a single thing to buy! Manager had no problem with that, so I just followed him. He bought a bicycle, a dozen bras and underpants for his girlfriend, including some other stuff which he didn't even know what was for. I returned only with a fine pair of men's shoes.

Later in the evening we went to the most expensive bar, a few streets away from the Republic House. We felt fairly small among the other guests, whom to us looked like the elite of Uganda, so we decided to raise ourselves above the rest, with a little lie. We told everybody we could get to listen, that Manager was a son of the Vice-President Kiseka and that I was a son of Salem Saleh, Museveni's brother. Then we bought beers, drinks and roasted chicken for everybody present, and a party was thrown. Everything was great, until three half-drunk guys entered the bar. They simply refused to believe us, and started stealing every-body's attention. When the humiliation became too great, we demanded an apology, but they just laughed as deep as they could. We left but promised to return. We became the bosses again, when we returned with our guns. We told them to kneel down and beg us to rule them, while aiming between their heads. The party had ended with a rush of adrenaline and we knew that somebody might call the police, so we rushed back to our quarters, while laughing our heads off. When we got home it was time for bed, if we wanted to be worth anything the following day. Just the thought of it annoyed me, so we decided to continue our night parade.

We convinced one of the bouncers by tripling his monthly salary that we were old enough for the disco. The place was crowded with people, and the music was loud. We were getting drunk, and soon Manager got angry with me, after I had stolen the fourth girl away from him without noticing. He told me that he was sick and tired of going to the disco with me. 'You can't even use them for anything!' he finished, as he almost cried. Then I came up with an idea: I told him to choose a girl. Immediately he pointed at one sitting alone at the bar with her back towards us, and I approached her like a strong and proud young man. When we got home, all three of us were drunk, and Manager said goodnight as the woman and I went to my room. I told her to go to bed with the lights out and left the room pretending to go for a pee. Manager stood outside the door, drooling like a hyena. We waited there for about ten minutes, swapped the keys for our rooms and went to bed. The following morning I woke up in Manager's bed, to his shouting from outside the door. When I opened, he told me that the woman was very old with no teeth. He started crying, and I had one of my life's best laughs.

A Home

A week or so went by as I tried to figure out of what to do with the money, that could provide me with houses and cars. I came to think of my mother without a home of her own, and a movement order was granted to me by my platoon sergeant. On my way I stopped by a shop and bought ten loaves of bread, because I knew that I couldn't arrive empty handed. I arrived by bus and walked the last 500 hundred metres where I found my mother gossiping with another woman outside her door. Without any greetings I pulled her by the arm and we went inside, and this time I noticed how poor her home looked. When I handed her the bags of bread she surprised me with her big smile followed by tears. I wondered what would happen when I gave her the money, so when I gave it to her I walked outside for a while to avoid her reaction. When I returned she was holding it to her chest as if she feared it to fly away; and her smiling lips, and shut eyes were turned towards the ceiling, as if she was about to fly to heaven. I woke her up by asking if anyone was selling a house, or a piece of land, and with excitement she grabbed my hand and kissed it, before lying to me that I was her favourite child.

The following morning, my mother was the first to get up, and as we ate the breakfast she took my hand and spit in it. When I asked her the reason for this, she simply said that it was for my protection, though I found it hard to believe. I still said: 'Thank you Mother.' Soon Mother took me to a young man, who was selling a piece of land which he had inherited from his father. A small house was included in the price, as well as a banana plantation, and two huge avocado trees. It was a fair deal, so we took it. The next few days my mother was completely impossible, giving me too much unwanted attention. She dragged me around, showing me to everybody, telling them what I had done, embarrassing me with loud praising, so I decided to end it in one blow by throwing a party. She invited everybody in the area and the most of the evening and night I sat against the wall that surrounded her new home while observing my blessed mother doing everything she could to keep the people happy. That was when I realised that God gives a good heart to those who have nothing to offer. Before I left my mother I made it clear that if I found her with a man she would be chased away.

A few days later, Manager and I stood at the gate, when as from nowhere, a truck with a load of child soldiers arrived. Suddenly the place was swarming with RPs. Without a word they grabbed us and threw us among the other children. The other passengers looked grim, with big eyes which seemed never to have seen the light of the day. Most had just been taken from the north front, and we learned that we were being taken to Simba barracks to start school. I looked at Manager and said: 'We don't belong here!' Even when we ditched the truck, no one followed. These child soldiers seemed dead and all of them were quiet, with hands on their chin. They looked at us without blinking, and I could see a question-mark in their hearts. Today I still see their faces in my dreams, and I'm too scared to think of what became of them. The pain is too strong, and I don't know how I can express it, but I know one thing: I miss all of them. I wonder whether I will ever see them, because I cannot return to my country, but I haven't stopped counting the days. These kids stayed at most six months before returning to their units. They could not stay at Simba barracks. They were dumped there to plant maize, but not to study. After getting tired of this, many decided to go back to their units.

Everything went back to normal, and one Friday my platoon leader, Warakira, was going to a wedding as his brother's best-man. He entrusted me with his walkie-talkie and pistol and told me to follow him to the wedding. I went in the car with a civilian driver and followed him close behind but, because of the walkie-talkie and the pistol, my head suddenly got twisted, and with excitement I convinced myself that now I was a big chief! With my gun I ordered the driver to turn away from the escort and go to my sister's address. Now I would show her landlord, the old woman, who had the final say. Unfortunately the landlord wasn't around, and Margie had lost her job. In fact she didn't have the slightest trace of food in the house except for biscuits, which she claimed to have been living on for a week. So I bought the coal along with some food. At one o'clock I remembered that I had to drive Warakira home from the wedding party. Suddenly I was the same little China again, and I continuously pushed the driver on through town, while remembering all the scariest punishments I had seen through my life. All my hopes of receiving a mild lecture ran out, when I found that he already had gone. Suddenly I was torn out of my sleep and dragged out of the door and ready as the morning sun without touching the ground, I saw the RPs on each side of me in full march towards Warakira's office.

Warakira ordered me outside, and the RPs gave me twenty blows with a stick. After the punishment, I went and sat in front of the offices to forget the pain. I did not sit there for long, before senior officer Ahmad Kashilingi arrived in a Mercedes-Benz. I stood up straight and saluted him, but he swept the salute away with his hand. He waved me over, and told me to get into his car. We drove to his home in Kololo, the rich quarter of town, where he had a small mansion surrounded by a big fence. As we came to the gate he honked the horn, and an armed soldier saluted and opened for us. We had lunch together and he told me that he wanted me to be his bodyguard. I almost choked in my food. Merely the word 'bodyguard' had the associations of abuse, and with disgust I acknowledged that God's assaults had stuck in my mind. 'Still,' I hoped to myself, 'Kashilingi would be different from God.' I stood up, and saluted him, before saying: 'Yes sir!'

Paradise

That day in 1988, Kashilingi sent me back to the Republic House with one of his drivers to get my stuff. My heart was beating too fast, and the sweat on my forehead just kept on running, as I only hoped for the best. Nevertheless, I managed to pack and return without any fuss. Kashilingi gave me a room, and most of my worries were now over. A short while after having put everything in place, Kashilingi returned to my room and invited me to his house. As we walked through the house, I kept on seeing kids running and crying, and I learned that most of them were his own but of different wives. We had a quiet moment with a soft drink and soon I had come to terms with my new duty. That evening I had supper with Kashilingi's family, and afterwards he told me that I would be eating in his home. I didn't bother to know his reason for this; I just saluted him and looked forward to eat the nice food. I walked up to my uniport, and stood there for a while, looking down at the fence that separated Kashilingi's residency from Colonel Julius Chihanda's and Brigadier David Tinyefunza's. Behind Kashilingi's house, there was boys-quarters consisting of four rooms, and in front of it there was a parking lot which could contain up to five cars. After having finished touring, I went to my room and slept with a good feeling about my new life.

I woke up in time for the morning parade, and got in line in my uniform as the only girl present. Lieutenant Patrick Kiberu approached us with the day's briefing, and then he gave me an AK-47, while introducing me to the soldiers. The day started and Corporal Katumba and I escorted Kashilingi to the Republic House. Proudly I went and stood next to the Mercedes-Benz, with my gun resting at my left arm, and soon Kashilingi appeared. He stood on the veranda for a short while, staring at me with appraising eyes. Then he walked down, and we waited until he had entered the car. We arrived at the Republic House without a word spoken, and followed Kashilingi through the main entrance, and up the stairs to his office. My excitement couldn't be larger when I saw the soldier's reaction in the corridor, as they saw senior officer and Director of Records, Ahmad Kashilingi approaching. Of course I knew that all the fuss was for him, but I still felt like an important person too – that now I could use his power to become feared and respected. When we arrived at Kashilingi's office, the administrative officer of his department, Chris, sat at his desk in the front room. Despite his higher rank I had become so aroused that I refused to salute him. I saw the reaction in his eyes, which had become all but friendly. Katumba knew everything I needed to know, and told me to get a chair to sit with him outside the door, in the hallway. There we had to sit as ordinary guards, until our boss would leave his office.

One o'clock Kashilingi left, and we followed him in the car. I did not know where we were going, but I was afraid that it was illegal to ask, so I just had to keep my eyes open. Finally all the mystery vapourised as I found myself in front of a restaurant, and as we sat ourselves after Kashilingi, I was told not to be modest, and choose whatever I wanted. No escort had ever been bragging to me about this, and I had spoken with many, so I felt like the most important escort in the world. Four o'clock his work at the office were done. We returned home, and I thought about the day that had passed. The only exciting event had been the lunch-break, while the rest of the time had required a lot of solid patience of sitting outside a door, only disrupted by a few toilet visits. Though I rarely allowed myself to miss anybody, I couldn't help thinking about Manager, and the great times we had before. I gave in to let the good memories join in my mind, while I tried to find a conclusion to it all. When he came down the stairs from where he had been calling, Kashilingi stood in civilian clothes. He told me to get my gun, and then we drove to Kabaragara where I learned that most of his friends were going to drink. I was told to stay in the car, and keep an open eye on him. Thereafter he sat himself outside the bar on the veranda to join his civilian friends. I could even hear them whisper from where I was sitting, and Kashilingi was now the centre of their party, as he told them about me. Kashilingi talked about how dangerous I could be, and said that if one of them would insult him, I would shoot them all. After he had said this, I tried to judge myself in that situation and seriously found that I only would shoot the one responsible. Soon I was getting tired of listening to their chit-chat, and I felt restless in my legs. Our leaders would forget us in their cars for hours. Sometimes we would fall asleep, and they would beat us. Few of the officers cared about their bodyguard, but others treated us like dogs. I was getting bored and hungry. I remembered the bag that Kashilingi always had by the gear leaver. When they had stopped talking about me, I slipped the bag on top of my lap and opened it, while staring at some invisible point as far away from it as possible. I felt the shape of a pistol sliding through my fingers, and all around it there was a mass of paper notes. I stopped my search, and picked up a note. Then I pushed the bag aside and went out, as if I was going to the toilet. In the shade of the car I looked at my catch, and to my joy the note was enough to buy a nice amount of chicken. I made a sign to a man who was grilling some a few metres away, while showing my arms as wide apart as I could, that I wanted a big piece. His kindness couldn't have been greater, as he hurried over with a leg, and quickly we made our secret exchange. Now I just had to eat it as fast as I could, but that was no problem, because I munched it in as if it had no bones. I went back to the car, and sat myself down with a satisfied stomach. The mission was over, but still I couldn't stop licking my fingers.

The following day Katumba felt that my training was over, and left me to guard alone. Then he went to visit his many friends around the building, and I felt a bit sad. The problem was the immense boredom I felt, just by sitting myself down, while Manager had a much better time down at the gate. I broke off only a few minutes after having started the day, and rushed down to greet him, but as we talked, I suddenly remembered my gun. I had left it outside the door. I ran back only to find an empty spot. I almost panicked because I knew from the battlefield that I could get killed if I left it there, and the fear forced me away from reasoning between a combat soldier and an escort. Quickly but discreetly I asked Katumba, who referred me to Chris. Chris's lips turned into a demonic smile. He picked up the phone and called the RPs; then I remembered the incident from the day before. They arrived in a minute, and took me to the warehouse of the Republic House. They ordered me to roll in the mud, until my uniform had become all wet. After having returned from changing, Chris gave me back my gun with a triumphant face, and I saw that he understood my eyes, that craved for revenge. I left the office, carelessly dragging the AK after me, as I waited for a comment. With my mind darkening I went back to my chair full of mean thoughts, and planned how to revenge Chris.

When it was lunchtime, a woman stopped us at the gate. Kashilingi ordered me to sit myself in the back seat, and I felt as if my rank was being stripped off from my shoulders. We carried on with the woman in front, and stopped at one of the many restaurants in Kampala. As we had sat ourselves, Kashilingi asked for the menu and handed it over to the woman, while asking what she desired. Her eyes got bigger, as she shifted between looking at the menu and Kashilingi. The waiter started looking at his nails, while the rest of us zoomed in on her. 'Menu,' she finally said. Kashilingi looked back at her, not quite understanding, and she repeated herself, 'I thing I would like the menu'. That was too much fun for one day, but it wasn't appropriate to laugh at Kashilingi's girl, unless we wanted ten blows or so with a stick. Katumba and I started to sound like two steam-engines, with our mouths tightly closed, as the pressurised air toyed with our chins, until it steamed off through our noses. The neighbouring seats didn't have the same problem, so they started laughing while passing the scene on to others, making waves of laughter roll through the place like the waves of the Victorian Nile. A little confused without getting an explanation to the sudden change of mood, she ordered something else. While all of us waited for our food, Kashilingi allowed us to clear our laughing voices. Officially we laughed at everything else in the restaurant, but we laughed even more as the woman joined in. After lunch we dropped the lady off at the tax-park, and went back to the office. Only an hour passed, and Taban, one of Kashilingi's drivers, arrived. He was on his way to the army clinic, at the first floor with one of Kashilingi's kids who had got sick. As Taban waited for the kid to return, he told me that he was more than sure, that I soon would get the full rank of Corporal. I couldn't really believe him, as I saw him as this great heroic figure, who merely had decided to compliment me. He was a Kakwa coming not far from Idi Amin's village, and I was always impressed with the way he walked. He decorated himself with weapons of all sorts: a bayonet on each side of the belt, a pistol tugged down in his trousers at his back, and then he for some reason had a rope at his right side. He was small but still he required the space of a bull. The first thing I did when I got home was to visit Taban in

175

his room, and ask him of how he got the rank of sergeant. He told me that once he was in Idi Amin's army where he was trained as a commando. This I believed, and hoped one day to be as tough as him.

Ramadan started. Kashilingi and his family had to fast because he was a Muslim, which meant that they couldn't smoke, eat, or drink as long as the sun was still up. The first day when the sun was about to descend, I sneaked into the dining room and saw a beautiful laid table with lots of different dishes of food and drinks. The downside of it all was that I couldn't have a taste of it, because I had not fasted. Those who had not fasted were served regular food, while the others enjoyed the rest. I waited until Kashilingi had finished eating, before I told him, that I too wanted to fast. He smiled and said: 'Sure, why not?' and then I started Ramadan together with his family.

During the Ramadan, every morning at four o'clock, Kashilingi's daughter Kobusingye would come and wake me up for Daku [food, before sunrise]. At midday my lips were drying up, and my eyes were getting even smaller, and I guessed that to be the same reason why Kashilingi went home to get some rest at this time during Ramadan. When going home, Kashilingi turned his eyes on me and smiled, telling me that I didn't have to fast in order to eat the good food with them. But I couldn't stop because I was afraid that his kids will laugh at me. I told him that I would not eat, until the breaking of the day's fast. I was convinced that my little lie had worked on him, because he nodded with a satisfied face. He had just went to his room to rest when I hurried down to the nearby shop. I bought myself a litre of milk and a huge piece of hot-loaf, which I hid in my bag until I reached to my room. Happy with my secret cache I warmed the milk on my field-stove, put sugar in and started eating the sweet bread as if I never had eaten before. When my stomach was relieved from the worst hunger, I started looking around the room, and then I noticed him standing in my doorway. In panic I hid the milk and the bread in front of his amused eyes, which changed me into a crying child. I begged him not to tell his children, but could only hope when he turned away and left me alone with my food.

The following day I woke up early, brushed my shoes and ironed my uniform, before walking down, where I met Taban, busy washing the car. He had a bandage on one of his legs, and when I asked him why, he told me that he had caught a snake on its way down his boot. It sounded so exciting that I almost wished that it had been me, but then I met Katumba, on his way out of the house, for the morning parade. He suggested that maybe Taban just had fallen over his own two feet, in a drunken moment. Taban was a Muslim and a commando. I didn't think that he could lie about such a thing. But still I sneaked into his room to see if Katumba really could be right. I came across some empty whisky bottles in a box, and later when I asked him, he told me that those had been for his medicine.

Soon Katumba and I became good friends. He entrusted me to bring letters for Kashilingi's daughter, Kobusingye. I was already busy thinking about how Kashilingi would react if he caught me, when Kiberu too began with the other daughter Aisha. I felt like a postal worker, as I received letters from those boys every second day. This courier business lasted for about a month, until one day I was having a cigarette with Kashilingi's niece, Regina, when Kashilingi called me. I stopped whistling when I saw him standing with a determined look, while holding his daughter Kobusingye's hand. Slowly he took mine too, and dragged us to her bedroom, threw her pillow aside revealing all her letters, and banged our heads together. I didn't want more of this, so I explained that I never knew what the letters were about.

Quietly he said that he was sorry for hurting me before shouting. 'But don't bring any more letters into this house!' Secretly I passed the message on to Katumba and Kiberu, but they seemed determined with the girls.

It was time for Idi, the celebration at the end of Ramadan. Two days before the celebration, the family were sent in Kashilingi's mini-tax to Rukungiri, the village of Kashilingi's parents. Katumba and I stayed behind with Kashilingi, who still had a few more days at the office. Finally we followed the family in one of his Mercedes-Benz, and because of the civilian number plates, we were stopped on a military road-block. I admired the MP sergeant's uniform in red and white, especially his barrette, as he demanded Kashilingi to identify himself. I waited for his reply with excitement before he said: 'I am senior officer Ahmad Kashilingi, and Director of Records.' The sergeant's face went limp for a second, as if he used all his capacity to replay the words he just had heard. When he realised that he had heard right, he almost fell when removing the stop signs that blocked the road. On our way we stopped at a restaurant, that suddenly was changed into a fuss of table rearrangements. The manager appeared from his office, and the waitresses buzzed away from the other customers, and came to welcome Kashilingi. As usual when he was in a good mood, he slapped a few of the waitresses' bums, so I was only stopped from beginning to laugh because of a distracting plate of chicken that was being placed in front of me. When we arrived at Kashilingi's, Katumba and Kiberu started connecting the music and television, while I played with Kashilingi's children.

The holiday was over, and soon we were on the road going back to Kampala. When we arrived home Kashilingi invited me to the living-room, because he was going to play a movie for the children. Kashilingi was in a good mood,

China reporting for duty.

China with Ruben Høi and Nanna. Ruben supports FC Copenhagen, China on the other hand is a fan of AB Gladsaxe. Photo taken in China's Danish apartment in 2001.

In May 2002, China addressed the United Nations Conference on Child Soldiers. The resultant meeting with Nelson Mandela was an emotional moment for China. At the far left of the picture is Harrison Ford.

China with Bill Clinton and Whoopi Goldberg.

A free China at Copenhagen Central Station.

sitting in his big sofa, with a glass of beer on the table in front of him. Then he told Kobusingye to fetch me a beer too. I had never been drinking in front of him, so I refused at first by telling him that I never had been drinking one, but he insisted.

The Savage Heart

The following day before going to the office, Kashilingi and I had breakfast, while conversing about this and that. But when he asked about my parents, the food in my hand froze. Slowly I began telling him about my father, but I couldn't finish because of the tears behind my eyelids. Kashilingi breathed out heavily, before telling me that he joined Idi Amin's army, because of his father's mistreatings. I looked into his eyes without blinking, and asked to his mother, but she had passed away before he could remember. In the same moment we stood up, left the breakfast behind, and walked down to the car as if our destinies had made us one. I had just been sitting outside the office for an hour, when Kashilingi came out, while stuffing his pistol into his trousers. Katumba and I followed, and we drove to Rubiri barracks, where we found a battalion of recruits ready for inspection. Kashilingi and senior officer Peter Karim started inspecting them, and I followed behind, posing with my pistol at their side. It was a poor line-up with worn-out uniforms, mainly of boys who I noticed all had their eyes on me. Kashilingi told me to choose three recruits, and I surprised myself as I felt a shock wave through my stomach. Now I stood face to face with those hungry boys, and I got confused of whom to choose, because most of them had heard what Kashilingi just had said. I almost drowned in sorry faces, so I had to close my eyes in order to hide away from the reality. When I opened them, I focused at the boy in front of me. 'My name is Benoni, sir!'

he replied to my question, and I told him to step in front, all flattered by his way of addressing me. But the reality of pity came crashing down again, when the boy next to Benoni whispered 'Take me, please, Afande!' and I couldn't resist. Later he nicknamed himself 'Sharp'. When I was about to pick the third one, Katumba called me over, and showed me a kid named Jamiru. He told me that Jamiru was a Muslim, and he would be of much help in slaughtering Kashilingi's hens. I felt like laughing, but when I saw his young age I hesitated no more.

Back at the Republic House, Kashilingi told me to call Taban, so that I could take the three boys to Mbuya in the military store, and get them some uniforms. Among these three soldiers, I became fond of Sharp, because he was funny, and full of jokes. He never stopped calling me Afande China, though he was a bit older than me. With Benoni it was entirely different. He was in his mid twenties, and to him a woman belonged to the kitchen. He was aggressive, and denied to recognise my rank. He was merely a recruit which meant that, even though I was only thirteen or fourteen at that time, I was years in front of him when it came to military experience. I was annoyed about having to find brutal ways to get his respect and say 'the magic word' Afande. Jamiru was atop of the world, but apart from that I can't say much. Jamiru and Katumba had found each other and were now brothers. Katumba seemed to be a man of constant pain, and like me, he had been raised in the army. Jamiru was now learning everything he could of Katumba's ways, and soon this little twelve-year old kid turned into an ancient warrior who thought to be superior in everything.

A few days had passed, and I got promoted to the rank of sergeant. I couldn't believe my ears when Kashilingi then appointed me to be the chief escort. It was nearly impossible to hide my excitement, but again the fear rose inside me, as

I looked at the grown-up men, who now had to live under my orders. My way of walking quickly changed, and at supper time Kashilingi told me that he would attend the morning parade, to see how I was managing. Early morning he arrived in full uniform, and told everybody there to respect me as their new chief escort. I was the first to approach if any questions should emerge. My whole body trembled as he said this, and I felt like jumping in the air but then he walked around us, and told Katumba to pack his stuff, for then to find his way to the office. Katumba was going to be transferred to the north front, just like all the previous bodyguard.

All of Kashilingi's bodyguards who had an affair with his daughters or told about his affairs to his wife were all sent to the north front. Many of his bodyguards were kids just like me, and later I came to meet one of these bodyguards, and his name was Silas. Silas was now living at the officers' mess in Kololo, near Kashilingi's home, but now Silas had been shot more than four times during the battle in the north front, and he was becoming thin every day. Silas was light in colour, and he resembled me a bit, and this made us become friends. Now it was Katumba's turn, and maybe tomorrow mine. The last time I saw Katumba he was blind, and that was a mystery for me, because I could not understand why.

Now that I was the chief escort, I wanted to be treated like one, because there was nothing on earth I was more afraid of than being looked at as a coward, and I was frightened to give up. I had the rank and title to decide for the escort, but I was a young girl at the same time, who was afraid that one day they would disobey my orders. The desperation was closing in on me, and it seemed that I had to do everything I could to be feared. Four o'clock we were back from the offices. Kashilingi hurried into the house and I followed, but waited near the living-room. Soon he came out from his

181

bedroom and told me to get Jamiru ready. When I had seen them off, I went to the kitchen where the house girl Namaganda was busy washing the dishes. I remained standing there with my hands resting on the hips beside my pistol and bayonet, waiting to be served. Then I realised that she simply had decided to ignore me, so I took a plate of food from the oven, and hid away my anger.

When I was about to pick some food, Namaganda grabbed the plate out of my hand, like an eagle capturing a new-born chicken. I turned and smiled, before asking her the reason for this. She explained that this was the last food, and she was saving it for Kashilingi's nephew, Julius. 'You mean, you didn't save any food for me?' I burst out, and I would have slapped her if she hadn't been so much bigger than me. I hated to be the loser, so I took a firm grip of the plate and we started pulling. Both of us lost the grip, and the plate fell to the floor. Her size didn't matter any more, so I kicked her in the stomach. She bent forward to the blow, and I turned around, walking outside. Standing a few paces from the doorway, I heard quick footsteps at my back. I turned around, and saw Namaganda approaching with a kitchen knife. 'Do you want to kill me?' I asked, while I drew my pistol. I remembered my bayonet, so I put away the pistol, and there she stood waving the knife. I kicked her hand and, before the knife landed, I had cut her arm. I left her screaming and went to my room.

Later I heard a knock on the door, and it was Jamiru, still in his uniform. He told me that Kashilingi was calling me, so I dressed up and followed him. Everyone except for the little ones were waiting in the living-room. Beside Kashilingi, Namaganda sat with her arm in a bandage, and I sat myself down as far from them as I could.

'Do I leave you here to terrorise my family?' he roared.

'No, Afande!' I replied and explained to what had happened.

'I always tell you that this "thing" is dangerous, but you don't seem to listen. One day, I suppose, I will find all of you dead,' he said, referring to me as the thing.

After these few words he let me go, and I fell asleep, pleased with his judgement.

That night I woke up late, because it was Saturday. Outside I met Aisha, in front of the house. She was sad and when I asked why, she told me that her boyfriend Kiberu was being transferred to another unit. I was happy as I didn't like him, being a lieutenant who always obstructed me from carrying out my duties. Still, I pretended to be sorry. We continued our conversation, until I got a chance to tell of my problem with her. I got jealous watching Aisha's breasts bounce up and down whenever she ran, and I wished that I would grow up faster, and be able to do it better. She told me to pull my coming breasts for a couple of minutes each morning, and in a few weeks they would be just like hers. I really looked forward to that day, when I would be bouncing them into the air. I left Aisha still standing there, and went inside to the breakfast-table.

Julius and his cousin Emanuel were having their breakfast and, as I joined in, they told me about a party at their college. None of us were allowed to go anywhere at night, even I was not allowed to be near the gate after six. We decided to sneak out anyway, because we knew that Kashilingi would be home late. In the evening after supper, Julius and Emanuel went to dress up, but I was already dressed in my military uniform, and the reason for this was that I wanted the boys at the party to fear me. Before we left, I told Sharp, who had the night guard, not to tell Kashilingi, in case he returned before us. When we arrived, the men at the entrance got us in without having to pay. Most of the people wanted to speak with me, and I got everything for free. Soon I was getting tired because of Julius and his cousin, who kept on introducing me to everybody. We returned home at round five o'clock and, as I was about to fall asleep, Taban knocked on the door, and told me that Kashihngi was calling. When I got to the living-room, Kashilingi was dressed in his nightgown already busy shouting at Julius and Emanuel.

'Yes Afande,' I saluted.

'Didn't I tell you never to go out at night?' he asked.

I couldn't really find the answer, but when I looked down, he ordered Taban to drive the three of us to the military jail in Mbuya barracks.

In jail, many of the guards didn't like me, and the reason for this was my proud attitude. They told me that, in the morning, they would make me sweep and clean in and out of the jail. But I didn't care, because I knew that I had enough money to buy their anger. Eight o'clock the next morning Kashilingi arrived. He told the guard commander to give me a hard job, and so he left with Julius and Emanuel. I was hurt, because I thought it wasn't fair to save the two boys and leave me behind. I came to think whether I meant anything at all to Kashilingi, who decided to leave me in jail with one pair of uniform, knowing that I was a girl who needed to change. As soon as Kashilingi had left, I stayed in the cell and watched through the window. The guard commander approached, and said: 'You see. Even Kashilingi want you to be punished, so I am now going to make you work, until you look like a pig.' After he had talked and finished, I put my hand in my pocket and showed the sergeant some money. When his eyes widened, I told him that I would give it to him, if he promised to let me be. At night, Sergeant sent one of his comrades to buy some beers, and, as it had been my money, he invited me for a drink. We sat ourselves out on the grass and drank, as we watched the stars. The sergeant was now my friend, and as I was about to return to the cell, he said:

'I hope Afande Kashilingi picks you up, because I'm off tomorrow.' After a lot of thoughts had crossed my mind, I slowly laid myself on the concrete floor and slept. The following day I was more than sure that I would be released, but after dawn I still hadn't seen Kashilingi and gave up for the day. In the evening the third day, he arrived with Jennifer and Jamiru, and when the guard commander brought me out, Kashilingi became angry when he saw that my uniform still was clean. He called the guard and told him to beat me with a stick, and as I was about to lay down, I heard Jennifer tell him that I already had enough. Kashilingi called off the punishment, and ordered me to enter the car. When we arrived, I ran to my room, where I remained until the next morning. After breakfast we drove to the office, and, before lunch, Kashilingi came out and told me to call his lover, a lady who worked as a secretary to Rwigyema, who was now a major general and the Minister of State for Defence. When I got there, I met Rwigyema's bodyguards, and one of the boys named Happy was my best friend, so I began gossiping, suddenly forgetting what I had come for.

Rwigyema appeared from his office, and took me by my hand, while saying: 'I can't work to that noise!' I almost panicked as we stood in front of his desk, where he told me to sit in his chair. 'You are now the minister, so go on and sit!' and I nervously looked to his secretary who just smiled. After a while he told me that I was free to go, but he had to report the incident to Kashilingi. I felt the pressure of the minister's promise, and without looking I slipped through the door, and soon I was back on my chair. I waited for the major general's arrival, but fortunately he never came, and I was relieved from yet another punishment. Rwigyema and I became friends. Whenever he caught me making noise with his bodyguard, he would take me by my ear and pull it, until I once more promised never to make noise again. I turned from admiring him as the senior officer I once knew in the bush, to love him for his kindness. He never forgot who made his power, and remained among us blunt as ever. I hope that anyone who saw and felt this love of his will remember it always.

A House of Tragedy

Kashilingi was a big fan of theatre, particularly the troop Jimmy Katumba. He watched their plays most of his week-ends with Jennifer, because his wife lived at his hometown. One of those week-ends he left me behind in charge of the house, with the words: 'Do not kill anyone, understood. Take care of them ' I stood on the veranda with Regina, and Alex, an escort who just had been with us for a couple of months.

As we stood there, a civilian driver named Tumwine arrived, whose job was to drive Kashilingi's children to school. The two boys looked threatening at each other, because both were in love with Regina. A moment later, they argued about where the Thirty-Fifth Battalion had been transferred.

Tumwine asked Alex how he could be sure, when he couldn't even spell his own name. Alex replied by calling Tumwine a cow. I heard a clap and when I turned, I saw tears in Alex's eyes, and that was it. He walked down towards his room, saying: 'Now I'm even being beaten by a civilian.' I went inside the house, leaving Tumwine and Regina there. Shortly after having spoken to Jennifer, I met Alex who had made his way in, using the back entrance. He had an AK-47 with three magazines taped together. I could see that he was ready to shoot, but I had no choice, so I told him to leave the house. I could hardly see his eyes, as he pointed the gun at me at close range, and asked: 'Do you want to die?' Since I was the chief escort, I felt that I should take full responsibility, even if I had to give my own life. I stood there in front of the barrel all sweating, and I could not give up begging Alex. The more I begged him the more he got upset. I thought of screaming, but again I became afraid. Suddenly I saw Tumwine walk slowly behind, and when he grabbed Alex from behind, the first bullet struck the wall close to the bedroom where the children were asleep. I realised that this was only the beginning. Jennifer walked from her bedroom, but disappeared again. I stood there all confused, but soon I had to join the struggle. My main worry was the magazines, and I tried until I managed to remove them. Now my only worry was one bullet, which was left inside the chamber. Suddenly from nowhere I saw Regina pulling Alex's gun. I shouted while telling her to 'piss off', but it all fell on deaf ears. Too late, the second shot was heard, and I saw Regina fall to the floor. Before I could reach her, the blood had already covered the floor where she laid. I turned to Alex, and he too had been shot.

Regina was badly damaged on one of her legs, and she was bleeding more than Alex, who had been shot by the same bullet. The bullet had penetrated her thigh, and the muscle had been shattered. The house was in panic. The kids were crying, and everybody's hope was on me. After having tied Regina's leg, I decided to take her to the hospital but not Alex. I was upset and I didn't care whether he died or not.

Tumwine and I carried Regina outside, and as we were about to put her in the car, Colonel Chihanda walked out of his house, stood himself behind his fence with his arms crossed, and said: 'Are you busy killing yourselves?' for then to walk back inside. I couldn't get why he had come out in the first place, but I wasn't surprised, as this was a typical reaction of most senior officers. Besides, Chihanda was known to most as a brutal Senior Officer, who had burned some of our comrades alive during the bush war. When

Regina was aboard I thought about Alex, and realised that I might have done the same as Alex, so I changed my mind about leaving him behind. I ordered Tumwine to drive as fast as he could, and soon we arrived at Nsambya hospital. Regina was already in a coma, when I left her in the doctors' hands. Alex was hit somewhere close to his private parts, but it was not life-threatening. Tumwine and I stayed seated in the car, and I was terrified about how Kashilingi would react to this. I strongly believed that he would transfer me to the north, but if I was lucky, he would send me to jail. A doctor came and told me that Regina had lost a lot of blood, and they needed someone as quickly as possible to give some; otherwise she might die. 'Regina needs someone with the same blood group,' he added.

I stood there and looked him in the eyes, because I had no idea whatsoever about blood groups. The doctor was a kind man, and so he explained it to me. Once again we drove, and this time I ordered the hazard lights on. At home I furiously ordered all grown-ups to enter the car, and soon we were back at the hospital. The doctors checked our blood and, of all people I had brought, I was the only one who had the same blood group as Regina. I was taken to a room, and was told to lay down on a mattress. The nurse took my hand, and soon I complained when they explained that I had to fill up the bottle, which was at my side. After having finished, she told me not to get up, but I refused and, as I was about to get to the car, I passed out.

On our way home we saw Kashilingi's Mercedes-Benz from a distance, approaching in high speed. As soon as we had stopped, he started shouting at me, but I was still too weak to respond. I heard him ask Tumwine, 'What's wrong with this one? Is she also shot?' In the same speed he drove to the hospital, and I knew that it was not over between Kashilingi and me.

After some time Kashilingi returned and, from my bed, I asked for a doctor, though I was a bit well. When the doctor arrived, I told him of what was happening, and he helped me by lying to Kashilingi that I needed a good rest. I stayed home for some days, eating and relaxing, and that's how I escaped the punishment. Days later I went to visit Regina, and she told me that her leg was turning blue, and indeed it was. That day she asked me to sleep over, and all night I watched her as she cried over her leg. The next day shortly after leaving the hospital, a doctor came to Kashilingi's home. He said that Regina's leg could not be saved, and that we had to call Kashilingi, who was at work, to go to the hospital. At night in the living-room, Kashilingi told everyone that Regina's leg was to be amputated. Despite the sadness, everybody laughed when Kashilingi's niece, a little girl, begged that Regina's leg should be given to her. When asked why, she simply said: 'Because it has red nail polish.'

Months later, Regina returned home, and spent most of her time hiding. She turned herself into a chain smoker, and this time she didn't hide from Kashilingi. Alex was now in prison, since he was a soldier, and there was hope for Regina to be sent to Germany for further treatment. Every time I returned from work she would call for me, and mostly she spoke about what future she might have. Somehow her words and tears affected me deeply, and it made me start to think about my own future. I became troubled when seeing every day alike, and now I seemed to be losing my mind.

I came to the point of hating the Republic House, but what troubled me most was that I could see no end. Everything at home seemed against me, and it became worse when Kashilingi started ordering me to keep my door open. One of those days at the office, I asked Kashilingi for a transfer. He shouted at me, while threatening that if I really wanted it, he would send me to the north front.

The man I had hoped to be a father had turned against me, and I didn't understand him any more. I was beginning to be frightened of him, though I hardly knew why. Things were getting out of control, and I had to come to terms with reality. His abuse against me had started the day I became his bodyguard, but he was too powerful, and I was scared to think bad about him, because I thought that he could see what I was thinking. I saw no way out, and all that I did was to try hard and concentrate on the good things that he did. The reality became too strong, and I could not take it any more. It became worse, when Kashilingi started taking me to a nearby clinic called 'Kicement'. There is so many things which happened to me, and what I saw that I cannot really tell about. I'm too afraid even to face it, and let it only be known by my heart. I was like a sheep, who had to just say, 'Yes, sir,' all the time. My soul seemed to be owned by our Afandes, and I wondered if ever I will be able to own myself! All the time I had to say, 'Yes sir' or 'Yes Afande'. Today I can't say 'No'. Every time I want to say NO, I become afraid, fearing that I might be punished or hated! My stomach was paining me, but he still abused me. Whenever I cried and told him that it was painful, he would say: 'I will do it slowly'. Every night he came and knocked at my door, and once I pretended to be fast asleep, but in the morning he asked me: 'Why did you not open?' Soon he realised my trick, and I was ordered to keep my door open! I could not do anything. I was powerless, nowhere to turn to, and no one to talk to. I had to deal with it all by myself, and I wondered if there was anybody out there who felt my pain. I could not understand Kashilingi. He abused me in the night, and the following day he would send me to call his girlfriends. Other days, he would put me in jail. I'm so frightened of him, and I will always be, because I will never know what kind of a human he is! Inside me it feels as if he has power over me. I would lay in my bed, as I cried and listen to music until I would fall asleep. The music seemed to feel my pain, and it always calmed me down. Kashilingi knew very well how I felt, because every time he abused me, my tears would be falling, but he ignored them. I will never know why, because I was there to protect him, but he treated me like I was a machine.

One day I reported myself sick, and remained in bed. I was so upset, but I didn't know why. I needed to do something, but I had no idea what it was. I went to Kashilingi's house, where Regina was alone watching television. I passed her and went to the fridge, grabbed a beer and drank it, while she silently stared at me. I walked back to my room, and the next thing I remember was me busy shooting in the outside toilet with my AK-47. After the incident I heard Regina cry for help. I dropped the gun and hurried to help her. She was laying on the floor holding her leg, and when I asked of what had happened, she told me that she had fallen from the sofa because of some terrifying sounds. Deep inside I cried, but I could not tell her that it had been my fault. Instead I convinced her that it was the noise from the house being built nearby. Once again, Regina was taken back to the hospital for another operation, and I was allowed to stay with her until she was discharged.

Regina was never sent to Germany, but was taken to a local doctor who made her an artificial leg. She didn't like her new leg, and most of the time she preferred the walking sticks. Regina was getting fat, and that raised many questions among neighbours and friends. One day at the office, I was called by Colonel Julius Kihanda, who asked me if Regina was pregnant. I told him that I hadn't thought about it, but since the day she had returned from the hospital, I hadn't seen her with a boy. He looked concerned but before I left, he told me to investigate. After work I hurried to

Regina's bedroom, and asked if Kihanda's suspicion was true. She started crying, saying: 'All this is Kashilingi,' but I could not understand whether or not this was as her answer to my question. I left her crying, and went for a little shopping, and on my way back Lt-Colonel Moses Drago who lived in the neighbourhood called me over. My entire body shivered as if I had been struck by malaria, and the few things I carried became heavy. I stood still for a while, and after having breathed like a tired cow, I managed to approach him. He was sharing a few beers on his veranda with one of his friends Lt-Colonel Peter Karamagi. Drago asked questions but I could not answer, because of my paralysed tongue which refused to co-operate. Before I left he told me that he was not as dangerous as people thought, and all he wanted was my friendship. I walked away proud, as I thought of having spoken with one of the most popular war heroes. Most of all, I was excited about the cars that he drove, being colourful with horns that honked like animals. Now my greatest dream had become to get a ride in one of them.

When I got home I was still excited, so I went to Regina. She was still sad, making me keep quiet, so instead I offered her a cigarette. As we smoked she told me that, indeed, she was pregnant. I put pressure on her to tell who the father was, but she refused. A few days later, Regina gave birth to a girl. Later I caught Jennifer say that the child resembled Kashilingi. Since Regina had kept her pregnancy secret, and hadn't told of who the father was, Kashilingi's two daughters were now desperate for the truth. One evening when everyone sat in the living-room, Kashilingi asked Regina to tell us the whole story. Regina looked as if the world was about to end, as our eyes stared at her and the child in her arms. She broke down and cried, saying that, one day, a bodyguard of Drago's had raped her when she was alone in the house. I knew that she was telling lies, because no body-guards could enter a senior officer's home, because of the soldiers at the gate. Besides, she would have told me when she revealed her pregnancy. I got angry and walked away.

The next day was Saturday, and everyone slept late except for me. I went and knocked on Regina's window. I demanded her to tell me the truth, otherwise I would never smoke with her again. Regina told me that Kashilingi had forced her to lie, but still she refused to tell me of who the father was.

Later that day my sister Margie and her boyfriend came to visit me. Before leaving she told me that they were moving to Kabale. I was sad, but when she told me that she expected a baby, I found myself smiling.

I was beginning to enjoy my life, because of the friendship I had gained with Drago. He made me feel safe and relaxed, in a way no other man had done before him, and every time I was away from him, I missed his company. He spoiled me with everything, and seemed to understand my worst fear as my greatest pleasure. I came to know him, as a twenty-four-year-old, who could only write his name, but he was also a very unselfish man. Most of the places he took me, even a private felt free to address him as a friend and not as a Lieutenant-Colonel. One evening Drago and I were having an ice-cream at a café. In the middle of the conversation, he interrupted by suggesting that I asked Kashilingi for a transfer to his battalion, but I could only nod with a sad smile.

I was standing at the gate with Sharp when Drago came. He gave Sharp some money, to keep him quiet, and we drove off in his Land-Rover. He took me to a friend's house, where we watched some movies. The movie Delta Force made me forget all about the time, and it was midnight when I returned. At the gate, Sharp told me that Kashilingi had been looking all over for me, and to my distress he hadn't been able to keep quiet.

The following day, Kashilingi called for me and accused me of betraying him. This time he sent me to the 'bad guys' in the cells of the Republic House.

Eight o'clock in the evening, I heard Drago ordering the MPs to bring me out. He spent some time with us, and before leaving he handed some money out to each of us. Now the military police had become the 'good guys', and we spent the night drinking. When Kashilingi came to release me, I didn't really want to go. I smelled heavily of alcohol, and to protect my new friends, I hardly breathed until I got home.

My desperation increased for each day that passed, because of Kashilingi's behaviour. I began to notice a side of my personality which I couldn't really control. Many times I thought of running away, but I knew that he could use his authority to make my life a living hell. There were many things that I needed to think about, but I couldn't think straight unless I was far away from Kashilingi's reach, and I rarely got that chance.

In the morning at the office, I told Kashilingi that I needed to visit my mother.

When he refused, I started crying, so he changed his mind and ordered Chris to grant me a movement order. When we got home, I went to Drago's. Unfortunately I was told by one of the bodyguards Kabawo, that Drago had gone north to his unit. I returned home, with the promise of Kabawo, to take me there the next morning. That night because of my growing excitement, I went to bed without eating. I also needed to prepare my pistol as I knew very well that where I was going was a dangerous place. I equipped myself with five magazines. And so the journey began. When I arrived, Kabawo was waiting for me at the gate, and he too was ready with his AK-47. We walked to the bus park, and got aboard a bus which was going to Lira. When we reached

Karuma bridge, I looked down in the splashing water, trying not to remember what once happened. I was relieved when Kabawo interrupted me by showing me an elephant, which walked freely beside the road.

Soon we arrived at Dr Obote's home town, Lira, where many buildings had been bombed, and most people seemed cold and poor. The few people that I spoke to were rude; most just stared and walked away without responding. After having ate, Kabawo and I came across a military truck which was going to Kitugum. There were many soldiers, and all were desperate for transport, and it was hard, as everybody struggled to board themselves. There were two lieutenants, and both wanted to sit in front. Kabawo started arguing with them, because he wanted me to sit there, since the truck belonged to Drago's brigade. Corporal Kabawo struggled with the lieutenants, until they agreed.

Drago was very happy when we arrived, and he told Kabawo how much he trusted in him. After having changed our clothes, Drago invited us into a restaurant. Shortly after, we were joined by the district administrator, and he wanted us to join him at the dance club. When we arrived, the manager hurried to prepare a place for us at the end of the dancing floor, and we spent most of the time talking and drinking.

The next morning, Drago ordered the brigade administrator to slaughter some cows and pass some meat to each soldier. Drago invited all his men from the rank of sergeant and above to his quarters, and as the soldiers began preparing the fire, we took a short trip to town. The town was poor, there was not much to see, and the shops mostly contained sugar and salt. The only buildings that wasn't ruined was those I had seen the night before, and the roads in the city offered no better comfort than those in the bush. Many of the kids were naked, and most seemed not to have washed for several days, but still I could see a smile on their faces, as they passed me carrying containers of water. The troubled city and its weary inhabitants made me change my mind from going any further.

As we walked back to the barracks I met my uncle Caravel, who told me that he had been put under house-arrest. As we spoke, Drago stayed at a distance, and that gave Caravel a chance to interrogate me. I told him that Drago only was my friend, but he didn't believe me, and when I asked him the reason of his arrest, he chased me away. Drago seemed desperate to know how I came to know Caravel and, when I told him that he was my uncle, he invited him over. But the lieutenant who had been sent to call for Caravel returned alone. As we sat around the fire, Drago told everybody to stop calling him Afande, and I realised that he was getting drunk. One sergeant stood in front of everyone and said that he wished all commanders were like Drago. After he had finished talking, Drago and I went into the house, and we heard them sing until morning.

In the morning as we ate breakfast, Drago suggested that I stay for another day. I wanted to, but I had been granted only three days. After the breakfast, I walked down to Caravel, and, as we spoke, felt as if I would never see him again. The thought made my eyes wet, so I said goodbye.

After a while, Drago told me that I was to go back with a military aircraft which would be landing any minute. We said goodbye and all I could hope for was to see him again. Before Gulu we landed in the bush. There were many dead soldiers, and I couldn't believe my eyes. I saw the dead officers being sorted from the rest, and loaded into the aircraft. I cried in silence, when seeing the dead soldiers being buried in what appeared to me as a mass grave. Every soldier there seemed tired, and I was shocked when I noticed their behaviour, acting as if they didn't know who they were any more. Their uniforms were torn, and they smelled badly. The casualties were so many that some had to wait for another helicopter. After having unloaded the wounded at Gulu barracks, we flew to Kampala. By eight o'clock in the evening, I was in my bed. What I had seen seemed to have stuck in my memory, and I doubted if ever I would live without it. I spent some time thinking about the dead soldiers, and at the end, I could not find any reason for their death. The next day at the office, I noticed all the women that I always had passed. Women of different ages, who looked for their sons and daughters. I went and spoke to one of the women, who had been left standing at the death office. This crying, tired woman told me that she had not seen her son for some years, and that she had been coming to this office for more than a year. I knew for sure that her son was dead and left lying on the ground just like many others, but one thing I could not understand with the authority was why they did not tell the truth. On our way back home, I questioned myself if, one day, NRA would point out the graves of the comrades who had fallen so bravely in the battle of one man.

A Burning Farewell

A week had passed since my return from the north. It was a morning in 1989, and I was standing next to Kashilingi's Mercedes-Benz. I heard a car stop at the gate, and it was Chris. He stepped out and ordered me to call Kashilingi, but I refused, telling him that since I was the chief bodyguard, I should know why. Chris became angry and took my refusal as revenge, forgetting that I only did my job. We stood there and argued, until he finally told me what had happened. I ran and told Kashilingi the news, and in panic we all drove to the Republic House. There were senior officers all over, looking at the Republic House in full blaze, and a tense atmosphere of shock and panic filled the place. Everybody seemed to be asking questions to the person next to them.

The fire badly damaged the Directorate of Records on the last floor, and most senior officers believed the fire to have started from Kashilingi's office. As the Director of Records, it seemed his duty to have all the answers. According to Kashilingi, he had lost many of his private documents, including money from the safe.

Kashilingi was suspended, and he was troubled by this, seeing it as betrayal.

I asked myself if Kashilingi, as it was said, could be behind it, and if so, why?

I remembered Kashilingi having complained about his rank to someone I believed to be Museveni, in a phone conversation I had overheard about a month previously. I answered the call personally, and this person had asked for Kashilingi, *not* Afande Kashilingi. The rank issue and the way he had addressed Kashilingi made me rule out every higher-ranking senior officer as the caller, but the President and the Army Commander. Curious, I listened from behind the curtains, and after the conversation Kashilingi walked away in anger. After some hours of thinking, I found no reason for him to have committed this crime, and as far as I knew, the only person who had the authority to suspend him was the President. Maybe I jumped to the conclusion that the President just as well could be behind it, since he was a man who achieved his goals, spending immense sacrifices. I was convinced that he as well could have decided to lose the Republic House, just to frame Kashilingi, who Museveni might had seen to have become too powerful.

Kashilingi was no longer coming home late, and he wanted the gate closed twenty-four hours a day. Sometime during the day he would sit in his car, and that to me seemed as if he was hiding without knowing it. At some point, I became frightened for my life, as I had no idea of the outcome. There was this crazy ideas going through my head, of soldiers coming in the night to kill everybody. It made me scared, so I decided to cut a hole in our fence, which I then would use to escape.

One morning I was still in my room, when two senior officers arrived from Rubiri First Division, with one platoon. Bamwesigye was the brigade commander, and James Kazini, his second-in-command. Kazini was aggressive in his orders, and he seemed excited with what was going on. The two senior officers ordered Kashilingi to hand over all of his uniforms and AK-47, but not the pistol. For the first time, I saw tears in Kashilingi's eyes, and I was certain that this was his downfall. The bodyguards and I were lined in front of Kashilingi, and he was told to choose two and one driver. Jamiru, Bogere and I were staying, each with an AK-47 and one full magazine. The powerful man, who was feared by most, was now powerless, and his career seemed to be vanishing. That became a big blow on my own life, and I had to act before it was too late. I knew that soon I would be asked questions, which I couldn't possibly answer. In the evening I asked Kashilingi to let me take my stuff to my mother, and without hesitation he agreed. Early the next morning, Jamiru and Bogere helped me pack my belongings and drive me to the buspark. I arrived at my mother's safely, but many of my things had been broken.

The third day, I returned to Kashilingi, and things were never the same again. He was full of suspicion, and he spent most of the nights walking outside the house. I was getting bored because of staying at home every day and, without Kashilingi's permission, I went to town. There I met a mechanic, a friend of Drago's, who used to fix Kashilingi's cars. I stayed at his garage, watching movies until late in the evening, when he drove me home. At the gate, Jamiru stood on guard with his gun ready. When I ordered him to open he informed me that he had been ordered not to let me in. I tried to force him, but he said that if I continued, he would have to shoot. I was extremely hurt and disappointed at this man, who I had been protecting for so long. I saw him as a betrayer and found no other option but to get revenge. I walked away, letting Jamiru think that I had given up, sneaked around the premises and used the hole to enter my room. I went straight for my gun, but it had been taken away. Powerless I sat myself on the floor, and let the tears go.

Early morning I went to the gate, and ordered Jamiru to call Kashilingi. Kashilingi stood at a distance and asked of what I wanted. I asked him to tell me why he was doing this, and he said that I was being used to spy on him. There was nothing more for me to say, and before walking away, I said: 'Afande Kashilingi, thank you for everything!'

I went to Rubiri barracks, and I was taken to Captain James Kazini's office, who told me to return the next morning for deployment. I asked myself into which unit I might be transferred, but suddenly I imagined the officers waiting there with their drooling mouths. I was confused, and frightened and I didn't know where to go, so I decided to go to Drago's place, because it was better than a thousand lions.

Some days later, I heard that Kashilingi's home had been invaded by the military police. When Kashilingi heard of his arrest, he called the President, but Museveni was out of the country. Kashilingi didn't give up, so he called the new army chief, Mugisha Muntu, who denied to have any knowledge of the arrest. Now Kashilingi was afraid. He had asked them why specifically Rubiri barracks, and not Luzira or the military police headquarters. When the soldiers couldn't answer, he knew that if he surrendered to them, he would be slaughtered. Kashilingi stood in front of the armed soldiers with his briefcase, while begging them to let him drive alone to the army chief's office. The soldiers kept strict to their orders, until Colonel Julius Kihanda came along and convinced them to indulge Kashilingi. He drove in his Mercedes-Benz, closely followed by the soldiers and, when he arrived at the offices, he locked his car and walked inside, while the soldiers guarded the place. Two hours passed, and the army chief happened to be on his way for lunch. When he saw the building surrounded, he asked: 'What are you doing here? Am I under arrest?'

'No sir! We are waiting for Afande Kashilingi to leave your office.'

When the chief realised that Kashilingi had been missing for two hours, he simply panicked. Radio calls were made to all units of Uganda to be on standby, and the chief ordered a raid at Kashilingi's.

Few days later I met one of Kashilingi's daughters, who called the raid unforgettable. The military police, who had been sent there to watch the children's every move, turned bad and emptied the house. They kept the children away from going to school, and the house was turned into a military barracks. The kids were put under house-arrest, and they could only look through the window, as they prayed for their lives to be spared. Since the house belonged to the Ministry of Defence, Kashilingi's children were kicked out, and in a matter of days, they were wandering on the streets.

I was sad to hear of what had happened, and I couldn't understand why these children were treated like enemies. I had no time to feel with Kashilingi's children, because things were also turning bad for me. I was hunted by the intelligence staff, and all was asking the same questions: 'Why did you stay behind? To spy for him?' I was put under immense pressure by these men, who accused me of being Kashilingi's niece, and I wondered if that meant that I was guilty, as

Kashilingi was charged. In my heart I knew that they knew very well that I was not Kashiliingi's niece, but they were trying to blackmail me, in order to scare me more than I was. Almost daily I was harassed and, to stop that from happening, I was expected by most to give sexual favours. I refused to give in, fighting hard to keep up my spirit.

During those days, I met Colonel Julius Chihanda on foot and in civilian clothes. Surprised, I approached him, and he told me that he had been suspended for helping Kashilingi. When I began telling him of my situation, he told me to back off before he got into further trouble. People I had been counting on began to avoid my presence. I came to understand them when I heard that Kashilingi's childhood friend, a captain who had been suspected of aiding him to escape, had been tortured and beaten to death.

The most shocking news was that a dear friend of mine – a younger brother of Kashilingi – was chopped to pieces in his Rukungiri home. At that moment I knew, I had to do something drastic to avoid the same fate. Suddenly Drago came, and the following day we drove to his new brigade in Anaka near Gulu. When we arrived, he ordered his bodyguards to make fire, where we then sat and talked about Kashilingi. Drago himself didn't think that Kashilingi was responsible, though he couldn't understand why he had run away.

The next day the brigade was moved next to Idi Amin's birthplace. Koboko was a small town close to the border of Sudan. The next night we were Joined by Major Bunyenyezi and his brigade. Sudan, too, was on a build-up on the other side of the valley, which ran along the border. Few days later, even more brigades were brought in, and I came to witness a gigantic stand-off. The only good thing about this situation was an increased salary, and I was impressed to see privates eat chicken for breakfast. Both sides grew to a scary size, and there seemed no end to the lines of artillery. When the upcoming war was called off, many soldiers seemed more disappointed than relieved, because of the lost income. Drago's brigade was sent to yet another battle, somewhere in the bush of Gulu, but I was sent to his house at Gulu barracks.

After some days of boredom, I was called by the division commander, Colonel Peter Karim, who asked if I knew where Kashilingi was, assuring me that no matter where I went I would have to answer for Kashilingi. I could only look him in his eyes, salute him and shake my head. He let me go, troubled and tired of questions, and I began to wonder if there was any safe place for me. Weeks later Karim went to Kampala, leaving Colonel Stanley Muhangi in charge. I was inside the house ironing my uniform, when a soldier walked in and told me that Afande Muhangi was calling. With a scaring knowledge of what he wanted from me, I told the boy to go and tell Muhangi that I would be there after having finished my ironing. A few minutes passed before a lieutenant appeared in the door, ordering me to go with him. Surprised, I told him that I had to take a shower first, and he insisted to stay until I was ready. Muhangi was waiting behind his fence, but as I was about to reach the gate, I heard a helicopter. When I looked back at the fence there were no Muhangi. It landed in front of me and Drago came out, walked past me and right into Muhangi's house. Relieved I went back to the house, and after few minutes Drago walked in, and I thought of telling him, but I feared that he would not understand. I couldn't have felt more lucky, when a few months later, I heard that Muhangi had died of AIDS but I still couldn't help asking myself of how many female soldiers he himself had killed this way.

A few days later I returned with Drago to the front line. Since we captured power in 1986 Drago kept on, and he was continually transferred from one unit to another, and it was always to the battlefield. In Gulu we were always mobile, walking, hunting for rebels. But Drago wasn't the only one who kept on fighting the wars. Many of my fellow child soldiers kept on and they, too, were now hardened just like Drago, but the difference was that they were lower-ranked soldiers, and they were forgotten. Many of my fellow child soldiers were orphans. Their family were killed in the Luwero bush war. Since there was no one left to miss them or find them, they were left to fight the war until the end. Anyone who got shot or got their legs and arms cut off were sent to Mubende Casualty Wing. When Mubende became over-crowded with casualties, the government got rid of them, and now they were left to steal and were killed. Many Acholi people were considered rebels, and even if some of us knew that they were not, we still looked at them as one. The hate we had for Obote, the former Ugandan president, never changed, and the Acholi seemed to be paying the price. Drago's second-in-command spoke Kinyankole, and he took everything personal. To him every Acholi was a rebel, and they deserved nothing but death. Every time we captured an Acholi we had to kill them, and Drago hated this. Drago was a hardened war fighter, but when it came to civilians he wanted to keep his hands clean, but some of the leaders saw this as something else. Most of the interagency officers were only of one kind, and those who were not always watched. Our Brigade interagency officer spoke the same language as Drago's second-in-command, and this meant that Drago had to change what was happening. One day Drago returned from the State House, where he had gone to attend the Army Counsel with President Museveni, and when he arrived, there were Acholi men who were tied up in the most painful way, called Kandoya style. Some had died, and others were in a bad state because they were being beaten as their arms were tied behind their back.

They had no shirts on and you could see the chest about to go apart. There, on their knees, with no more words to say, as their eyes tried to ask for mercy. But ours turned, and looked away. I tried to ask God to turn me into a general so I could save them, but my wish never came. The bad thing was that every time you showed sympathy for the enemy, you would be accused of being on their side, so the best way was to hate them, though inside you knew that you did not.

Drago went berserk, and started fighting the second-in-command. After the fight, the major went to Kampala and, after some months, Drago was transferred from the north to Karamoja in the east.

When I look back, I see only a few of my comrades alive. Many have died in the battlefield, from AIDS, or the firing-squad, and others took their own lives. The good officers, such as Benoni Tumukunde, Julius Ayine, Muntu Oyera, Silver Odyeyo, Kanabi, Katabarwa, but to mention a few, died of car accidents, ambush, AIDS and chest pains. To try and forget them, I just take one cigarette and smoke, but is it enough? All had fought hard to save their country, and they had survived it all, but later to die on friendly ground. With tears and sadness, I search for them in the sky, hoping that, one day, I might see their faces again. With all this happening, we could not find any one to tell our fear. A person next to you seemed to be going through the same, and no one had time to listen to you. You had to keep your fear, and die with it. In the evening we were always lined up for hours by our unit political commissar, who told us of how to dedicate our hearts and soul to our leaders. We were also told that civilians didn't know anything, and we would not trust them. He meant that anything which took place in the army should remain in the army. It was a crime for a soldier to talk to a journalist, or tell anything to a civilian. But the journalists from our government-owned newspaper called *New Vision* was allowed in our military barracks with no fear, but they reported the opposite.

Some time passed, and something strange began to happen. Drago annoyed me, not only of what he said, but also the clothes that he wore, or the way he ate: everything seemed to disturb me. He tried to give me as much care as he could, but it all meant nothing. I packed my things, and left without saying goodbye.

Life under Injustice

I went to the military police in Kampala, and I was relieved to hear that Major Kaka was the commandant. He was a special friend of mine, and a good man who I had known since the rebel times. One of the guards took me to Kaka's office, and before I could salute him, he had already shook my hand. As we chatted, I told him that I wished to join the military police. Without giving it a second thought he grabbed the phone, called the Directorate of Records, and ordered my transfer. Everything went faster than I could have hoped for, and soon I was on my way to my new quarters, escorted by the administrating officer of the unit. After having packed out my stuff I returned to Kaka who took us to a restaurant. As we ate he asked me if I was a Rwandese, and I silenced in alarm, because I knew that answering such a question could be crucial. I could not figure out why he wanted to know, and he had no answer himself so I told him, that I was half. Kaka's smile remained the same though, and after lunch he took me to a bar. The place was crowded mostly with Tutsi soldiers carrying all ranks, but though it was a rare sight I didn't manage to understand the occasion. At the morning parade Kaka didn't show up, and the second-in-command informed us that he had disappeared with most of his bodyguards. I was almost crushed by the news, as this had to be a bad token. Just as I had thought to have found the right spot in my life, the most important person left. Once again everything seemed to go in the wrong direction.

Weeks later, when nothing had gone wrong yet, I found that I actually had a very good time with my new duty. There was nothing I loved more than my new look, with my red barrette and belt with red and white stripes, making me even more smart in the military uniform. I loved my new look, but others hated it. Non-military police, soldiers and civilians hated us, and they called us nicknames, such as 'Kanywa Omusayi' [drinkers of blood] and there was nothing on earth people feared more than being jailed at the Military Police headquarters. If you were brought to MP HQ there were possibilities that you might say goodbye to your life. I came to love military police, because non-MP officers were now afraid to abuse me. Because if they did, then I too might treat them badly if they one day were jailed at MP HQ. I took my job and my rank very serious, and soon I had the respect of most, and I began to hear stories about myself and Sarah at the most unlikely places. Sarah was a half something and half black. But many soldiers called her a half-caste. She was older than me, and she drove a green army-colour Mercedes-Benz of one Afande Doctor Ronald Baata who worked at the Republic House as Minister of Health. Sarah, too, was very smart in her military uniform, and she was very beautiful girl. When Dr Baata got another driver, things went bad for Sarah. Later I learned that she was staying with Captain Jafali. Later Sarah died during an abortion, just like many other girls.

One morning at the parade, Afande Biraro, the acting military police commandant, told us that Major-General Fred Rwigyema had died in the battle of Rwanda, and a shock-wave of surprise and sadness ran through the lines.

That same morning I also heard the reason of Kaka's disappearance. We were told that he was doing a fine job in Rwanda, along with half of the Tutsi soldiers from the Ugandan army, who had chosen to fight and start a new life in their motherland, Rwanda. Rwigyema's sudden death made me think of my two uncles, Caravel and his young brother M. M. I couldn't help swearing at Kaka, blaming him for not telling me, when having asked of my origin at the restaurant. But now that I had lost my opportunity to go with them, I had to find a way of establishing contact, and at least hear their last words, before it was too late.

I was wandering in town one day when I met Happy, a friend of mine, and a former bodyguard of Rwigyema. He took me to a shop where a woman took my letter, and told me to return in a week. Then I learned that Caravel had died on the battlefield. M. M. was now my only hope, and I tried to convince myself that he would survive. I was so anxious that, every time I thought of writing, the fear of getting bad news stopped me.

I was getting depressed, being angry at myself for not writing. I felt lost without anybody to talk to, and I began to feel as a spare who easily could be replaced. I found it hard to look myself in the mirror, because of a feeling that I had turned ugly and disgusting. When I looked at my stomach it had begun to grow in the most strange way, and sometimes I wished never to have been born. I carried on my duties despite all, driving around town with soldiers, checking movement orders, and soon even other people began to comment on my look. I often took the comments as mild insults, but one day an officer managed to make me laugh by suggesting that I was pregnant. I got hungrier than ever, and I couldn't stand anything but grilled chicken, making me throw up whenever I couldn't afford it. One day after work, laying on my bed, I suddenly felt a kicking sensation from inside my stomach. I thought that I could have some kind of parasite growing inside, because I blankly refused the possibility that I actually could be pregnant.

The next morning I went to the doctor, who demanded that I took a leave of six months. The doctor had concluded that I was pregnant. But one thing I couldn't understand was: 'How can a commando have a human being in their stomach?' It was hard to believe, but still my stomach grew, showing no intentions of stopping. Finally I forced myself to believe, and began nodding whenever people asked.

The leave forced me to find another place to stay, and Drago found it for me at his friend Musa. Drago was happy, and told me that if it was a girl I could have her, but if it became a boy he would get all his names, except for his rank.

Some weeks later Margie came to me with a letter from my sister Helen, who was dying of AIDS at my father's home. In the letter she told me of how much she loved me, and therefore her greatest fear was not to die, but to die without my promise of being there, at her funeral. She told me to be strong, hoping that I wouldn't be too affected by her departure. I was without words when I folded the letter, but inside of me, I too was dying. It was way too much for me to comprehend. So much, that I decided not to think about it any further. Margie and I argued, when I told her that I couldn't go. I was hurt by what she called me, but still I had to realise that she, too, had been hurt. The second day, before leaving, she told me that she would never see me again, but I knew that after some time she would forgive me.

A few depressing days passed before I was taken to the hospital for examination. The doctor had many patients to attend to and Musa told me that he would return later and fetch me. The doctor's surprise shone through his eyes as he examined me. Now he looked busy, and while backing up towards the door he told me to stay put. Shortly after he returned with nurses, who took me by the arms, and slowly we walked into the labour ward. I sat on the bed, amused by those women who acted as if they had been possessed, and all of them were much older than me. I couldn't feel a thing, though I had been told that I was about to give birth. I imagined: 'Am I just going to lay there and, when the time comes, are the child just going to come out?' I couldn't get it. 'Are these woman crying of excitement, or are they simply letting the whole world know that they are getting children?' A white doctor came, and examined me. He told the doctors who were standing by that I wouldn't be able to push out the child, so they had to help me when giving birth. The moment came when I too started crying, and soon I had removed all my clothes. I jumped all over the place trying to escape the pain, but it just wouldn't stop. Now I realised that I actually was the weakest among them all, because they still had their clothes on, and stayed in their beds. I bit my fingers, and pinched my body but all meant nothing. I suppose that I had decided to stop giving birth, but when I was at the stairs on my way to leave the labour ward, I was grabbed by a group of doctors and nurse.

At around eleven o'clock at night, 3 March 1991, I gave birth to my son. The difference between me and so many other women soldiers was that my child was born with a father who was ready to take a responsibility, and not discard us as a freak accident. I had seen so many women with more than three kids who hardly wore any clothes, and I blamed the NRA for that. Now I had a child who I loved more than anything else, so I came to believe that these women, too, felt this way. Most of us were too young to be mothers, but in the NRA there were no age. It was a crime for a child soldier to say: 'I cannot do this, because I'm a child.' Too many young mothers had to figure out how to be both mothers and fathers.

The next morning Drago and his family were all over the place, and I could see life in Drago's eyes, as he struggled to hold the child in his arms. Later that day my son and I were driven back to Musa's home, which were crowded with people who had been invited to the party. It meant nothing to me, because of my thoughts which were back at my father's. I left everything to the happy people and went to sleep. I loved my son so much and, whenever he cried, I would cry too. He gave me hope and strength, and whenever I was sad, I would look at his face and smile.

My six months' leave was over and, when I returned to my unit, I began to see these women with a new set of eyes. I approached a girl not much older than I. This lance-corporal carried two small children of nearly mutual age. She looked at my son for a moment, before looking at the one resting in her own arms, and said: 'I can only guess who their father is'. No one had asked these girls whether they were ready as mothers, nor had any among these officers any intention whatsoever to take their part of the responsibility. At the morning parades at the silent moment when the commandant and officers approached, you would hear infants and small children from within the quarters, crying for their mothers who stood in the line. But none of these officers seemed to hear these cries of their own blood. Soon every sound was taken away by our singing voices with happy faces that would convince most. Our faces was of a child's, but our bones was stronger than iron. But a careful eye would shy us away, afraid to reveal the weakening sorrow. Most passers-by would only hear our voices and see guns in the air. They would call it life, and wish to join in, not seeing what lived beneath.

The artillery unit at Bombo barracks was ordered to give space for a 'women's wing' of the Ugandan army. It looked as if somebody was trying to forget, by sweeping all these mothers away beneath the same carpet, like disposal you don't have time for. It might have been of good intention, but wouldn't you question why all this hadn't been prevented in the first place? If this was of a good intention, well, I didn't think that by putting too many broken souls together would solve anything. I imagined them from my own experience, blaming each other more than the very abuser. Nothing changed, and now I was convinced that the women soldiers of the NRA was nothing but Museveni's treats to the hungry lions in command. Soon the 'Women's Wing' got over-crowded, and many were forced to leave the army, with the absurd amount of 500 dollars and an iron roof. These 500 dollars seemed by the NRA to be too much for the women to handle, and therefore it was decided that they received the money in two payments. Since the NRA had forgotten to give them a land, they probably sold their roof the very first day of their civilian lives. An amount like this would provide a mother with two children, food and rent for at most two months. This method wasn't only used for these women, I have to add. Now that the war was not our biggest problem, suddenly there seemed to be many, who of different reasons no longer were seen fit to serve. Many of my child comrades were also sent away from the army, because many of them started losing their mind. They started shooting other soldiers before turning the gun to themselves. Many of them died this way, and no one among our leaders took notice of this, though it was happening right in front of them.

Actually I was one of the fortunate mothers of the NRA, with a busy but caring father to my child, and a duty to fulfil back at the military police.

We will never enjoy this world, and we win never see what others sees, even though we walk through the same road.

I got disappointed, though, to find Lt-Colonel James Kazini as our new commanding officer. Kazini had no respect for life, and if you looked in his eyes, you would see the thirstiness of blood. I suppose that he wanted this post and finally he was here. The chief before Kaka senior officer Silver Odweyo had been thrown from his office to stand in line at the Luzira prison's death-row where he died, after having been reported for treason by Kazini, then second-in-command of Rubiri barracks. James Kazini claimed that Odweyo had been about to achieve some radio codes, by attempting to bribe a radio operator. Odweyo was one of the many officers who had served under Obote's regime, and was therefore easy to frame. He denied all the allegations but Museveni seemed, as he always had been, easy to be convinced by Kazini. To my knowledge the questions is still, whether Kazini, for once, wasn't using the cheapest trick in the book to gain power, and whether Odweyo as a northerner, coming from an area of strong resistance against Museveni, really had been thoughtless enough to risk being caught in the act of betraying the very same.

Kazini had been busy changing the rule of the military police, including the prisoners' basic rights, which he practically had stripped of all decency. The health situation was almost in a state of emergency, but still he kept the prisoners away from the hospitals. The jails were cold, and he had made the prisoners to sleep on the concrete floor without blankets, and most of them, except for the senior officers, were left with their underwear. The food was already of a bad quality, and when I added everything up, I began to suspect him to be the cause of those prisoners losing their sight, and beginning to pee blood. Kazini's rule made me open my eyes, and I began to see the horrors of these jails, where many soldiers had suffered a long time before him. I learned that many prisoners had no idea of why they were being kept there, and most had been there for some years without trial. I knew many of these soldiers from the battlefield, and in my eyes they were heroes, who had fought so hard to retain freedom, and now they were beggars of cigarettes.

Many prisoners lost their lives, and torture was the favourite games of James Kazini. Kazini did this with the help of his bodyguard named Corporal Kinyata, who he had made his second-in-command. Kinyata was a young boy without education, and he was extremely brutal to those he didn't like. He controlled the entire unit in the name of his boss, and he even had power to beat and torture Kazini's own junior officers.

Kinyata wasn't a big problem to me, but the new regimental sergeant-major wanted to have a sexual relationship with me and, when I refused, he removed me from my old room, to share one with another female corporal. When I got a nanny, the room became too small for four people, and it became hard to breathe at night. My son's health was the major concern. and so I began harassing my lower-ranked room-mate, as I hoped that she would succeed where I hadn't in getting another quarter. The sergeant-major didn't give up. He still had to find a small mistake that I did. One day I had just ate, and forgotten to wore my beret again. He called me over and asked about my beret, and when I touched on my head, 'Damn,' I said inside. Sergeant-major called a sergeant and ordered him to roll me in the mud. After, I was given seven days' extra duty. The sergeant-major ordered me not to leave my post, and I couldn't even try, because he kept on checking on me. I stood there and looked at my military uniform getting wet from the milk of my breast. I thought of going and shoot the sergeant-major and his family, but the love of my son prevented me from doing it.

I had just returned one afternoon, and I was busy breast-feeding my son, when Drago suddenly visited me. When he saw the room overcrowded with beds and guns, he became angry, blaming me for not telling him. I was surprised to see him so concerned, and I hadn't even bothered to tell him, because of an idea I had that people only laughed at my problems. Drago wanted me to move to a friend of his, senior officer Peter Karamagi, who had a big house outside the city. Before leaving, Drago gave me some money, and told me to buy some furniture.

The very next day I dumped my stuff on the back of my pick-up, and left with my son and our nanny. The house consisted of five large rooms, apart from a shower, toilet and a kitchen. Behind the house was the bodyguards' quarters, where I felt free to go whenever I got bored. There was a Muganda boy called Tim, who Karamagi had taken under his wing. He lived in one of the rooms at the bodyguards' quarters, and soon we became buddies. Tim had lived in this house even before Karamagi, so he knew the area well, especially where all the voodoo men lived. I desperately wanted the rank of officer, so one of the very first days Tim escorted me to one of them. The first thing my eye met was the most spoiled cow I ever had seen. The garden was overcrowded with children, and I was surprised only to see two women. With big ceremonial gestures, he introduced himself as Muwanga.

I was invited into a dark and creepy bungalow, where he as the first thing told me to put my money on top of a cow skin. Before he began to tell me of what had brought me there, he spit on the money and all that I said was 'Yes...yes...yes', and at that time I was baffled of his incredible accuracy, and a strange sound and movement from behind a curtain. He told me that it was the spirits from behind that curtain, who was telling him to give me three different kinds of medicine: 'The first one, sniff the smoke; the second, mix with your bathing water.' He held his breath for a short while before he continued: 'The last one: hang it in a tree in front of the house at exactly six o'clock in the evening without anybody seeing you.' I was about to tell him the difficulties of the last task, when he warned me that any complaint would disrupt everything.

Before six o'clock I was in front of the house, surveying the movement of people. Just before time I started, as stealthy as I could to climb the tree, with a small bag of medicine between my teeth. Suddenly a twig broke below my foot, and I opened my mouth in alarm. The medicine dropped to the ground, so I had to climb back down, and search for it. I knew that I had been spotted by most, so I pretended to have lost my watch. Just after six o'clock, the medicine was hanging far above the ground. The bathing task was easy, but when I was about to burn the first medi-cine, I got embarrassed to let anybody see. Therefore I closed the window, and I almost suffocated in my room.

The next morning the bag had vanished from the tree, and at that point I was sure of a promotion, within weeks. I was so desperate of a high rank, so that I could escape the sexual abuse of our admin, and other officers. How much can I tell? It's hard for me, too, to confront my past, because the more I confront them the more pain. Three weeks passed though, without any sign of the promise I had been given, and soon I was back at Muwanga's door. After having talked, he left me alone for a minute, and I couldn't wait to see the spirits. I looked at the curtain, drew it aside and our eyes met. The dog was huge, and it seemed to have been laying there for centuries. It only looked at me for a second, before it appar-ently decided to ignore me, and laid its head back at its paw. Now I was angry, and I wanted my money back, including some on top for the embarrassment and, because of my uniform, Muwanga complied without hesitation.

One day Kazini called me into his office, and showed me a signed letter, while asking if that was the signature of Kashilingi. Knowing that this man could be up to anything, I told him that I could not tell if it was indeed Kashilingi's. He looked me in the eyes, before telling me that I was lying just to protect my uncle. Kazini knew very well that Kashilingi was never my uncle, but Kazini was always like this. Many who knew him said that he smoked a lot of drugs, and he could change any time, by saying things that were hard to understand. The signature was Kashilingi's, but I was afraid to tell Kazini the truth. Then he might claim that, since I knew his signature, I would also know where Kashilingi was hiding. Before leaving his office, he told me that Kashilingi had been arrested. I didn't believe his information about Kashilingi, but that mattered not, because what it really meant to me was that I had become a part of his primary target. Scared, I left, and all I could hope for was that I soon would be away from his mind.

The next day, just after lunch, I was standing at the MP compound. The sergeant who stood a few metres from me was reading the government-owned newspaper *New Vision*. When he looked at me, I instantly felt that something was not right, so I walked over to him. He stopped reading and hid the paper behind his back, but then he finally showed me the headline: KASHILINGI ARRESTED.

Shortly after, a convoy of military cars packed with armed personnel drove in. The cars were driving so fast, that I missed to see if it really was Kashilingi, and therefore I still had hope. I was afraid, as I knew that if Kashilingi was arrested, then I too might follow. Soldiers in the barracks were ordered to be on standby. Suddenly everyone started running up and down, and to me it looked as if Idi Amin was the one who had been arrested. I couldn't do anything but to remain where I was standing, because I simply didn't know where I belonged. Soon cars of senior officers started driving in one by one, and I got really frightened, as everything started to look like an execution. Most of the comrades were looking at me, and they all wanted to know how I felt about the arrest. Their questions made me more nervous, so I thought of hiding, but that would only have been like hiding in the lion's mouth. Instead, I sneaked to see Kashilingi, who was being surrounded by all the senior officers. He was handcuffed on both legs and arms, without shoes, only wearing what appeared to be a sleeping suit, as if he had been dragged right out of his bed. Kashilingi did bad things on me, but when you think that someone is going to die, you might even cry, not knowing why. I ran to the toilet to hide but, only a few minutes later, Kazini called for me. I stood bravely in front of the senior officers, and watched as they made fun of Kashilingi. One of the senior officers asked me why I never left with Kashilingi and, when I could not answer, he told Kazini to keep an eye on me, so I didn't help Kashilingi to escape. As the drama went on, they ordered me to look Kashilingi in the eyes, and tell him that he was stupid to run away. I could not see the end as the pressure increased but, when I cried, one of them told me not to cry for a man who had betrayed the NRA.

After the humiliation Kashilingi was placed in a tiny 1 x 1.80-metre cell without windows. He could not possibly escape, but still they kept him handcuffed. The only times I saw Kashilingi was whenever it was my turn as Orderly Sergeant responsible for all procedures to be carried out in the barracks.

A couple of weeks later, a prisoner came to me, and revealed a letter from his pants. It had come from Kashilingi. At first I could only hide it behind my belt, and hurry to a safer place. The letter was addressed to Major General Salem Saleh, and it instructed me to deliver it. I didn't know if I could trust this prisoner, as one possibility could be that he had already showed it to Kazini, looking for a pardon. I wasn't of much use that night on duty, so I prepared to deliver the letter to Saleh, who was a close friend of Kashilingi, and I believed Saleh to be the same breed of war heroes as him. Early in the morning I went home, and after having breast-fed my son, I joined Karamagi's girlfriend who had breakfast in the living-room. I sat beside her, and waited until she had finished, and then I showed her the letter, while telling her that I had to deliver it the very same day. After having calmed down, she convinced me that I should do anything else but delivering the letter, so I chewed it up and went to sleep. Some days later after the incident, one of the military police officers called me to his house, and told me that he and other officers had been in a meeting with Kazini, who had asked them all about me. At the end he had wanted to know if I was capable of helping Kashilingi to escape. Some of the officers hadn't thought so, while others had been without an answer. Kazini told them that he was going to trick me, to see how I felt about Kashilingi, but then he had stopped talking, and I could only guess of what he was up to. This officer knew Kashilingi, and I had seen him on visit several times at Kashilingi's, but I was one of the few who knew about this relationship.

Then the call came from Kazini, and this time I was determined to show him how I felt. He asked me if I wanted to visit Kashilingi, and I said: 'Afande, I hate Kashilingi just like you do, now that he have betrayed the NRA. I have nothing to do with him, Sir,' I saluted. Kazini remained seated in his office-chair, and started to swing from side to side, with his hands flat on the table. I stood perfectly still, watching the light skin on his face, as his eyes got smaller, just like a cobra about to spit. He then called for Lieutenant

Ruhinda, and when I heard the sound of a large bunch of keys, I knew that Ruhinda was on his way. Ruhinda was tall and skinny, with a long nose hanging on his long face. He was truly a friend to just about everyone, but only if you were not in one of his cells. Just as he appeared before us Kazini ordered him: 'Take her to Kashilingi. Unlock the cell, and let them talk in peace'.

At first I was too surprised by Kazini's persistence, and since it was an order I could only obey. The distance from Kazini's office to the cell quarters didn't give me much time to think, but as soon as Ruhinda had entered the cell quarters, I suddenly ran off, and stayed in town the rest of that day. Kazini's behaviour made me think of him as this sick man, who was trying to gain more rank through me, by creating a scenario where he personally would prevent Kashilingi's escape.

Only a few days later Kazini moved me out of Kampala to Karuma bridge, where the military police had its only detachment. When the administrative officer told me, I went straight to Kazini's office with my son, but, as I was about to talk, he promptly ordered me to leave. Karuma was still considered a dangerous place, not only from the rebels, but also because of the dense population of tsetse flies and mosquitoes. Kazini knew that very well, but apparently he didn't give a damn. Never mind about Kazini, but let me round it all up by saying that James Kazini was rewarded for all his deeds: in a matter of a year or two he managed to walk from captain to major-general, while those who were senior to him are still on the same rank

After a few months in Karuma. I heard that Kazini was promoted, and sent to Gulu to be a Fourth Division Commander. Kazini left his bodyguard, Corporal Kinyata in the military police, and this shocked me! Kazini used Kinyata, and he knew perfectly that everyone in the military police hated Kinyata, but he still left him behind. Kinyata was harassed every day by everyone, and I do not know what happened to him. Now Kazini is on the rank of major-general and the army chief (army commander).

One Heart, Separate Worlds

My son was about nine months old, and I didn't want to leave him to Drago's family, so I took him to my sister Margie. I told Margie of what was happening, and she accepted to keep my son, but her husband refused, because of the boy's age. Margie took me to an orphanage home, and there we met a woman who accepted the child. When we returned home, my sister's husband changed his mind, and the following day, I went to Karuma happy, and a little stronger.

The road from Karuma to Pakwach ran through a national park, where the rebels had one of their strongholds. Every morning we would wait at the other side of the roadblock for civilian vehicles to arrive. Our job was to escort the civilians, mostly going to Arua, in the hometown of Idi Amin. I loved Karuma, not because of its rebels, but because we had a good detachment commander. I had a good time with my fellow sergeants, and one of them later became like a brother to me. Stephen and I did the convoy work together, but still I could not tell him of my troubled life, because I knew that a friend could easily turn out to be the enemy. Our job was dangerous and it had already taken many lives and every morning my friends and I would eat half a chicken each before taking off, because we knew that any day could be our last. At some point I didn't care whether I died or not, but because of my son, I still tried to dodge the bullets. The convoy work was hard, and it required a lot of skill to control the civilians, who only seemed to care for time, forgetting about the danger. The convoy was extreme slow, because of the trucks, and it made those with faster cars to lose their patience. Every day we beat civilians who broke the convoy, putting everyone at risk, and we hated that kind of disrespect. Many comrades had lost their lives on this route, while protecting the lives of these civilians, so whenever they questioned our rule we would be furious. I was probably one of the worst, believing that beatings were the only solution to keep them sensible, and some would even stay away when they knew I had the shift.

The first priority of putting a convoy together was to minimise the amount of casualties in the event of an ambush. Therefore the trucks would go in front, then the private cars in the middle, followed by the large crowded buses. One of those mornings, just before taking off, a young soldier around twelve years of age came to me saying that he had something to tell me, but I was too busy to pay attention, though he kept following me as I ordered the soldiers aboard. That day we were ambushed and the very same boy was killed, spilling his precious blood on my uniform. I hated myself for not listening, and cried though I couldn't bring him back. I spent most of my time trying to figure out what the kid had tried to tell me, but I never got the answer. I was greatly affected by the death of that boy, and almost every day I thought about my own death. So I went to the detach[ment] commander, and asked him to grant me a few weeks off from the convoy.

Now my job was to make sure that the soldiers in Karuma did their duty, including the two roadblocks that guarded each side of the bridge. The detach[ment] had two girls, and I was the only sergeant outranking the corporals, who were a lot older than me, and I had to be as hard as a rock, to be able to do my work. One evening when I went to the roadblock, a private told me that the guard commander had left his post. I went to the centre of the village, where I found the corporal busy drinking. When I ordered him out, he threatened to shoot me, and in front of everyone, he told me to kneel down and beg. As I did so, his girlfriend started to laugh at me, and I could see in his eyes that, if I didn't do as he told, I would be dead. After some time of begging he let me go, and that was his biggest mistake. About to explode, I went back to the roadblock and ordered two privates to join him, steal his gun and bring him to me. The privates returned and said that they never managed, because the corporal had his gun around his shoulder. It was getting late and before returning to the camp, I ordered the soldiers to be ready with the corporal, the following morning. I could not sleep that night, I just kept turning in my bed thinking of this lower-ranked 'thing', who had humiliated me in front of a bunch of civilians, and I badly wanted revenge. Very early in the morning the two privates had brought me the corporal. I brought him to the parade and ordered him to lay himself face down in front of the parade. Then he was surrounded by several soldiers with sticks fresh from the bush, and they whipped him until they had used up ten sticks.

Few days after the incident, when I was sitting at the road-block, a white four-wheel drive pick-up arrived. The driver was a white man and, as the soldiers checked his car, he walked over to me, and introduced himself as Paul. After having introduced myself, he invited me for a drink. He told me that he was an American, and he worked with the World Food Programme in Kenya. Paul was tall, and he had long hair which made him look tough. He was curious of what had made me join the army, but I could not say because I knew that it was a serious offence to discuss anything concerning the army life with a white man. Paul wanted to know if I was happy with my life, and I said 'Yes' with a smile. I tried to change the conversation by asking him if he had any children, but that didn't stop him from asking how long I had been in the army. Paul's questions were getting too sensitive, so I told him that I had to go, but before I left, he asked me if I could meet him in Gulu, at the 'Acholi Inn'. I saw that this man might be my opportunity to get a better life, and I was sure that nothing was impossible for a white man. Quickly I ran to the detach[ment] commander and told him that I had received a message from Drago, who wanted me in Gulu at once, and without hesitating he granted me the day off.

I went back to the road-block, got a lift and soon I stood in front of reception. The receptionist looked at my uniform and refused to have any such person in the hotel, but before I lost my temper Paul showed up. He was surprised to see me in my uniform, so he suggested to buy me some clothes in town. Soon we were back at the hotel's restaurant which to me seemed like another world. Everything seemed to be in system, from the tables to the way one was supposed to eat. When I looked around, everyone sat with straight backs ready to leave at any given moment, while they, as if in a ceremony, ate their meals in slow motion, with their knives and forks. I ignored it all, and decided to use my hands as any normal person would. When I looked at Paul he smiled, and asked me to try out the knife and fork, but I gave up when the third piece of meat had escaped my fork. We went back to the bar, and there the questions began. He wanted to know everything, my age, the army life and when I joined. He was mostly concerned with my rank, which to him didn't match my age. In his country, he told me, a sergeant would be around thirty-five. Every question he had asked was the very same which we had been forbidden to answer, so I suspected him and lied in every answer. Paul said he would like to see me again, and asked me to wait for him at the roadblock, where he would pass through on his way from Sudan to Kenya.

Paul left for Sudan, and I returned to Karuma. I spent most of my time thinking about him, and I really looked forward to see him again. But my hope to be saved by him had vanished, because of the mistrust his questions had given me, but still I wanted him as a friend. I could forget everything else but the day where he had promised to return. By seven o'clock that morning I was already at the roadblock, with my eyes scouting towards Sudan. He arrived with a lot of presents, but I had no idea what to do with them. I stood with a variety of body and facial creams, a five-in-one torch, and a huge package of biscuits. He told me that he was going back to America, and he had no idea of when he was coming back. When Paul drove off, I was left in tears. I regretted and wished to have told him about the miserable life I had.

Soon I was back at the convoy, and the first morning there were a lot of old trucks. One of the drivers had a mechanical problem with his truck. I walked over to the driver, and asked him to stay and get ready for the next day's convoy, but he refused, saying that he only had a minor problem. Since the truck was slow, I put it at the very end of the convoy. Six soldiers, one armed with an RPG went with me on that truck, while Sergeant Stephen commanded the front. When we reached in the middle of the danger zone, the driver stopped and I saw him trying to fix something beneath the truck.

We had no means of communication on the convoy, which made it difficult for me to stop Stephen. I fired my gun into the air, but the convoy kept moving, and now the pressure was growing, because I couldn't risk to lose any of my soldiers. The driver was extremely slow, and I got angry, so I ordered the soldiers to beat on him, until he got his truck to move.

We drove on for some time until we came to the hill, where I was relieved to see the rest of the convoy waiting for us at the foot of the hill. Suddenly the driver began to panic, crying: 'Banange nze nfudde, brake silina' [Oh, I'm dead, I've no brake]. The truck was now out of control, and before us were many buses filled with people. I knew that if I didn't give my own life, the people would be squashed to death, or blown up by the RPG. With my gun swinging in my other hand, I grabbed the truck's side-mirror and told my soldiers to stay in the truck. The soldiers and I tried to make as much noise as we could but, because of the long distance between us, we could not be heard. Once again I decided to shoot in the air, but it was too late. My greatest wish was to make Stephen move the convoy, so that we had enough space to slow down. When we got closer to the convoy, the driver wanted to jump out, and to make him stay, I pressed my gun at his neck, and told him not to, or I would have to shoot him. At some point I wanted to jump out too, but I knew that if I survived and others died, I would face a heavy punishment. The driver was so scared that all he could do was to cry. He made me see how brave I was, and the differences between a civilian and a soldier, that a soldier had other things in their mind than death. Stephen realised our trouble, but there was no way he could do anything. He could only stand, just like everybody else, and watch our deaths. At that moment I didn't know what to wish, or say to my son who was so far away. And believe me, I could see my own end appear in my eyes, and with tears I ordered the driver to cut off into the bush. He did exactly as I ordered, and I do not remember how I managed to survive that ordeal. I only remember myself standing in the middle of the road, watching the boy who laid dead there with a fractured head and broken body. Then I noticed the civilians with their hands in their pockets, looking at him as if watching a dead bore. I felt that these civilians were responsible for his death, and I desperately needed to kill them all, but my gun had been taken by one of the Mercedes bus drivers, Ramadan. I demanded it back, but Stephen told Ramadan to keep it away from me. Then I tore a branch off a nearby tree, and began to beat every civilian I could reach, as I cried like a child. I collapsed to the ground, and the next thing I remember was when my comrades carried me back to our camp.

My right knee was badly hurt by my own bullet which I had triggered by accident after my warning shot. The wound was deep, and my blood showed no sign of stopping. That's when I knew that I would lose my leg, just like Regina, and I thought that this was the end of my future. I was then laid on to a mattress, behind the Land-Rover, and driven to the hospital, which was about ten kilometres away from our camp. There a doctor named Odongo came and gave me a painful injection in the wound. I accepted this but, when he started stitching me up without cleaning it, I complained. His only reply was that, if I thought that it was so important, I could do it myself. As he stitched the wound, it felt as if he was doing it with his eyes closed, and when I told him to stop, he told my fellow comrades to hold me. After the doctor had finished, he told the soldiers to take me to the hospital bed, where my leg was strung up vertically.

In the evening the pain grew stronger, and soon Odongo appeared at my bedside. He had come to ease my pain with another injection, but I refused, as I feared that he would have given me an overdose. The reason for my suspicion was the way he had been treating me, with such a disrespect of my future health. Furthermore he was a Lango, coming from Dr Obote's tribe, and during the bush war, we were told always not to trust the Northerners. That could have been his main reason for having no sympathy for me, being an NRA soldier who many Northerner girls had accused of raping them. But there was also another reason for Acholi people to hate us soldiers. We were seen as letting the rebels abduct a lot of their children, who were then turned to serve as soldiers and wives of the rebels. Odongo stood there and shook his head, while saying: 'Soldiers', and I could only cover my head and tell him to leave.

The next morning two soldiers arrived, and I was very happy to see them, because I needed so much to be taken to the toilet, which was outside the hospital. The soldiers stayed for a while, and I had a good time as they drove me around in the wheelchair. In the evening they returned to the camp, and once again I was left alone, and nobody at the hospital was able to assist me. The thing was that I had to hold my leg straight with one of my hands, making it impossible to manoeuvre the chair around, and that night it took me an hour to reach the toilet. When I finally got there, my need was long gone, so I laid myself besides the toilet and laughed at it all.

Soon I got tired with this place where everything smelled or tasted of medicine, and I badly wanted to move out. The next time the soldiers arrived I persuaded them to smuggle me out. I was dumped into the back of the Land-Rover, and soon I was back at the camp, where I was welcomed by a crowd of soldiers' wives who saluted me with their high-pitched rhythmic voices. The detach[ment] commander invited me to his quarters, and later my fellow sergeants made a small welcoming party for me. We spend the rest of that evening drinking and everybody seemed happy to see that I hadn't lost my leg.

The next day, I was granted permission to go to Kampala, in order to get further treatment. It took me about half an hour to get to the roadblock, and there I got a bus, which was driven by the very same hero, Ramadan, who had prevented me from shooting at the civilians. I stayed with Karamagi for a week, before going to the company which had the driver responsible for the accident. There I met a man who introduced himself as the manager of the company. I showed him my knee, after having explained of the accident. He told me to wait, because he wanted the driver to be present, and with patience I waited. The driver was then told by the manager to take full responsibility, and therefore pay the compensation for my injury alone. The driver was still in a bad condition, and I could see that he had no chance of paying such money. Though I thought of him as a man responsible for the accident, I decided to pressure the manager until he gave me what I had come for. I was paid by cheque, and for the first time in my life I cashed it in a bank. I walked all the way back home smiling, with 300 dollars in my pocket. I didn't come across this kind of money every day, and I didn't want to waste it in grilled chicken. I sat in the living-room for hours, thinking of what kind of business I could start.

Few days later, I returned to Karuma, and I was now working as a roadblock commander. I enjoyed my new job, because of the bribes I was offered, but the detach[ment] commander didn't know about this. He was content with what the army provided, and he didn't seem to have any intention of leaving. Beans and posho was the only thing he could imagine, while the privates who were considered the last on the army food-chain ate chicken, and laughed. My post gave me an opportunity to meet various businessmen, who often didn't pay full government tax. These men tried to befriend me by offering money, and in return I could let their trucks pass without checking the goods. Soon I became so business minded that, whenever I was off, I would go to Gulu near the border of Sudan, and buy powder milk from the Sudanese refugees for then to sell it in Kampala. I'm not sure if it was a crime to buy or sell this milk, but it was brought only for the refugees living in Sudan. The milk prices in Kampala always differed. Sometimes you would win and sometimes you would lose. It wasn't only milk that one could buy from these refugees, also fish oil, which mainly came from the USA.

Soon one of my friends in the military police bought a share of my business, but it didn't take long before I lost all our money. I thought of telling him, but I couldn't figure out how his reaction would be, so I kept on telling him that business was booming. Every time I bit my tongue as I even tried to convince myself. I was still trying to recover from my loss, when a French man introduced me to his friend who was coming from Switzerland. The Swiss had a company which was specialising in coffee and sunflowers. At his home near his main office in Kampala, he had an African girlfriend, who I hated without even knowing why. Though one reason might have been that I knew he had a wife back home. Since this girlfriend of his knew Major-General Salem Saleh, I had to pretend to love her with all my heart. Later, the Swiss man established another office in Arua, which was responsible for buying coffee and sunflowers direct from the farmers. The Swiss and I became good friends, and I tried to help him as much as I could, by making sure that his trucks were not checked at the roadblocks. Months later, he seemed tired of bribing me, and suggested to give me a 1,000 dollars, which he wanted me to use in business. After having signed an 'I owe you', he told me that it wasn't just a gift, because he would want them back after some time. I felt a pressure but it became hard for me to give the money back, now that I had it in my hands. Besides, I was desperate to buy a watch, which I had seen in town. Happily I went to town and, when I got home, I had already used half of the money.

I couldn't believe what I had just done, but my mind seemed too tired to think about it. So many things occupied my mind, and they all seemed important, but I didn't know what to consider first or which really troubled me. Finally I was struck by a headache so strong that Drago admitted me to a private clinic. He was so scared, after having seen me like this, that he urged me to send our son in his care. I laid there in a hospital bed with intravenous drip for three days.

After two weeks in Kampala I returned to Karuma, where I made a deal with an officer, who had been left in charge of the detachment. He allowed me to go to Arua, and there I met with my friend, the Swiss, who happily invited me to the hotel which he shared with his African girlfriend. After a few beers, I told the Swiss that I had to leave, but he insisted me to stay, while promising to cover all the costs. The hotel was very expensive, and the food which they served was strange, only covering one tenth of the plate. I didn't have to pay, but still the price angered me, making me look at him as a waste of money. Besides, luxury had never been my way, and I believed that I would get exactly the same hospitality from a cheaper hotel. I almost asked the Swiss to give me the money which he meant to pay for me, but I decided to be advised from his girlfriend first. She laughed, and called me a typical soldier, so I decided to give it a miss.

Around eight o'clock the place got busy, and the brigade commander of Arua, Lt-Colonel Katagara, arrived. Since I was dressed in my uniform, I stood up and saluted him, but he didn't return my salute. He knew me from when I had been Kashilingi's bodyguard, and I knew him well because of the massacre he had carried out in a place near Karamoja. He drank his beer standing, and I noticed him staring at me through all the time. Fortunately I didn't have to be humble and I certainly did not have to run away, and once again I thanked Afande Kaka for having slipped me into the military police. Then Katagara called me over, and whispered that he wanted me to go with him to his quarters. And when I answered 'No, sir!' he suddenly turned everything upside down. 'What are you doing here with a white man? Are you spying?' I smiled and asked him what he himself was doing there. Katagara was annoyed with my reply, and before leaving he told me that, sooner or later, I would have to answer the question.

After Katagara had left I became afraid, but I couldn't think of what he might do, so I only took his words as the threat of a coward. Shortly after, the Swiss, his girlfriend and I went to their room. The Swiss offered me a cigarette, but I refused because of the packet I had in my pocket, but again he insisted. While smoking, the two started laughing at me, but I only thought that they were drunk. The Swiss asked me for the very same cigarette which I had between my fingers, and I wondered why, because I always had thought that only soldiers shared. After having given him the cigarette, I noticed that something was wrong. Everything in the room started to move, including them. At first I managed to shake it off and I returned to normal for some time, but I really had to concentrate. Suddenly everything came back in a rush as if I had been caught off-guard. I could not tell them of what I was seeing, because I thought that I was getting mad. Their faces had grown, and it became worse whenever they laughed. When I started laughing, the Swiss asked me to pretend to be a bad soldier about to kill. I stopped for about ten seconds, but it didn't work, and I was told to try again. This time I closed my eyes, and now I could see everything that I have ever done, and it all seemed real, but still I couldn't stop laughing. I felt as if my eyes were getting bigger, and when I tried to cover them, the lips too demanded more space. I was tired, and they told me to lay on their bed. I couldn't feel myself, and my body had turned light as paper. Suddenly I realised that something terrible was wrong with me, and I was getting seriously afraid of my own sanity. At last they admitted that I had been smoking marijuana. Relieved, I laughed, but promised myself that this time would be the first and last. I very much loved the Swiss as a friend, of whom I had trusted as a responsible and thoughtful man. Now I felt betrayed of his thoughtlessness, this man who I had relied on with my very soul. That night my respect for him vanished. He was gone, and instead there was a irresponsible shell of a man left.

The next morning I left without saying goodbye, afraid of him seeing the reality which had begun covering my eyes. In town I was told that people in Lira were desperately in need of food, and were now buying anything. I hurried to a broker who told me that in a matter of days he would be ready with dried corn. Now all my money was in corn, and everything was ready to be transported, but in my eagerness I had forgotten to save money for hiring a truck. I needed to be in Lira as soon as possible, before the corn prices would fall. I hurried to the Swiss' offices where I met his friend, the Frenchman sitting behind the desk, and with his huge stomach he stood up to greet me. The French and the Swiss man seemed to be working together, but I did not know if they were partners, or if the Swiss merely hired the French's trucks. Outside the office there were trucks, and many of them were owned by the French. I told him how desperately I needed a transport to Lira, but I also made it clear to him that I could not afford to pay. He told me that he had heard that there was plenty of the sunflowers in Lira, so he would give me the transport, and in return I would help the driver to buy sunflowers. When I asked him of how the Swiss would react to this, he said that of course he wouldn't know, but he was sure that the Swiss would understand.

After having loaded my corns, the French gave the driver some money, and told him that it was for buying sunflowers. Many customers were already waiting as we arrived in Lira and, in a matter of minutes, I had sold the whole cargo. Tired but satisfied, I checked in a hotel, leaving the job of finding the sunflowers to the driver. A while later he returned and told me that there was no sunflowers in all of Lira. The profit from the sunflowers was supposed to cover the transport costs, and though the loss seemed to be for me to cover, I didn't have any intention to pay. While trying to come up with a plan, the driver suggested us to go through the district of Mbale, where he believed we could get to transport people's goods to Kampala. Those monies would then pay for the diesel which the truck had used. It sounded like a good idea, so I gave the driver 'go ahead'.

In Mbale we tried in all the stores, but everybody seemed just to have transported their goods. We drove to Kampala with an empty truck, and decided to let the driver go to the Swiss man's stores alone.

After a day or two in Kampala I met with a man in his late fifties. He was a coffee dealer, but he didn't have enough money to work on his own. He told me of how coffee could make people rich overnight, and you should have seen how excited I became. He seemed honest, making me trust him with all of my money, and besides his honesty, it wasn't only me, but also many other people had entrusted their money with him. The old man was the only one who knew where the coffee was, and he could not tell any of us, even if he was threatened with death. Before leaving, he showed us a store where we would meet when he returned. He promised to return in two weeks' time, so I reported myself sick, because I wanted to return to Karuma after the old man had returned.

A week passed since the old man had left, and every time I thought of my profit to come, I would skip a meal.

Two weeks and a day passed – without any signs of the old man. I contacted the other 'shareholders', but nobody knew where the old man lived, so I could only pray. Few more days passed, and when I went to the stores: the old man and the coffee had arrived the day before. I was too embarrassed to look him in the eyes, because of the bad names I had been calling him while he had been away. The coffee price was still high when we sold.

The old man suggested us to make one more investment, but I didn't want to risk any more, so I took my money and bought a minibus. A week later I realised that the bus was in a very bad condition. I took it to a garage but, whenever they finished with one problem, there would only be another, the very next day. The bus I had bought for business seemed to be in love with the garage, and now I was in big trouble. The bus had ate all my money, so I had to return to Karuma.

I learned that the detachment commander had been waiting for me, and shortly after my arrival, he called for the radio operator. He was ordered to read me the message, which he had received from Lt-Colonel Katagara:

All units stand by: Look out for Sergeant China of the Military Police. During her stay in Koboko, she have disarmed the bodyguards of the Sudanese Rebel Leader, Colonel John Garang. Up to now it is not known where those guns are. Therefore I, Lt-Colonel Katagara demands, that she hand those guns over or be arrested.

'Will my life end this way?' I questioned myself, but when I looked at the detachment commander, I could see that he believed my innocence. But that didn't matter because I was aware that his words could not beat those of Katagara's, and I knew that I could not defend myself, because of the low rank that I possessed. After signal having finished, I didn't wait for tomorrow. I asked the detachment commander to grant me permission so that I could go to the military police headquarters, and explain why Katagara was after me. The commander gave me a go-ahead, and all that he could wish me for: 'I hope you win, because I do not want to lose you, Sergeant.'

In my heart I was more than sure that I would return to Karuma, but I did not know when, or how. I got into the bus and my eyes could not stop looking in the window, sad-looking for what they were leaving behind.

When I arrived in Kampala I decided to go to my friend, the Swiss. He invited me to his house with a warm welcome, just like always. He waited until I sat myself, and then he pulled a stool, and sat very close in front of me. I looked once in his eyes, and he was not the Swiss that I once knew. His face was pale, but when I told him that I had not the 3,000 dollars, his face turned red. Nothing else, he wanted the money he had borrowed me, and the money that the truck had lost in Lira trip. I was frightened, because I had no money, and he needed it now or tomorrow. The money that I was left with was the bus that I had bought. I thought of giving him the bus, but again I changed my mind, because I didn't know what was my next move. With his girlfriend sitting next to him, he told me that I should not forget that she knew Major-General Salem Saleh. Since there were my friends, I had told them everything, and I only realised, that very day, that I had done a big mistake for having told about the land I had bought for my mother. And now he wanted it for his African girlfriend. He ordered me to stay in the house, and if I decided to leave, he would then punish me. Now I was under house-arrest, and I could do nothing because I had no gun. I sat in one place until the evening, and everybody had been told not to speak with me, even the gardener or the housegirl, both had been told not to.

The next day we started the journey, and no matter which words I used to beg, I could not get them to feel sorry for my mother. We drove 300 kilometres, and the only words I got to say, were those I used to beg them. I wasn't really hurt by the way the Swiss was treating me, but I was by his girlfriend, because she knew the ways and the pain. My mother was very happy to see us. I watched her as she ran to hug the Swiss. I'm even not sure if she remembered to greet me before she proudly hurried to call the neighbours. She returned with an old man who carried a pipe between his teeth. Mother left us with her neighbours and began preparing some food. But she already sensed that I was in trouble, though I pretended to be free of worry. My mother's neighbour was a funny-looking man and, while I sat alone in pain, the Swiss and the girl were busy taking snapshots of the old man. The others ate, but I could not find my appetite, and soon time came to show them around. As we walked, the girlfriend said that the land was too small and, besides that, she had never liked its surroundings. I learned that she had reckoned the land to be huge enough for ranching. I took her hand, and begged her to accept it, but she refused, and referred me to the Swiss. I could not look him in the eyes. I was getting weak and now I looked at him as my commander. I stood with my head down, when they told Mother. My mother started crying, and I cried too when she begged them to forgive me, because I was her only child being able to support her. I felt that once again we would be forced apart, and I feared that this time it would be for ever. Sad but true, I was right.

PART FOUR
A New Life

Zero Count

While driving back to Kampala, I suggested the Swiss to take my salary until I had paid him back, but he hammered on the steering-wheel with both his hands, and told me to shut up, before he promised me jail. When he mentioned this, I got really hurt, but the safety-belt which I squeezed in my hand took away my wrath. At midnight I arrived at Karamagi's, and while in my bed, I remembered Paul. Now my head was thinking of one thing: America.

Early morning I went to a boy who had just returned from Italy. After having told him my trouble, he told me that all I needed was a passport under fake names. He got the application forms, and we filled them out together: *Name of bearer* – Kyomujuni Innocent. *Occupation* – secretary. I had to bribe my way through three levels, before I reached the district administrator's office, where I bribed the secretary to put my forms on top of the pile. Then I went to the passport office, where I had to bribe two more officials to prevent my passport from being stuck for months. Everything needed money, so I decided to sell the bus. The engine was in a poor condition, and I had no patience, so I sold it for 1,000 dollars. Nearly all of it went to the passport, and when I left Karamagi's home, everything started to be expensive. I moved in with a family which I had known through Kashilingi and, since I lived there for free, I had to buy the food. After some days I received my passport, and now I just had to get a visa.

I knew some Baganda boys, and all were ready to help me in everything but money. I was taken to Babumba, a manager of a team which was going to the Ninth Special Olympics world games of 1995. Babumba and I had met each other several times at the Republic House, and when I asked him to help me, he looked as if he just burned his fingers. He told me that he could not risk his life by helping a soldier to get an American visa. 'Oh, Mr Babumba, you mean my sister who worked at the Republic House?' I said. Fortunately he believed me, and said the visa would cost me 920 dollars. I looked down for a while, before asking him if he could lower the price. With a smile, he told me that his office was not Owino [one of the biggest market squares in Kampala at that time]. I left my passport in his care, and promised to return soon with the money.

That day, I walked all over Kampala, and all the people, that I once had helped when in trouble with the traffic, could not help. Everybody told stories. I was getting tired and hungry, but as I was about to give up, I met Justine's husband Ronald. When I told him about my trouble, he suggested to sell him my mother's land. He had the money ready, and there was nothing I could do but to sell. As we walked up the stairs to his lawyer, my tears began wetting my cheeks just like the day he attacked me. I was so confused that I did whatever I was told, but this time it was different. A wound for life. I went back to Babumba, paid, and thought that this was all I needed to get to America.

When I returned home, they told me that Kashilingi was going to be taken to court, and eight o'clock in the morning we went there. Kashilingi was standing in front of us, and I could see that he was desperate for freedom. He had spent nearly four years in jail, and this was his first time to appear in court. There was a few of his friends, and one news group:

the *New Vision*. It didn't appear to me that the government had decided to give him a fair trial, but that Museveni was now convinced that Kashilingi never would stand on his feet again. At first, Kashilingi was being charged with treason, and later a deserter. The government claimed that he had been captured at the battlefield, fighting along with the rebel Allied Democratic Forces Group (ADF). In court Kashilingi insisted to have been kidnapped from his hotel, in the Republic of Zaïre [now Democratic Republic of the Congo]. His own friend, Major Kyakabale, who then had been a brigade commander in Kasese, had arranged the kidnapping. Shortly after the arrest of Kashilingi, Kyakabale had been promoted to the rank of Lt-Colonel, but later he, too, was sent to prison for some very obscure reasons.

Kashilingi's case lasted for two days, before he was released. All of his riches was now gone, and his name was forgotten, but maybe one among his sons will some day bring it back.

A few days after Kashilingi's release, I left the family that I had been living with. I went near the military police barracks, and lived with one of my cousins. I knew that it would be much safer for me, because they would not suspect me to be right behind the fence. I didn't tell her that I was on the run – it was too dangerous for her to know. Besides, I feared that she might get frightened and chase me away. I told her of my plans to leave the country, but she didn't believe it. I guess she believed that I was too troubled a child to be capable of such a move.

On my way to check on my visa, I met Stephen, who I had not seen for some time. He wanted to know about the business, and I told him that I had bought a brand new minibus, which had just arrived at the port of Mombassa in Kenya. I felt really bad, when lying to him, and all I hoped for was that some day I make it up to him.

Babumba told me that the visa had been granted, but the Olympic team was going through Entebbe International airport, but there I feared the security agents, so I told him to give me my passport. I had to find the way on my own. As I was walking back home, I remembered that I could not travel without a ticket, but I didn't have such money. I had sold the land, what more could I sell? After some hours of thinking, I decided to go to my father, though I didn't know what I was going to do there.

In the bus I met a woman who was a friend to Maggie my sister. She told me that she had met Maggie who told her that Grace my other sister was dead. I looked at her and smiled, and that's when she started saying: 'Grace died in Rwandan genocide.' The Hutu came to her home, killed her little daughter and then her husband. Grace was taken to the road, where she was killed before being tied on the tree. And these were the words written on her chest: 'Anyone who don't know how a Tutsi look like, here is one.' After listening to this woman, I asked her of how Maggie came to know this. Maggie was told by my grandmother, the mother to my mother, who had returned to Rwanda in 1982 when Obote chased away Tutsis. I tried as much as I can to laugh at my sister's death, because I was afraid that I might get confused. I avoided to think about her death, and so many other things helped me a bit from losing my mind.

When I got at my father's, I found him very sick. He had divorced his wife. My stepsisters and brothers were no longer going to school, and they hated Father for this. The kids wanted us to go to their mother who rented a house of two rooms ten minutes' walk from my father. My father was deserted, and he had not eaten for days, so I decided to cook for him before leaving. My stepmother tried to make herself as the good person, and Father the evil, but I refused to give my father all the blame. She had no money, and she wanted her children back to school, but she had no more power to sell the cows. She was beating around the bush and it annoyed me, so I said: 'Just say what you want me to do.' She told me to sell three cows and give her the money, and it sounded as if she believed to have all of us in her hands.

I was hurt to see that my father was dying without anybody at his side, when his family was so large. Everything that father had owned was vanishing, and I believe it all went in my stepmother's stomach. I knew that no matter what, I was going away, though I didn't know if it was to the grave or to another life. There was so much I wanted to tell her before I left, but I couldn't, because I was still afraid of her. I asked her to go with us to our father, and she agreed. When Father heard her voice, he struggled to get out of the bed and, when he couldn't, he called for me. After having sat himself, he asked all of us to sit and listen to what he was about to say: 'Baby I'm so sorry, but it was never me. I had married this woman, and now I have lost all of you. You are the only child I love, and if I die, everything is yours.' Suddenly he almost stood up: 'Don't give anything to them. They are not my children!' Again, he relaxed: 'But I regret one thing: . . . ' He looked at me and stopped talking. My stepmother went mad, as if she had been stung by the bees but, before she could attack him, I stopped her. Slowly Father went back inside, and I regret to this day that I listened. He confused me, and left me in suspense. His deeds throughout my childhood were never consistent with his last words. He had washed his hands and left the guilt for me. He remains a mystery in my life.

We agreed, my stepmother and I, to sell three of his cows without his consent. After my stepmother left, the children and I went for a short walk. Since I knew that I was going away, I needed to say goodbye to my old friends – and enemies. We went house to house, and the last house was where Rehema had lived, but sadly she was not there any more. I was surrounded by so many people of my past trying to remind me, but I failed to listen and my heart failed to say goodbye, because of the dangers which awaited me. It was a goodbye in silence to my friends and family, and I feared our meeting to be the last. At around ten o'clock we returned, and I sat myself at Father's side, but he was in a deep sleep. I remained looking at his face, until I had memorised every detail. I went to the children's room, and watched them play. They seemed too innocent to see their own trembling future.

Early in the morning we went to the farm. My grandmother was now blind, but still she knew me by the touch. 'How is he? Is my son dying?' she asked like an innocent child.

'No, he will be all right, but he wants to go to the hospital. Therefore I have come to sell some cows,' I answered.

'Greet him from me,' she only said, before going back inside.

The cows were busy grazing at the field, and when three of the cows had been loaded on to the truck, I said that we needed a fourth, but the kids refused, and suddenly I felt ashamed. We drove to the meat park, and sold the cows to one of our neighbours' boys, and I put the money in my pocket. We went to a hotel, where I told them to eat whatever they desired and, while they ate, I planned my next move. Finally I told them that I had changed my mind about giving the money to their mother. I asked them if they had passport photos, and they told me that they had them at home. 'I want you to listen carefully. Go home and get the photos, so I can open an account for you,' I said and told them where we should meet. When they were about to leave I felt broken inside, so I called them back and gave each some money.

When they were out of my sight, I hurried to the bus-park, and took off to Kampala. I had all the money, but it was still not enough, so I hid in the bus and went to Arua. There I went to a Muslim family who once originated from Asia. I had helped the man and his children one day at Karuma. He had run out of petrol, without having money, and I had borrowed it for him. He was one of the few left who I trusted to help. He told me to wait, and the fifth day, he gave me a sorry amount of twenty dollars. I thought of Drago, but I loved him too much and feared him to be as the rest. I was desperate more than ever. The three months' visa was expiring, and I was left with eleven days. The tenth day, I told the house girl of my cousin's neighbour to go with the kids and buy two hens. My cousin was still at work. I took her largest bag and forced her small television into it. I was about to leave, when I realised that her neighbour's could fit in as well. I struggled my way to the mini-tax with both televisions on my shoulder. I was close to panic when I found that there no buyers were for black and white televisions. I thought of returning them, but I wasn't sure if they would have understood the importance of my theft. The eighth day I sold them for fifteen dollars to a man who fixed radios. The money was enough to buy a ticket, but since I was going through Kenya, I needed money for transport.

I was in panic because my visa was left with nine days to expire. I went to a Ugandan travel agent and paid for the ticket, but the man told me that he would not give it to me. I would get it from Kenya, where they had another office. He called Kenya, before giving me a note which had the address and telephone numbers. The very same day, I went to where Drago and his girlfriend had a shop, but he wasn't there. Rita was there, but we were never good friends. Drago had put my son in her care, and now I had come to say goodbye to my son, who wasn't there. I felt pain but, as always, I have never liked to show my weakness and pain in front of anyone. I sat myself in front of her desk, and looked in her eyes for a while, before telling her: 'I'm going, and I ask you to look after my son until the day I would return.' She never said a word. She just kept her eyes on me until I walked out. Outside I met Drago's brother Eric, and I told him that I wanted to see Drago, but he told me that he had left him at one of his friends' wedding. The word 'wedding' made me realise my trouble, and I also tried to imagine where I was going, and it seemed as if I was going to never-ending darkness. Drago had money, and he was becoming powerful too, but the surroundings he lived in were so much different from mine. It was only that he cared a lot about other people than himself, and that was making him famous and loveable among soldiers and civilian population.

There was never problems for me to walk around in town. Most people recognised me better when dressed in a military uniform, because I really never wore civilian clothes. Again, I went and begged from those I had once helped, until I got them to give me transport money. The ninth day, I went to the mini-tax park and boarded one going to Busia, on the border between Kenya and Uganda. In the tax I met with two civilian boys who I knew, and they promised to help me go through the border. I had no bag, only the clothes on my body and some photos of me and my former friends in a military uniform. I was so frightened, but one thing that I promised myself was not to be captured. I was prepared to lose my life, because I knew the danger when captured.

At the border I showed my passport. The man looked at my face, before asking me of why I hadn't used Entebbe International airport. I didn't know what to say, so I kept quiet. He stamped my passport, and told me to go on the other side, where the Internal Security Organisation (ISO) had their office. I knew very well that many of these security men knew me, and so my heart began to beat. At the border gate, there was a policeman, and that made feel safe because no policeman knew me. My friend didn't know what to do, so everything was up to me to solve. Suddenly I saw a latrine on the other side of the security office, and I said in silence: 'If this toilet do not save me, it will kill me.' I walked to it and stayed there for a while, and when I came out I went straight to the border gate where I then successfully passed. When I had my foot on the Kenyan soil, I sat down and I do not remember who I thanked. My friends could only look, and shook their heads.

We then boarded a bus, and early the next morning we arrived in the Kenyan capital, Nairobi. Things there were very different from where I had come from, and it was like I had come from the jungle. Everyone seemed busy, and the cars were hooting all over me, though the two friends were holding on to my hand. Together we walked to the travel agency, where I had to pick up my ticket. There a man asked my passport, and I gave it to him. He then told me that the American Embassy had asked all travel agencies to send people who would be travelling to America to the Embassy, before issuing them tickets. I didn't think that that was a big deal, and on 2 August 1995, I went to the American Embassy in Nairobi Kenya, and the visa's expiring date was: 9 August 1995.

I entered through the gate and, when I got to a small barred window, I waited there with my passport in my hands. A woman in her late forties came and took my passport. She looked at it and gave it back to me, while telling me to wait for another person. A man came and he, too, was in his late forties. He was a small but strong man, with a big stomach and short hair. He, too, took my passport and, after having read it, he told me that the games had already been started: 'What else are you going to do in America?' he continued. He told me that he would have to cancel the visa. When he grabbed a stamp, I shouted in panic for him to

246

stop. As I took out my photos and movement orders from the envelope, my tears started falling, as I looked at the man who was about to reject me. I gave it all to him, and, as he looked through the photos, I was busy crying while asking him to help me. When he looked at the photos one more time, I began to explain everything, and, at the end, he told me that he was sorry, and cancelled my visa. The barred window made it difficult for me to at least reach out my hand and touch his. He had stamped twice, and now he walked away, leaving me in tears. When I looked at the visa page, I got the only explanation, as if I just had understood the words:

CANCELLED
WITHOUT PREJUDICE
AMERICAN EMBASSY
NAIROBI.

I went and stood a few metres away and cried. Everything were turning into darkness, and I couldn't get my mind to work. I walked to where the two boys were waiting for me, and told them that my visa had been cancelled. We returned to the travel agency, and when I asked them to refund the ticket, they told me that they couldn't. If I wanted the money, I should go back to Uganda where I had bought it. For the first time in my life, I let anybody know how I felt, and told the boys that I was going to throw myself in front of a car. 'I'm not wanted in this world, so why should I live?'

But they looked at me for a while, before one of them reminded me of how much I had endured. Then he asked me why a 'commando' like me would go and kill herself because of a cancelled visa. Despite him misunderstanding my reason for committing suicide, he showed me that he, at least, thought that I was worthy of living.

The boys went their way, and like a mad person, I found my way to a hotel. I ordered some food to make them leave me alone, as I tried to gather my thoughts.

'China!' a voice said, I turned and my eyes met with 'Boxer', a former fellow soldier who I had known when I worked at the Republic House.

I will never know how I felt at that moment. I was sitting by myself in a foreign country, and suddenly an angel had come to me, from nowhere. I told him everything, and he made it clear that, without money, nothing could be done. Boxer was now a different person, he drank everything from home-made to beers, and at that very moment he was drunker. He and I walked around in town, while talking about our past. He also told me that Kenya was a dangerous place to be, because ISO had offices there.

In the evening of that day I returned back to Uganda. I had decided to risk my life, because to me death seemed the same, and it didn't matter any more how I would die. We arrived very early in the morning, and I found it easy to get to the travel agency. They refunded my 1,000 dollars, and I went to the buses where I stayed until the time came to drive back to Kenya. At the border of Busia, I handed my passport to a man, who then started questioning me. He wanted to know why I had returned and why I was going back so quickly. He was very surprised, as he told me that since he had worked there, he had never seen such a move. When I told him that I had forgotten some money, he demanded to see it, so I showed it to him. After having counted it, he took 100 dollars before telling me that I was now free to enter the Kenyan border.

When I arrived in Kenya, Boxer was waiting for me and, as we walked, I asked him to take me to a cheaper hotel. After having finished to pay, he suggested that we go buy a fake passport. It would then help me travel on a visa, free to

England. All this time Boxer had been trading in fake dealing, and he knew most of the tricks. All I did was to walk behind him like a lost sheep. He took me to a studio, and I took identity photos. We went to a place, and there were many people sawing with the machine. Many of them greeted him, but he only spoke to one of them, who was in his late thirties. I didn't hear what they talked about, but I could only guess. Then Boxer walked back to me, and asked 100 dollars. After Boxer had been handed the passport, we went back to my hotel, and there I got to see the passport. The passport had been, I supposed, stolen from a Malawi, and in the passport she was thirty-seven years old, with dark eyes. After having read it, I looked at Boxer and told him that anyone could see that I wasn't thirty-seven years, and besides, I have brown eyes. He laughed before telling me that I shouldn't think about that. I looked at the whole thing as a mess, so I asked him to take it back and bring me my money, but he refused, while telling me that it didn't work that way. This time he promised me to find the right passport, so I gave him another 100 dollars. He returned after an hour, and he had a South African passport, and it also belonged to a lady. As I carried on reading, I discovered that this one had blue eyes and, when I told Boxer, he looked in my eyes and said: 'I didn't know, you too had blue eyes! Look at me, ja, you have blue eyes,' he continued. I laughed before asking him if he had another idea besides passport. 'Yes, you could go to South Africa, and you could even use your own passport.'

It sounded like a good idea, but then I realised that I had nearly used half of the money, because I thought that the cost of the ticket was the same in the whole world. Boxer told me that I could get to South Africa by road, but I found it hard to believe him. He assured me that if I help him to get to South Africa, he too would make sure that I get there safe.

249

I had no choice but to take this last chance. I gave him some money, and told him go buy bus tickets. Boxer had already sold his Ugandan passport, so I gave him 100 dollars to buy himself a fake Ugandan passport.

On 4 August 1995 Boxer and I left Kenya for Tanzania, and arrived late in the evening. We spent a night in Dar es Salaam, the capital city of Tanzania, and early morning we boarded a bus which was going to the border between Zambia and Tanzania. We arrived in the evening, and on 7 August 1995, we left and arrived in Lusaka, Zambia, early the next morning. There we took a bus going from Lusaka to Zimbabwe, and we arrived at the border with Zambia and Zimbabwe, early morning on 8 August 1995. The bus rushed through the country, and on 9 August, we left the Zimbabwean border for South Africa.

The immigration workers were surprised to see that we have travelled through all these countries. Fortunately, they were happy to meet any Ugandan, because of our nation's support in the people's fight against apartheid. They only asked us one question: 'Why are you here, and for how long?'

I told them: 'For a couple of weeks' and in my passport a 'temporary residence permit' and a stamp was added: 'valid until: 1995-08-23'.

At around nine o'clock a.m., we boarded a minibus and arrived in Johannesburg four p.m. The moment I stepped out of the bus, my body began to freeze, and when I looked around I only saw African people. No one wore a jacket and I simply failed to understand. Boxer and I stopped a cab and asked the man to find us a cheap hotel. He drove us to 'Chelsea Hotel' in Hillbrow. At the reception I paid 100 Rand for both of us. Even the room was extreme cold, so I walked back again and asked for more blankets. Raja was from Mauritius and he was curious about where I came from, and I told him. I was running out of money and told Boxer that I only could support him for two more days as we had agreed. Boxer, a man in his early thirties, began to cry and told me that I was like his mother. I had already seen that he was being destroyed by too much marijuana, and I was overwhelmed by pity, so I decided that we stayed together until all the money I had was used up. I couldn't afford to buy food for both of us, and Boxer had found an even cheaper hotel named 'Poor man's Hotel', without security and breakfast included. He came and told me that it could be a dangerous place, so we agreed that I stayed at Chelsea. Every morning Boxer came, and I offered him my breakfast, because I had decided that a cup of tea and an egg was enough for me.

The second day we went to Home Affairs, where I met the first Afrikaans. Tinus Van Jaarveld was between thirty-five and thirty-seven. I handed over everything of which I had shown at the American embassy, and he reacted positive to this, and with a smile he called for his colleague: 'Hey, come and help this rebel as soon as possible!' Boxer, too, had a photo of himself where he looked just like Rambo, carrying a large machine-gun (LMG). They photocopied our photos, and gave us a three month's stay permit. The man then told us: 'We don't give jobs, or housing. We only give you the stay permit, so it's up to you to find your way.' I didn't care, as long as I had escaped my pursuers.

Boxer told me that we should look for 'Red Cross'. When we got there I explained my situation to the woman there, including that I was pregnant. She gave me an address of 'The Woman's Shelter'. It was a huge room with a cemented floor, and this very floor was crowded with all sorts of people. I was angry and it seemed as if others destroyed what I was trying to build. Shocked, I stood and looked at where I had been sent, to a place of drinkers, drug addicts and insane people. I felt that I had been compared with them. I didn't despise any of them, but I feared that, if I stepped inside, I would be lost for ever. I went back and counted my money, and I was left with fifty dollars which would give us shelter for five more days.

It was a fine morning with sunny weather, and I was sitting outside in front the hotel trying to solve my situation. The man next to me had a pistol, and I was sure that he neither was a cop or a soldier. I suddenly became afraid to see this civilian with a gun. This would never have been allowed where I came from, and I believed that it was for a good reason. Then a woman in her late twenties came walking up the sidewalk, and stopped next to my table. She wore a very provoking miniskirt, which was a totally new experience for me, but before I could get her attention, a man approached and without as much as a 'Good day', I heard her ask: 'Have you come for business?' He then took her hand, and two of them walked inside. I was curious, and I wanted to know what the girl was selling. I went to the reception, and asked a young white boy, who laughed and asked where I was from. I rather felt stupid, and as I was about to enter the elevator, a middle-aged man placed his hand on my shoulder. He wished to know who I was and, before I could speak, he invited me into his office. He introduced himself as Morocka, and he was Jewish. I nearly collapsed when he told me that he was the owner of the hotel. I saw a speck of hope, and I only wished that he liked me. We spoke for a while where I explained the difficult situation Boxer and I were in. When he had finished his whisky, he called for the white boy from the reception: 'Bryce, come here!' he said. Soon the boy arrived, and he told him that, from now on, the both of us should live and eat for free. I didn't know how to thank him, but when I was about to kneel before him, he reached out the palm of his hands, and said: 'No, you don't do that!' Morocka left his office, and I watched him enter his white BMW.

A few days later we were hired. I was made a barmaid, while Boxer became a part of the security. The bar was divided into two parts. One downstairs was just a regular bar, but the one I had to work in bore the name: 'Sex Shop'. At one end there was a porno shop with movies and all sorts of weird objects. At the other end was a topless bar with a big screen at the ceiling showing non-stop porno movies. I was paralysed, and for the first couple of days I didn't speak. They expected me to be topless, but fortunately Raja accepted my refusal, and made me 'bar-helper'. One of the bar ladies, Dee, was nothing but an angel, she really cared for me. After work she always asked me out along with Ryan, her boyfriend. We went to cinemas, restaurants and everywhere we went, she covered my expense. Of course she was paid a lot more than me who got fifty dollars a month, while she had 180 dollars a week for working topless and striptease. Dee lived next to my room at Chelsea hotel, and her door was open for me at any moment. Nicole worked there as well, but she was very different from Dee. She was paid the same as Dee, but she seemed to love money more than herself. She had a boyfriend, but still she sold herself to the customers who came to watch strip shows.

One evening after work, Nicole invited me and some others to her birthday. As we had finished eating the cake, Nicole gave me her keys, and told me to get her a bottle of whisky. I did as she asked, and later I left them drinking, and went to sleep. Early morning, Raja shouted at me to open the door, and he entered with one of the guards. I was shocked when he accused me for having stolen Nicole's fifty dollars. I started crying, not because I was being accused, but the humiliation which I felt in my very heart. I showed Raja my salary, which he himself had paid me the day before. He believed me, but still we had to go to Nicole's room. She was sitting on her bed, holding a big teddy bear in her arms. I looked straight in her eyes, before I asked her why she had to lie. She couldn't answer, so I said: 'Nicole, you know the truth, and I hope that God will punish you for that.' I then gave her my salary, but she looked down and refused to take it. When Dee heard about this, she became angry, and promised herself never again to speak to Nicole.

Two weeks later Nicole left her boyfriend, and I noticed Nicole with a boy who had come to drink there. After closing time, Nicole and the boy left together. The next morning when I woke up, I heard someone screaming from the reception. When I got there, I found the security beating the very same boy who had been with Nicole. Nicole was standing beside two boxes full of porno movies, and I was told that the boy had been caught stealing from the sex shop. The boy had already been badly beaten, but still they kept on. I was frightened, because it was my first time to see a white person being beaten. All along I had thought that a white person wouldn't survive a beating, because of their fragile-looking skin. Suddenly Morocka arrived, and I was relieved when he stopped them. Morocka wanted to know what had happened, and when they told him he turned and said: 'Innocent I trust you. Tell me what you saw.'

'Mr Morocka, when I came down here, they were already beating him, and all that I know about this boy is that he had been drinking in sex shop,' I said.

Morocka didn't think that it was the boy's fault, so he let him go, but fired Nicole.

Weeks later, Dee and her boyfriend started smoking cocaine, and I was greatly affected with sadness. She was a beautiful person, but I could see that the drug was killing her. I tried to tell her that she was turning into something bad, but it seemed too late for her to act. Dee's money were now going to cocaine, and sometimes I even had to borrow her my own, which I knew she wouldn't pay back. I really didn't mind whether she paid me back or not, because of everything she had done for me without expecting anything in return.

My stomach was growing bigger, and I was getting desperate. Because of this, I started to smoke more than forty cigarettes a day. Soon my health turned bad, but I couldn't tell Morocka or anybody else, because I feared that I would be fired. I worked with pain, and believe me, this was different, but I'm not going into details for the sake of someone's future life. Dee was getting destroyed by the drug, and now there was no one I could tell or share my pain with. A month later Dee quit her job. Now I was the only one left to take care of the bar. The sex shop was losing customers, and I was afraid that I would lose my job. To stop this from happening, I started to serve double up. When the customer paid for a drink, I would give them two.

Soon Raja found out that the alcohol was disappearing, as he was responsible for the stock. He didn't wait for my explanation, and went straight to Morocka. He called for me, and I found him seated behind his desk, drinking a glass of whisky. 'Innocent! Have you eaten?' he asked.

'No, Mr Morocka,' I replied.

He took a phone, and ordered a couple of omelettes. I couldn't tell if he was angry with me, but I knew that I had to tell him the truth.

'Innocent! Are you stealing from me?" he asked.

'No, Mr Morocka,' I replied once more, and explained why.

At last he smiled, and told me not to do anything without having asked him first.

The omelette arrived, but I couldn't swallow. My throat

was dry, and I hoped him to leave me in peace. My wish came true, and it only took me a minute to finish up.

I continued working and, around four in the evening, Boxer came and told me that Lt-Colonel Moses Drago had been killed in an ambush. Slowly I walked and stood against the wall. My life seemed to leave me, but I had to be strong because of my son, Moses Drago Jr. I went down the stairs, and asked Raja permission to borrow the phone. I nearly collapsed when Drago himself answered the phone, and that was the first call since I left Uganda. When I told him that someone had told me that he was dead, he laughed, and told me of how he was stronger than ever. I was confused, and didn't know if I could believe him because of what Boxer had said. Drago, too, had been told that I was no longer living, and I think he got the news from the two boys in Kenya. He was very happy to hear that I was alive, and he begged me to return, but I told him, 'No'. He promised that he would talk to the NRA and explain about the whole thing, but I knew the NRA, and I would not risk my life. Besides, I knew that Drago could never give me what I really wanted: freedom. Before saying goodbye, Drago wanted me to promise him one thing: that I would look after his children some day. With a smile, I said, 'Yes', and told him that I would call the next day.

Around six o'clock, I called and the phone was answered by his young brother, Eric, because Drago was gone. The first thing I wanted to know from Eric was why Drago had not told me. But Eric had no answer, and I couldn't speak any more. I started crying still with the phone in my hands, with a faint hope that it all had been a lie. Then I heard numerous voices of people around Eric, and I realised something had happened. My last hope was taken away. I called Eric the day after, but I never found out what killed Drago. Three brothers-in-arms, of one tribe, Lt-Colonel Moses

Drago, Lt-Colonel Bruce, Major Moses Kanabi, in a matter of four years, all three were gone.

Drago was my son's father and, for that reason, everything about him has to be good, for the sake of my son. But those who can overlook, they might understand. My childhood was long gone, and now everyone that I loved was melting away. My mother and my sisters were gone, and now I was alone, and I needed love, but I could not know from who or where, as long as I could put my head in someone's hand. I knew very well that, no matter how I cried, I will never get any of this back, so I forced myself to hate everyone who have died away from me, because the love I felt for them was killing me like a lethal injection. I tried to forget, but it was hard, and soon I found it impossible. I was surrounded by drugs and I was tempted more than once but, every time, my eyes saw the painful effect in the one who offered. Instead I drank heavily. I was fired and at that point I realised that I was losing.

I decided to go to a man who I considered my friend. This man used to come to watch striptease where I worked, and when I could not find anywhere to go, I gave him a call, and told him that at work they had some problems, therefore, I had to stop working for some time. I thought that if I told him that I was no longer working, then he might take advantage and abuse me. I stayed there for some time, and soon the man changed. He told me that he was tired of feeding me, and got nothing in return. He went on, 'You are staying in my house for nothing, and I think it's time for you to start opening up your...'. I decided to run away from this man, and since I had nothing, I decided to take some of his stuff, and I wondered if he was hurt by this. This kind of things happened to me, and it really hurts to sleep with people just to live on. I had to do everything, good and bad, in order to keep myself, because that was all I was left with, and it would hurt me so much to let the last proof of my existence, my body, melt away. After some time being hurted by people, I asked myself: does people have feelings, if I do the same, would anybody feel hurt by it?

A Time to Be

Four more years had to pass before I finally found a way out. I had desperately needed time to process what I had been through, without finding it.

I was alone. I didn't know why I was going. I just walked. I had a letter in my hands, remembering only to deliver it. I entered a huge building signed 'United Nations High Commissioner for Refugees'. At the reception I talked, but the girl didn't seem to listen. She only stared with her mouth wide open. I was an African dressed all in white with a white scarf,like a Muslim coming from Mecca. I handed her the letter, and when I saw her hand accepting it, I suddenly cried. She made a call, spoke briefly, and a minute later I followed a lady into her office. Her name was Pamela, and I sat down without having introduced myself. She had just read the letter, when I was asked to begin telling everything. The way she had asked was the key I had lost, and in a split second everything appeared before my eyes. I couldn't speak. I was released by this person which seemed to care so much. I crouched down deep in the chair, so deep that everything turned into darkness. She couldn't handle my reaction, and told me that she would be back. Pamela returned with a man, who took my hand and led me to his office. He asked me if I smoked, gave me a cigarette and told me to let it all out. Then he quietly looked into his desk, while I cried like a child. When my tears had dried, the man introduced himself as Burt Leenschool. Burt wanted to know how I got this letter, and I began:

'Some months ago I met a Ugandan man, who told me that he lived in England, but travelled all over the world in order to promote his organisation which was fighting against Museveni's government. When the man mentioned Museveni, I remembered Drago, my friends, and myself. I joined his group. In the South African Group, he had fifteen members, of whom most were ex-Museveni soldiers. The group leader was a Muslim, and he told us that we were not the only ones. I was so desperate to join the struggle, that all suspicion was forgotten. Once again I would be able to do what I was good at. This time it would be of my own free will, and I knew very well what I would be fighting for. Later the leader rented an office in the middle of Johannesburg, and during most meetings we would watch movies to commemorate Idi Amin's words. Particularly one was ready to go back in the bush. During my fifth meeting, I heard the comrades talk about Major Kasaija, who was in the Ugandan army. Kasaija was a very good friend of mine, and I wanted to know more about where he was at that particular time. When I heard that he had been brought to work at the Ugandan Embassy in South Africa, I simply couldn't wait seeing him. I thought that he would understand me, and therefore I wanted him to tell me what to do to get back home in peace. I started looking for the embassy's telephone number, and when I got it, I decided to call. I spoke to Kasaija, but he couldn't remember me, but I was sure that it was him, because of the language he spoke. To refresh his memory, I roughly told him about my whole history in the army. He invited me over to his office, though I knew him well, I still didn't want to risk my life, so I went with a Zambian man, who I told to wait at the reception. 'If you hear me scream, please run for help,' I said.

'When I entered Kasaija's office he was a man I had never seen before. Kasaija stood up and greeted me with respect, I suppose, because of what I had told him about myself. The instant when I had laid my eyes on him, I had seen that he never had been a soldier, but he claimed to know the real Major Kasaija. He offered me tea, but I refused anything without a capsule. It was after closing time, and I was alone with him and his secretary. I felt safer, but my eyes still couldn't stay in one place. Kasaija told me that he believed I was a victim of a big mistake. He was convinced that I truly was a hero who deserved better.

'Now I believed that he was on my side, so I decided to tell about my new involvement, as I tried to explain the consequence, when betrayed. Suddenly he changed. I was impressed to see what he had been hiding. Now he was prepared like a soldier going to war. He demanded me to deliver my comrades in return for immunity. I could only laugh inside at this man who believed me wrong. Besides, I didn't believe in his immunity. He gave me some money, and I promised to return soon after my research was done. I knew that I had convinced him well, and that he didn't know that I had earned his money for nothing.

'Weeks later, I invited myself to the party which Uganda airlines had arranged. At around eleven o'clock, I was joined by some guys who promised to drive me back to Johannesburg. I was drunk, and I'm not sure what I talked about concerning Museveni's government. But I'm sure that I used my past to earn their respect. Around twelve o'clock the three guys and I drove off. I couldn't really tell whether or not we were going in the right direction, because I didn't know Pretoria that well. They suddenly stopped at a building, and two of them dragged me to an apartment. I was ordered to strip myself naked. They searched my clothes, and when they asked for my passport I told them that it was at home. I was asked if I was in contact with Kashilingi and I denied.

'Early morning I had sobered up, and two of them took a firm grip on me, while the other slowly began to stab me in my backside with what could have been like an ice-pick. They knew who I was, and they wanted to know of how much I had been talking and to whom. I gave them my side of the story, of why I had run away, but still they called me a deserter. They assured me that this was nothing compared to what would happen when I was taken back. After they had taken away my last sense of dignity, I was tired and told them to take me back to Uganda to face whatever they had decided, but they could not because I was very weak and sick. I saved myself by making myself even more sick. Every time they said that it was time to go, I would make myself even more sick, and this trick saved my life, but time came. When we stopped at the first traffic-light in the busy Pretoria, I decided that this was it. Just when the driver reached for the gear-lever, I distracted them by punching the rear window, when they looked at it I had already opened the door. I was out.

I went straight to the hospital, and my wounds on my bums had healed, but my mind was broken. I had been under their rule of terror for some months, and to me it still feels like years. I couldn't have been much more than a ghost to them, when I reached at the reception. After an operation, I went to Home Affairs where Tinus Van Jaarveld received me. 'Rebel! What happened to you? You look like a ghost!' He was truly shocked when he saw the marks. I gave him the letter from the hospital, and managed to tell him of what happened. He took me straight to another office, where he in brief repeated my words to the woman there. Heidi listened carefully as I told her of my life. and how I became a child soldier. It was hard to talk, and I realised for the first time that I was no more in control. Since I became a child soldier, no woman have ever saw me cry, but now here I was, crying in front of a woman. I also hated to cry in front of a civilian, because I thought they were too stupid to understand things. But I had no choice, because now it was only civilians who were in control. When I had finished, she nearly forgot about me, looked down and began typing a letter as if she was angry at somebody. She put the letter in an envelope addressed to United Nations High Commissioner for Refugees.'

I had finished and I was back at the UN building in front of Burt. I looked down, and there was silence for a while. Then Burt told me that he would like someone to check my wounds. He called for a lady, Victoria W. Stofile, who checked me for him. The next day I was sent to the trauma clinic in Johannesburg. The woman I met there was very kind, but her questions nearly made me mad, maybe I already was, and I felt this voice inside of me, begging me to ask for help, and along with that, I really had to control myself as not to jump around in front of her, screaming and shouting. I was so afraid to remember, because I asked myself what would happen if they suddenly rejected me. I came to love her, because she was the one who would listen to me for hours, but I was still in control. I tried not to let anything I told affect my soul. I knew that I was a fighter, because I had managed all along, but now I was in someone's hands, and I didn't know in which direction they would throw me.

The woman didn't give up. She tried to convince me that not everyone wanted to harm me, and step by step I began trusting in her. I was overwhelmed with emotions by so large numbers, that I had to let as little out as I could. I had become the gatekeeper to my consciousness, but the pressure was so high that I had to give in. I lost control of myself, and everything erupted in my mind at once, twenty-four hours a day. There was nothing I was more frightened of than whenever I learned that she wanted me back for another consultation. I felt like saying: 'NO' in a big voice, but I feared her reaction, and I didn't want her to be upset with me. In my past, I had only learned to say 'Yes', even to the most terrible thing.

The trauma clinic found me a psychiatrist, and now I was seeing both. UN had booked a hotel room for me, and every time I was going to the psychiatrist, I was picked up by a Land Cruiser with UN flags in front. The psychiatrist was Afrikaans, in his late forties. He was a tall and strong-looking man, with his face covered with beard. I was put on medication, which replaced my nightmares with far-out dreams. Now I could laugh in my dreams, and not cry. The psychiatrist seemed to be helping me in many ways. I started excepting of who I was, and learned that the bad things I did was never my fault. I also started coming to terms with myself, by opening up a bit.

It was ten in the morning, and I was standing in front of the hotel, when a car arrived. I realised that it was for me. I approached the driver, who told me that he was taking me to Burt. Just as I had stopped in front of his desk, he asked me which country I wanted to be resettled in. I thought I had heard him wrong, and when I asked him what he had meant, he said: 'I want you to tell me which country you would like to live in'.

'United States of America,' I replied.

'Do you know anybody there?' he asked, and I said 'No'. He told me that he didn't think it was a good idea, but he was sending my statement to Geneva, and he was sure that they would decide what was best for me. I couldn't believe my ears, but all I could feel was a tingling sensation all over my body. My chair was turning hot and, excited, I stood up and screamed. Not because I was going to another country, but because of the rights I had been given to make a choice.

I had too much excitement, and I didn't know what to do with it. If I wasn't afraid of Burt, I would have hugged him, until some of his bones had broken.

Now we had to talk about my son, who I hadn't spoke to since his father's death. I didn't know where to begin, and where to end. I had a phone number of a friend of mine. Burt allowed me to call my friend. I did send him to the junior officers, who also knew Drago. My friend told me that, before Drago died, he had decided to leave my son in care of his girlfriend Rita. Rita was now with Drago Jr, and she didn't want to let him go. I think she loved him, because since I took my son from my sister Margie, it was Rita who had taken care of him, but at that moment, I didn't care about how Rita felt. All I wanted was my son.

When finally UN offices in Uganda had managed to get in contact with Rita, she told my son's family. They didn't trust her, and accused her of trying to steal Drago Moses Jr. As a consequence of this, they decided to take over the care of Moses. Rita had never been an easy person, and she couldn't just give in before having tried them in court. She lost the case, because she was not related with me, or Drago. Burt told me that he was doing all he could to reunite me with my son. Everything seemed to go in the right direction, and all I could do was to wait for Geneva to decide my fate. The love and care which I had received from the people at the UN offices made me feel like a child. My smile which I had lost was beginning to come back, and my trust in people was dramatically increasing.

The medication which I had received from the psychiatrist made me restless, and I felt an urge to tell about my past to everyone. But I still felt ashamed to tell the real me, because I thought that people would laugh or run away. Since I desperately wanted to talk, I decided to tell a different background of me. I told that I was a Canadian, who was on holidays, and when they asked what I was doing, I would say that I studied. In my country most people usually lies about who they are, and it does not matter if they have slept without food, they will still smile and say: 'I'm OK'. Many prefer not to talk about it because no one wants to be ashamed. One day someone told me to write my name, and as I wrote, the person broke down and laughed. When I asked him why he was laughing, he said that I wrote my name starting with a small letter. 'Oh', I looked down before telling the truth. The problem was that, I always told these lies without thinking, and since I didn't know myself, it was easier always for them to find the true 'China'. Some of them opened my eyes by telling me that if anyone liked me, then they should accept me for whom I am. I believed in their advice, but to be me would take a long time, no matter how much I pushed myself.

One morning I went to see Lori, and before I could enter her office I met Burt. He looked happy and invited me into his office. 'Guess what, you have been accepted by Denmark.' When he mentioned Denmark, I became sad, and when he asked why, I said: 'Mr Burt, I do not want to go to Denmark, because it's near Africa.'

'Oh no, I'm truly sorry I should have told you first that Denmark is very far.' When he finally said that it was bordering Germany, all my fear was gone. I left Burt's office, and sat myself down in the waiting-room. I asked myself: 'What kind of a country is Denmark, which have decided to accept me, when I have a broken life, and with no education. Have they felt my pain, even though they are so far away?' I couldn't be answered, so I walked back to my hotel, where I sat alone and tried to imagine the country: Denmark.

Two days later, I was taken to the Danish Embassy, and given a travel document. Back at the hotel, I met a German

man named Alex Kugler. Kugler was among a German medical group, which had come to practise at a South African hospital. Kugler was a Christian, and he spoke a little bit of Swahili. He had learned this on a tour in Kenya and Tanzania. He had the same wish as I had. He told me that, after finishing his studies, he would like to live in Africa and help the children there. I admired him for this, and soon I told him that he should let me know when he would be going to attend the prayers. In the evening Kugler came into my room, and told me that someone was waiting to drive us to the church. Outside a BMW was waiting, and when we entered, a man introduced himself to me as Wily Van Wyk. When I realised that he was an Afrikaans I became afraid, but just like always I decided to take a chance. On our way Van Wyk told me about Jesus, and how much he had improved his life. Since Van Wyk drove an expensive BMW, I sort of believed his testimony, though I believed that God had the last word. It was a huge church where black and white worshipped Jesus together. I sat next to Kugler, and on the other side of me an old Afrikaans couple sat. I was never used to sit in one place for long, and I was getting bored, but I managed to stay put until the service was over. Before returning to the hotel, Kugler had a cup of coffee, while I had a piece of cake.

The next day in the evening Van Wyk came to fetch us again, but this time he took us to his friend's house. It was a very cold winter's evening, but the house was warm enough that we didn't need to wear our jackets. I was the only black person, and when a Chinese girl walked in, I was relieved. The prayers started with a song, and afterwards we were told to take off our shoes and socks. I became embarrassed because of my socks which were full of holes. I tried to remove them as careful as I could, and I managed to do so without any notice. An Afrikaans lady had the water

266

ready, and she told us that now she was going to wash our feet, just like Jesus did to his disciples. Just after she had spoken, I nearly asked for a cigarette, as I felt like running away. After our feet had been washed, we were told to pray in silence, but I couldn't, because of all the hostility I had heard of between black and white. Was this love or was it a coincidence that I had come the ceremonial day, when they washed their feet, I questioned myself. I saw no hate, none of the remaining apartheid that always used to lurk around the corner. These people seemed to have grown up in an entirely different South Africa, but I just wasn't sure. Back at the hotel Kugler told me that he and some friends would leave the next day to camp in the mountains, but he assured me that he would return, before I could travel to Denmark.

In those days I met a German girl, named Judith Osseforth. She was in the same group as Kugler, studying medicine on her last year. Later on, she introduced me to Alexander Müller and Eberhard Reithmeier. I had a good time with them, and the day before my departure, they took me to a restaurant where I enjoyed my last meal. After having finished our meal, we had an ice-cream before we returned to the hotel. I couldn't fall asleep that night. I sat on my bed, and thought about this country which I was now going to leave the very next day. I had had a hard time in South Africa, but I still felt pain because I was leaving it behind. It was indeed a remarkable country, but my heart and soul refused to look at it as the past.

The next day, I was feeling sad and excited. I couldn't think or be in one place. It was very cold, but I was feeling hot. My heart became troubled, and at some point, I thought that I was getting a heart attack. I was standing at the reception when Kugler suddenly arrived. He hurried to his room, and after having dropped his luggage, he returned and we walked to the famous South African Union building. We walked all over the place taking photos, but I do not remember what I saw, because my mind was not with me.

Six o'clock in the evening, Pamela arrived in a United Nations car, and took me to the airport. She made sure to clear everything for me, and when she said goodbye, I cried, because at that moment there was no difference between her and my sister Margie, who I hadn't seen or talked to for four years. I walked through the hallway, until I came to a huge place filled with chairs. Some of the people were already seated. I asked myself: 'Is this a plane or a theatre?' I still couldn't understand, so I decided to ask one of the girls standing there. 'Is this a house, or a plane?' All of them started laughing, and I could only join them. They showed me my seat, and soon I was joined by two Spanish.

When the plane was about to take off, I noticed that everybody had a small table in front of them. I tried, but I couldn't find mine. 'How come, everyone have got one, but I don't', and no matter how much I searched for it, I could not find it. I thought of asking the Spanish, but I was afraid that they might laugh at me throughout the journey. When they said that we should put on our belts, I once again started struggling, but one of the guys noticed, and helped me with everything. Early morning, we arrived at the Frankfurt airport, and there I boarded another plane which then took me to my destiny. I arrived at Copenhagen airport, twelve o'clock, 21 June 1999. I came out of the plane, and before I could start walking, a tall man called my name. After having greet me, he took me by my hand, and straight to the police office. They cleared me, and after he handed me over to a lady, who stood waiting with a man. The lady introduced herself as Birgitte Knudsen, and her colleague Karl Erik. Three of us drove to their office, and I was introduced to another lady named Pia. I had never before felt such care, and I couldn't really find anything to give to this country, but I knew that I some day would come to love it with my very soul. After a while, Birgitte and Karl took me and showed me around Copenhagen. After the tour, they took me to a place called Diakonisse Stiftelsen. I was given a room, and everything there was new to me. I ate my lunch from a huge dining table, so luxurious that it felt as if I didn't belong.

When I looked back, and looked at where I was, it seemed as if I was at the end of the world. It could take some years to call a new country your home, because everything is so different from what you used to see. Whenever I turned my eyes and looked to the right, I would meet a different eye, with a different movement far from any I knew. If a person is not strong, he would easily call the movement of the very eye, hate, and sometimes feel rejected, and that's one of the reasons one can never stop thinking about the past. The past don't necessarily have to be good or bad, but because of your mind which is thinking about the motherland all the time, makes the past hunt you each minute of the day. When you come in contact with a native and start talking, you can easily misunderstand one another, because of the way you're expressing yourselves. Even the jokes they tell are different from what you know. When they laugh you too start laughing, and sometimes you don't even know why. If you don't let them compare colours and excuse them for every question asked, you will stay ignorant to each other. But, for me, I found it a little easier to adopt the ways of the Danes, because I had been a stranger before. If you give up, you will never learn more, and soon you would call good bad, and bad good. If you don't give up, you would learn the ways of others, just like a cat and a dog which once hunted each other, now laying in each other's arms. This world I had come to had been as an image of heaven before, and I was surprised to see that not everything was so. I have never seen and I have never expected to see a white person having to clean for a living. I was surprised when one morning I found a white man cleaning the kitchen, which was beside my room at Diakonisse Stiftelsen. I had hurried back to my room, and took a deep breath, before saying to myself: 'Indeed, there's a lot you need to take off your mind.'

Two days later, while I had breakfast, a man in his late fifties came and started making his coffee. After having finished, he offered me a cup. Though I didn't drink coffee, I still couldn't say no, afraid that I might offend him. The coffee was very strong, so I closed my eyes and drank. We introduced ourselves, and his name was Knud Held Hansen. Hansen was married and had three grown-up children, Jette and two twin boys named Carsten and Jens. Hansen lived in Aalborg, and he was in Copenhagen for some business. I liked the way he had approached me, in a very frankly manner. His ways made me relax inside, and my defences loosened up for the first time in a very long time. I noticed him looking at my head, as if something about me was missing. Just before finishing our coffee, he suddenly asked: 'Where is your hair? When is it coming back? I think you would look pretty with hair.' I found it easy to talk with him, and I felt as if I had known him for years. When having finished the coffee, he asked me if I wanted to see Copenhagen, and the first place he took me to see was the Little Mermaid. On our way back he asked me if I wanted to see 'Bakken'. As everything else, I had no idea of what he was talking about, but I didn't want us to part yet, so I agreed immediately. We parked the car, and walked on to a broad dirt road which leads through a forest with big old trees, and all around there was happy people walking or being driven in horse carriages. I was enchanted by the coachmen in strange uniforms driving the horses forward, which walked as if they were in a pleasant dream. Inside the clearings of the wood huge fires burned and Hansen told me that they were burning the witches. I stood and focused at one of the bonfires, but I saw no witches, and I was even more mystified. Finally we entered an amusement park, and I heard him compare it with 'Tivoli', which to me was a video store in Uganda. The place was overcrowded with people, busy amusing them-selves. Then I saw the huge machines swinging people into the air and down again. All of them were laughing and shouting, and for me it was heaven. I couldn't wait to join in and, just like a father, Hansen stood and watched me swing, like a child. I was wild with every game there, and he thought it was funny.

When I had taken the peak of my excitement, I was really hungry so we went to an Italian restaurant. As we sat wait-ing for our pizzas, a couple beside us greeted us. They talked very different from Hansen and those from Diakonisse Stiftelsen, and I was right when I told Hansen that they weren't Danish. Swedish was their language, but still Hansen understood everything they said. In the evening back at Diakonisse Stiftelsen Hansen had his strong coffee, while I enjoyed a cup of tea. As we sat there, his cellular phone rang, and I got the opportunity to talk with his wife and daughter. The next day Hansen returned to Aalborg, and I was left in tears, though I knew that I would see him again. He treated me like one of his children, and from then I took him like my real father. Hansen's love through those days made me think that USA's refusal of me was of a higher reason, but since I did not live there, I cannot really tell of what would have become of me.

In Denmark life is treated different, even an animal has its rights. Now I was no longer ordered on whom to kill or hate, as in the army but, the most beautiful of all, was that I no longer had to live my life for others, and no force makes me act against my will. But even with all this freedom, I still have the fear that I had to carry every day of the desperation that I saw in almost any soldier. That desperation often betrayed the innocent, as everyone struggled to find favours among the superiors. This is my final humiliation to speak of myself about shameful abuse and inferiority, because that's the only way I can save my friends. I was there, and I don't need to imagine their pain. I know it, and I still feel the abuse, and humiliation, scars which my body and soul will carry for ever. My fear seems to be permanent, and it feels as a mark for life. In my sleep I still see the shadows of my fellow child soldiers and friends, who ended their own lives with their guns in order to escape. Most of my pain is over now, but the war is still on, because there are many children who I believe are still crying for our help. The battle is not over, so lift up your voice and demand the glory.

Y. K. Musevini

Here I am wondering.

When I look in the mirror, it's your face I see. Even when I go to sleep, in my nightmares, it's you with that old gun in your hands, from the times when you talked and I was trapped by convincing words to shed my own blood for you.

I played your game, but I didn't know the rules. I saw your face shine, while mine lost its colour. Too tired to wash my face, because of that gun weakening my arms. While I was doing all the dirty work, my soul would ask me questions that only you could answer, but you couldn't, because you were hiding at a place I was denied to come. You were afraid of my soul and told your bodyguards not to let it in, and when I tried to force myself, you ordered them to catch me and steal it. I was running like a fugitive all the time, away from those guns you ordered for me. I tried to raise my voice for you to hear, but the hunt had already begun. Now that you got what you wanted, you don't even know my name. It's so strange, we don't play any more, why? I often cry. Didn't I raise my weapon high enough? Maybe it's because you got what you wanted. Why didn't you keep your promises? I have spent years trying to find the reason. Is it the high walls where you live, or is it the men with the guns around you twenty-four hours a day, that make you ignore the cries? Do you not remember? The children you promised a life when they needed it most, together with you at the enemy lines? Many got killed and you say it's not that bad, but still our parents are looking for us. I wish I knew then. To put my life in your hands is like falling in love with a lion.

I remember one mother coming to you, looking for her son. She gave you his names, and when she saw your reaction, she gave you the description of that little kid, who you knew hadn't stopped wetting the bed. But you had already given him foreign names, those of distant actors and buried the real. She looked down and cried, telling you that where she came from there were no such names. You would tell her that you had no more time, because of the road you were about to build. I watched her tears, and when she reached the stairs, her legs let her down. I guess that later you realised what you had done, but while passing her you chose to look the other way. I guess that I can't pat myself on the shoulder for a job well done, dodging bullets in the bush with you, in those times when your pockets still had no holes. These crying games we played, it's your time to cry. But you can still come back, and you don't have to give your life just a tiny piece. Others would follow your example, if you can give the mother back her child.

– from your Child Soldier